GLEN BURTON

IN HARM'S WAY

SOLDIER.

BODYGUARD.

MENTOR.

IN HARM'S WAY

NOTEBOOK
PUBLISHING

First published in the United Kingdom in 2019 by Notebook Publishing, 20–22 Wenlock Road, London, N1 7GU.

www.notebookpublishing.co

ISBN: 9780993589898

Cover Photograph taken by Nolan Conley.

A CIP catalogue record for this book is available from the British Library.

Typeset by Notebook Publishing.

For Poppy:

To my beautiful angel, the day you arrived into the world was the happiest day of my life. I have been blessed with each and every moment that we spend together. You truly are a gift that brings so much joy into my life. I always tell you and others how proud I am of you; of your unselfishness, your politeness, your cheery and happy attitude, and your caring and loving nature. I'm so proud to be able to call you my daughter because you are growing into a fine young lady.

You are the reason I'm here today.

I love you so much.

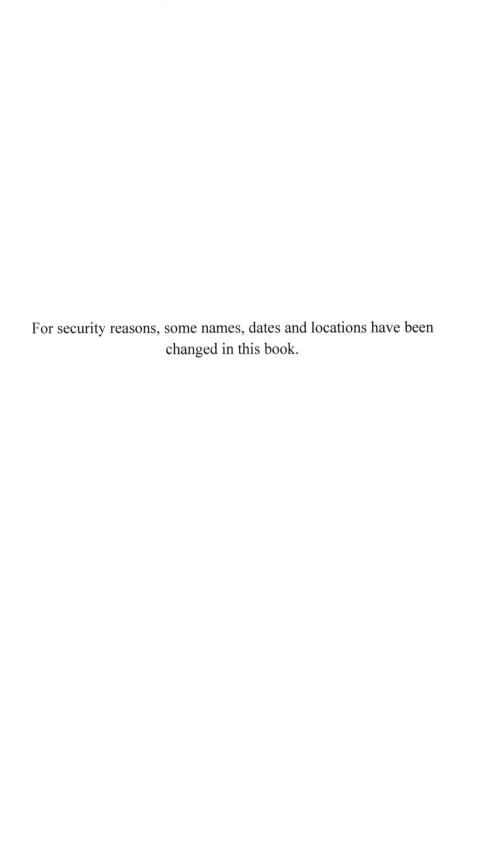

For security reasons, some names, dates and locations have been changed in this book.

CONTENTS

A NOTE FROM THE AUTHOR

MY ENTIRE LIFE TO date has involved a higher level of risk than most people face. That risk has presented itself in varying forms, whether through my lack of focus at school and potentially not having much of a career, leaving home at sixteen to join the Army and not making a success of it, or moving to a new country thousands of miles away with little money and minimal work options. As if all of that wasn't risk enough, I then ventured into harm's way as a bodyguard, not knowing whether I would succeed on my chosen path.

That risk-taking is, by no means, something to brag about, however. It is simply the journey I've taken through the choices I've made—and it is what helped me to achieve self-satisfaction in everything I do. I want to make it perfectly clear that what I've achieved in life may not be substantial from a monetary standpoint in the sense that I've made millions—I've done okay—but that has never been my goal, nor will it ever be. I am where I am today because I learned and embraced three key things that helped to change my life: *Performance, Motivation and Mindset.*

These three are the underpinnings that have enabled me to be always moving forward in everything I do; allowing me to take risks and grasp every opportunity coming my way. I have always needed to perform at the highest level, regardless of the objective. I was motivated to be the very best that I could be; as a person, in my career, and as a doting father. More so, I adopted a mindset that has enabled me to attack the hell out of everything I do until I excel at it. From a very young age, I was able to encourage myself—somewhat easily, I might add—to be the very best version of myself that I could be—well, apart from school, that is! Once I binned that off, the British Army then became my School of Life, and it carried that role for the next ten years. It was becoming a professional soldier that provided me with a platform to build from as I matured and grew into a leader, motivator and international operator. Discipline and respect were drilled (and sometimes beaten) into me. They were some of the key fundamentals of becoming who I am today. I've taken knocks, but each and every time I've got right back up again and bettered myself, both personally and professionally.

Let it be said, I expect nobody reading this book to follow my path. In fact, I'm a firm believer that education has grown to be more and more paramount over the years. If, however, you can learn from my journey, risk-taking and life choices, or if you can gain the motivation needed to help drive you to the next level where it helps you in some way, that will do me. There is, however, a flip side to that coin...

When I joined the Army, I was escaping a lot of negative things. I wasn't happy with hanging around on street corners after school, getting into mischief. I knew it was only going to be a matter of time before I'd start getting into trouble with the police, and so I recognized, very early on, that I needed to make some adjustments.

The Army doesn't embrace you talking about your feelings and emotions, so you can often bottle a lot up. It's like the coolest club in the world, the best gang to be a part of. But everyone is expected to be the hard man who will front up anything. That means, as soon as anyone talks about anything in regard to feelings and emotions, you're told to "Shut the fuck up and grab a beer". At the end of the day, they're training people to be well-oiled fighting machines, and so it goes against the grain to have soldiers talking about things that don't fall in line with that.

That was in the 1990s, and so I'm sure that things have evolved a great deal since then—one would hope so, anyway. When I came back from Bosnia in 1995, I felt completely fine but, looking back, the things I witnessed and experienced did me no favors whatsoever. Yes, it was the most amazing and astonishing period of my life—which you'll have the opportunity to read about in this book—but I was 21 years old, working in a volatile warzone, and it was a dirty and nasty war. I was out on the ground with the top man, and we'd often be witness to some atrocious events and incidents. I hadn't been trained, whether emotionally or mentally, to go to a place like that or to see some of the things I did. I was a trained professional soldier, yes, but I, nor anyone else, had ever been through an induction prior to being exposed to that type of environment. Nothing can ever truly prepare you for that. Nothing but the real thing. Boots on the ground, listening to the noises, smelling the air dense with shit and death, and then seeing, first-hand, the true horrors of war. Yes, I loved my time out there with the team I was working with, but it caught up with me later in life.

For the best part of 30 years, I've been in the business of protecting people, and it's something I've thoroughly enjoyed and taken pride in, but in so doing, I never made myself the priority. I could never be accused of being selfish, but in making sure that everyone else was okay, safe and taken care of, I should have done a damn sight better at looking after myself. What do I mean by that? Well, in the Army, you have an obligation to your team-mates and your regiment or corps. You are there to go into harm's way when called upon and take care of business, to be an asset, to be a well-trained and well-oiled machine. That's all part and parcel of what you sign up for. You know you aren't off on a Jolly Boys outing when the shit hits the fan. You're sent off to be peacemakers or you're asked to inflict as much havoc and damage upon the enemy as is possible. You witness so many things and go through so many emotions—but finding the inner strength to adapt to and overcome those things is a completely different matter altogether.

Following my Army career, I went into the private security business. This was a journey that took me to almost 90 countries. My job was to keep people safe and out of harm's way—and to do so at all costs, including if threats were made against them. In that role, your job is to take a bullet for your client, and if you don't have that mindset, you shouldn't be in it. It really is as simple as that. Every time I was on a job, I was completely zeroed in to making sure they were good to go, that they could go about their personal or business matters incident-free. I'd keep them on time, make sure they remained safe, ensure their reputation wasn't impacted. I'd manage their international travel, meet with their hosts and, as a representative of my clients, lay out a smooth trip for them.

I cannot underestimate the pride and satisfaction I took in doing this, and I'm proud to say I've been able to keep each of those that have called on me safe. I'm not glorifying this in any way, but when it came to being *In Harm's Way*, I've had, or will have, no problem with being in the thick of the action in order to protect my clients, my team mates, or myself. If that means pulling the trigger should a particular situation warrant it, then no problem,

I've done it and have no remorse. What was the alternative? I'll tell you what it was: me or those I was with ending up in a box.

Since the age of 16, my life, in part, has been absolute mayhem where it's been constantly under threat. Yes, I've witnessed and experienced great things that most people could only dream of, but I've also seen and gone through things that would break most people. The one thing that has enabled me to overcome the tough parts is my ability to find and then maintain mental strength.

I've no idea where it came from, but I'm sure as hell glad I found it. Maybe the Army laid the foundation for that or maybe it was some of the things I witnessed during the travels that followed my Army career. It's been that mental strength that's gotten me through some real bad shit. There were even times when I felt invincible, mentally—a dangerous mindset if ever there was one! I've seen people suffer and struggle for much less than I've gone through, but one thing I've learned over the years is that we all deal with things differently and that, no matter who you meet, you don't know what they might be going through. I'm no exception. For many who know me, they've seen me as a soldier, a tough-minded no-nonsense bodyguard who has done some pretty cool things and worked with some big names. But, to be honest with you, I couldn't care less about that. It was my job to protect and to take care of people. I was paid well to do so and, as a result, have been extremely fortunate to work with some pretty amazing people and meet other wonderful folks along the way.

Behind the work image that many have often seen, though, there is a person who has feelings and emotions. I'm saddened when I see a squirrel run over on the street, for fuck's sake. I've been impacted emotionally during some events I've witnessed, whether directly or through others telling me. I've been devastated when I've experienced heartbreak in relationships so, yes, I'm a real person. Some from back home say or think they know me but, no, they don't. The reason for that is because I've never allowed anyone to get close. I've shut up shop when it's come to most things outside of work, and that was a mistake. Many don't know that I was diagnosed with Post-Traumatic Stress Disorder due to some of the things I've witnessed and gone through in my Army career, and then later working in the security industry.

There will be some people reading this now who will say "What?" while others will probably say "That makes sense" by my admission, but I'm actually okay with it, though it's taken me some time to say that "It's okay to not be okay". It really isn't surprising that I've got PTSD; my time in Bosnia aside, over the last 30 years, I've lost colleagues and good friends, been exposed to extreme poverty-stricken environments, seen kids dying of Aids, come across mass war graves and witnessed death first-hand, as well as hearing plenty of bombs and bullets. I've also gone through my own personal losses, whether in relationships or family. I've seen a lot of the world and enjoyed much of it, but I've seen and experienced a lot of bad, too.

I was born and raised in Middlesbrough, 'The Boro', in the north-east of England in June 1974. At the age of sixteen, I left home to start basic training to be a professional soldier in the British Army. What followed was an intense and often brutal forty-three-week-long challenge, during which I needed to muster as much mental and physical strength as possible in order to achieve my goal. Some back home didn't think I'd last five minutes in the Army, though once I realized my purpose was to be a soldier, I never stopped trying to fulfil it.

I went on to have a successful ten-year career in an Infantry Battalion, conducting operations and training in some of the world's most challenging environments. My colleagues and I all shared a common bond in serving something greater than ourselves. It was a brotherhood that tied us together, and that bond is what allowed us to willingly walk into harm's way together. In April 2000, I would leave the Army as the most operational soldier in my Battalion. At that point I knew: it was time to pursue a new career.

It took me seven operational tours to become the operator I was when I left the Army. Getting off the speeding train was difficult, partly because I was heading into a world that was, to some extent, completely alien to me, and in which my skills, I thought, might not even be applicable. Nonetheless, upon leaving the Army, I focused on pursuing a career in the private security industry and, having successfully passed my Close Protection course during my resettlement training, started a new stage in my career, feeling ready to give it my all.

I was a 27-year-old young man who, for the previous ten years, had been surrounded by teammates, been fed three times a day, made a decent pay check, and been doing a job I'd been highly trained to do—and so what I was then faced with was a whole new world. That first year was a struggle, with only a few small gigs, though I spent most of the time doing a number of driving jobs as well as some bricklaying. I hated both, especially during the winter months. It was a monotonous routine of bricklaying, driving, drinking and football—and all the way knowing I could do so much more.

I was close to joining back-up when I suddenly found myself in Los Angeles, where my life and career would take a positive turn. The day I arrived, however, couldn't have been more tragic. It was September 11, 2001, and the terror attacks that took place on the East Coast that morning overshadowed any excitement. Little did I know at that time, but America would soon become my home.

"In Harm's Way" is the story of my life to date, from conducting operations against the IRA to being part of an unofficial smuggling operation in Sarajevo during the Balkans War. It was an operation that helped save hundreds of lives. I was wrongly accused by some in the international media of kidnapping a baby from Africa for a celebrity. I've been shot at, had a bounty put on my head in Iraq, lost good friends, and protected some of the biggest names in the world—and all whilst traveling across close to one hundred countries. When it came to venturing into harm's way and protecting those I worked with, as well as myself, I entered into a completely different psychological space. Whether it be on the streets of South Armagh, in the deserts of Iraq, or roaming around Moscow, Bogota or Sao Paulo whilst protecting a high-profile figure, the threats were ever-real and the risks huge. Nonetheless, at all times, I was fully switched on from the moment I landed in whichever country.

Throughout my career both in the military and the private sector—notably, careers that have spanned almost thirty years—I have witnessed a lot of good and bad, but I've also learned a great deal, both from those I served with and those I worked for. For that reason, this book has a focus on leadership and motivation lessons from the battlefield to the boardroom. So, if you're looking to find that inner belief that you may have struggled with in the past, or if it can help you to develop a more positive mindset, then this might be ideal for you. You can decide. What this is not, however, is a tell-all book. I have no interest in penning details about the personal or business lives of those I went on to work with and who would entrust their personal security, safety or business dealings with me. What I'm not going to do is see all the hard work I've put in to date lead me into tarnishing my own reputation. Besides, I've enjoyed and respected all who I've worked with, and felt the same in return. If I didn't, I wouldn't have worked with them.

With that said, however, I do discuss my work with Madonna, specifically our time together in Malawi. Given the media exposure and stories that were released during and following our visits, I simply want to set the record straight, but in no way does it compromise security or disclose secrets.

This is my story.

PREFACE

IT WAS GRIM AND bitterly cold, and soldiers nearby were carrying AK-47s while suspicious-looking characters, dressed in long macs, lurked nearby watching our every move. I suddenly felt as though I was immersed in an old Soviet Union war movie, but reality soon kicked in. This was no movie. It was as real as it gets. This was Sarajevo, Bosnia.

We could have been forgiven for not delivering pleasantries as we stepped out of our two armored Range Rovers. Serbian warlord Radovan Karadzic walked towards us, surrounded by his monstrous bodyguards, each with a hand on their hip pistols. I had no doubt they'd be quick to use them should a threat appear against their boss. We had a boss, too, and pistols, and Heckler and Koch MP5s. We, too, were prepared to use them. We were well and truly in harm's way, positioned in the heart of a brutal and gruesome warzone. It looked, smelled and felt every bit the part.

Bosnia, in the summer, was pretty grim, but during the wintertime it took the piss. Out on the ground, I would often cast a thought to the warmth and comfort of The Gables pub in Middlesbrough, an old hangout in my hometown, or the delightfully smelling kitchen of my mum's on a Sunday afternoon as she cooked a roast. All of that was a far cry from where I was now. It was close to Christmas, but there were no festivities here. Instead, a high-level meeting was taking place at a hotel in the remote mountain village of Pale, eleven miles south-east of Sarajevo.

On one side of the table were the leadership of the Serbian government and military, responsible for the killings of thousands through military and genocidal action during the Balkans War. On the other was one of the most highly decorated and respected British Army officers, General Sir Michael Rose, accompanied by his key advisors.

General Rose commanded a great deal of respect, both prior to and during his current role as the head of the United Nations Military Protection Force in the Balkans. As the former Commanding Officer of the Special Air Service, as well as 'Director of Special Forces', he'd had a career to be admired, and once I started working with him, I found that he backed up everything he said. He was a well-spoken leader, a General who cared about people, but he also took no shit, no matter who sat opposite him. It was just one of the traits in him that I would grow to admire.

The drive to the Panorama Hotel had taken us out of the city and up into the mountains, passing the many Serb trenches dug in along the way. We were familiar with the drive and hotel—we'd been a number of times since being in theatre—but we always maintained a high degree of vigilance in the event of the *What if*, knowing it could come at any time and from either side of the divide. With the bitterly cold conditions and roads deep in snow, we cautiously made our way up the mountain and past soldiers, sat huddled around small fires drinking hot coffee—or, most likely, their preferred drink of Slivovitz, a fruit brandy made from damson plums, produced in Central and Eastern Europe. We all tried it once but found it to be far from desirable. It seemed that every one of them smoked; rarely ever would you see any one of them without a cigarette hanging from their mouths—and that applied to the men and the women. Many seemed to be young teens—way too young to be out in the cold weather, let alone fighting a war.

Now and again, one or more of the soldiers would move out away from their little encampment and fire off a mortar or two down below into the Muslim stronghold. It would never happen when we were in the area, least of all because we were with the most powerful man in Bosnia at the time. Rose wasn't their boss, but he had the authority to drop a bomb and take out a position, and all sides in the war knew it, too. He wasn't afraid to do so, and I'd witnessed him more than once make the call, soon followed by the sound of a couple of jets on the radio flying in low and fast to take out a position that had violated the 'Demilitarized Zone' or carried out something against the rule book. It was a common occurrence.

While General Rose was impressively dedicated to establishing peace in The Balkans, to help him achieve that safely, he was protected by a small team of shady looking men, all of whom did everything with the utmost professionalism. It was a team I became a part of and one that fast-tracked me from boy to man. Given the environment I was in and the team I was a part of, there was no room for error and no place for bullshit. If I'd have delivered either, I'd have been shipped back to England in a heartbeat, probably after being filled in first.

Needless to say, I didn't get filled in, but what I did get from working with the General and this particular team was an experience that would never ever be forgotten. We were involved in, and subsequently witness to, things that would break most people, both mentally and physically. It was an emotional rollercoaster of a ride in a war zone that was sickening yet rewarding. I became mentally strong based on the things I saw—

death, poverty and extreme destruction. I was involved in an unofficial operation that smuggled people out of their hell. That operation became known as 'Schindler's List' and is one that helped hundreds of people. I was twenty-one years old, working in a war zone, doing things I had never imagined doing, and working with some of the finest soldiers in the British Army. I was surrounded by leaders—and it's *those* leaders that gave me a solid platform during my time in Bosnia and for the years that have passed since our time together.

This time gave me the ability to grow as a person, as well as in my role as a soldier, and working with this highly trained close protection team gave me an insight into that role. I studied each team member, listened, learned and asked questions, and we trained and socialized together. We witnessed devastating sorrow, sadness, death and destruction, but through it all, we stuck together and helped others. And although this was unintentional, in most parts, it helped us. I played my part in working with them to protect the General and each other. It was a team that truly had each other's back. Given the threats we faced daily, it was the only way it could be.

STEPPING OUT OF
THE COMFORT ZONE

I KNEW AT A young age that my path would have me moving away from home, and as I got closer to the required age for military service, I also knew I'd not come back a quitter once I'd taken the steps to join. I wasn't doing great in school, but it hadn't been helped that I'd already checked out mentally halfway through my last year.

I'd been at Newlands FCJ, a Catholic school for boys and girls, for the past few years and was preparing for my final exams. I'd spent the previous couple of weeks studying for a Religious Education exam—why, I've no idea—but found myself instead thinking of the brochures I'd picked up from the Army Careers Office. Think of that scenario for a second: I was studying for something I had absolutely no interest in, and all while being side-tracked with something that I had complete interest in. My head and my heart were into joining the military, and so I learned how to chase my own dreams, despite being such a young age. I didn't bounce my thoughts off anyone to get feedback; I simply went with my gut instincts and, because that worked for me, I've been able to carry it through my adult years with confidence.

I have to admit, though; the British Army do a great job with their marketing. As a young fifteen-year-old, I was completely enthralled by the pictures, from jungle operations to ceremonial parades, the intense fitness training to white sandy beaches. Ah, yes, the beaches... I'm sure they include those in all their marketing to capture the imagination of youngsters like me.

Religious Education didn't have much of a chance once I had those brochures in my hands. It had been my introduction to the Infantry. *I'll have some of that!* I had thought to myself as I turned the last page and hid the stack of brochures under my bed.

It had been a warm sunny day when I nervously entered the Armed Forces Careers Office on Albert Road in Middlesbrough, my hometown, in the north-east of England. I'd walked by the office many times before, whenever I was in town, but the last few times were with the intent of joining the Army—or certainly with the intent of finding out more information. Struggling to find the courage to go in and speak with one of the recruiters, I'd bypass each time and continue on. Now, however, I'd decided. I was going in. I was determined more than any other time, and my anticipation was getting too much. Besides, I just wanted to become a soldier. I had no idea what it would take to get there, but I was eager to find out and prepared for the challenge ahead.

A low-pitched bell sounded as I pushed the door. I walked inside before taking a seat, where chairs ran along the nearby wall.

'With you in a minute, lad,' came a voice from one of the four desks, where each had a teenager similar in age to me, speaking with a uniformed recruiter on the other side. I tried listening in on the conversation taking place with those sat at the desk closest to me, but it was no use. I didn't know what to expect at all, and so I sat nervously waiting for my turn. I could have walked right there and then, but I'm so glad I didn't. I knew how many times I'd passed by the place before actually walking in, and I didn't quite fancy going through all that again. Once I sat down, however, I felt quite relaxed, actually; it seemed like a whole different world—one I was keen to explore further. And I could feel it: my military adventure had begun.

Ten minutes passed before I was called forward to join one of the recruiters at the desk. He was a Sergeant from the Green Howards Regiment.

'Okay, take a seat,' he told me. 'What can we do for you then?' He placed both of his hands on his head to adjust his beret.

'Yeah I'm interested in joining the Infantry,' I said.

I had no clue what to call him. I didn't know anything about military rank just yet, and so I was caught between 'mate', 'pal' and 'fella', but I kept it straight to the point with nothing added to the end of my statement. I didn't quite fancy being launched through the wall for showing such disrespect. So, even at an early age and without any military discipline, I started to understand respect and thought it through. It was far more appropriate for me to play it safe than to address him as any of the above.

For the next forty-five minutes, we chatted about everything Army; what it was like, the different jobs and various regiments, as well as the pay and the travel, which I later learned was used often as a selling tool to young lads like me, with great effect. From a tough council estate to white sandy beaches... 'Yes, okay, let me think about that and get back to you!' Don't get me wrong: I'm very proud of where I'm from and happy with the way I was raised but, no disrespect to the north-east of England, Redcar it was not in those brochures. I wanted a challenge and some travel, and so I went in search of it—helped, of course, by those beaches.

I had plenty of questions for the recruiter, and as I prepared to leave, I was handed a bunch of flyers and brochures to take away with me.

And that was it. That was the start of it all. I didn't get my arm twisted into joining a specific regiment, though I knew that the Green Howards recruited heavily from my area. It had just been a good chat with a recruiter who answered the list of questions I'd prepared. Having been in the office and learning more about the Army, I left with even more enthusiasm for pursuing my goal. It was all on me from that point forward, I realized, and I was determined to follow through with chasing my dream of becoming a soldier.

I was penciled in for an aptitude test that was scheduled to take place in October. This meant I had a number of weeks to study and get some fitness under my belt. The test was set to measure suitability for the wide range of roles available in the British Army, just like it would with the Royal Navy and Royal Air Force. If a candidate knows what part of the Army they want to go into, they may have a specific role in mind. The outcome of the aptitude test would dictate whether or not they'd be permitted to progress their application for that role. Alternatively, if they didn't have a role in mind, their specific aptitude test result would provide them with a list of roles for which they would be deemed suitable.

In essence, therefore, the test had two purposes: it filtered out unsuitable candidates and then aligned suitable ones with their most appropriate roles within the Army, Navy or Air Force.

I hadn't really thought much beyond going into the Armed Forces Careers Office and then studying for the aptitude test, but it was a damn sight more exciting than studying for Religious Education. I just wasn't overjoyed that it would be a number of weeks away before I could even take the test. I spent some time beforehand to look up everything about my chosen three choices that I'd need to provide.

The famed Paras had been heavily involved in The Falklands War in 1982. I'd seen them on television jumping out of planes, and they had a big reputation with a very tough basic training course. The Royal Marines' training matched that of the Paras and also had a great reputation as a strong fighting force. Then there was the Guards Division, made up of the Coldstream, Scots, Welsh, Irish and Grenadier Guards. I felt comfortable that I'd get into at least one of the three, but I really had no idea. What I did know, however, was that, if selected for any of them, it would be tough as hell and I needed to be ready.

A few weeks before taking the test, big developments had been coming out of the Middle East. Iraqi troops, under the dictatorship of Saddam Hussein, invaded Kuwait; British and American troops were placed on standby to deploy to the region as diplomatic relations were seemingly breaking down at a rapid pace. Military intervention was becoming a reality.

Before taking the aptitude test, I had to inform my parents of my intention to join the Army, but I wasn't seeking their approval. The Army didn't see it like that, though, and so there would need to be signatures with me being under eighteen. I wasn't overly concerned about letting either of my parents know what I was planning to do: I was sure my dad would be fine with it as he was in the Territorial Army; my mum, however, I wasn't too sure about. I spoke with my uncle Martin but, outside of those three, I couldn't have cared less what anyone else thought. I was preparing for a bombardment coming my way from one of my nanas, who was keen for me to go to college, but me doing that was never going to happen. I knew at a young age what would be a good fit for me—and college was nowhere even close to making an appearance on my wish list!

When the test day finally arrived, I caught the bus and made my way to the town centre. I felt fit and was dressed in smart Farrah trousers, even if they were two inches too short. My shirt had been neatly pressed, and I thought I looked great. In reality, however, I looked like a bag of shit. There were other candidates already there when I arrived at the office—males and females of a similar age, who were taking the same test. I was to thankfully find that I wasn't the only one looking like a bag of shit, however, and so I felt somewhat at ease immediately. I wasn't nervous, and actually felt full of confidence that I'd get a decent score, but as I sat down at the small desk, I couldn't help thinking of the *What if I fail?* scenario. I'd built it up in my head for the past number of weeks so much that I hadn't thought of being rejected until this point.

Thankfully, my confidence outweighed my fear as I turned the page to begin. It was time to focus on my first military-related task: passing the test. There was complete silence throughout, with not one of us daring to speak or even sniff out loud as a couple of the recruiters paced around in their crisp green uniforms and big black boots, looking down at us. They instilled fear into us from the get-go, yet we were all there because we wanted to be a part of their world, whatever that entailed. After an hour, a few people held up their hands to show that they'd finished, and I soon followed.

'If you pass, what do you want to do?' asked one of the recruiters as he picked up my papers.

I gave him the Parachute Regiment, Royal Marines and The Guards in that order. I didn't have much interest in the latter, but one of the other applicants, George, told me 'The Second Battalion are off to Kenya for an exercise next year'. *Kenya,* I'd thought to myself. *I wouldn't mind that,* but I had no idea how he knew.

I waited impatiently for a couple of weeks before my acceptance letter arrived, which gave me two dates: one was to take the Oath of Allegiance; the other was my joining date, which was set for January. I'd made it in, and I was chuffed to bits. I had just less than three months to work on my fitness, though I was feeling pretty good about the levels I was achieving. I'd been covering some long hours, pounding up and down Roseberry Topping, as well as the Cleveland Hills not far from my home. They were both wonderful landmarks and excellent places for me to get my head into training hard.

I'd fill up my backpack with food and water, and make my way through various distances, setting myself challenges along the way. The terrain was rough, and the weather was grim; it was ideal preparation for the intense times ahead. It was exciting and I was enjoying it, especially with the potential for war with Iraq, though it wouldn't have been filling my parents with deep joy, I was sure of that. Even so, I put everything into my build-up training to prepare myself as best I could.

It was still dark as I made my way to Darlington train station on the morning of January 14, 1991. I was heading down to London, before making my way on the tube over to Waterloo Station. From there, I'd take another train to Brookwood in Surrey.

George, who had taken the aptitude test at the same time as me, was also joining the same regiment, and so we traveled down together. We were heading to Pirbright Camp to start basic training for Her Majesty's Coldstream Regiment of Foot Guards. They were known officially as 'The Coldstream Guards', notably a regiment of the British Army that formed part of the Household Division within the Infantry.

Despite giving my choices of the Paras first, Royal Marines second and Guards third, it was the latter I would be joining, dependant, of course, on me successfully completing basic training. It had been the trip to Kenya that had swayed it, but the Coldstream Guards came with a great reputation, just like the others.

After almost six months of doing my own build-up training, I was about to embark on forty-three weeks of pure hell. I was ready to attack it and win irrespective of the challenges ahead. I knew it wasn't going to be a walk in the park—if I thought that then I'd have stayed at home in my comfort zone, but I'd wanted out of that. I wanted to take on a challenge and, for me, I could think of no greater one. I was ready to go and give it all I had to become a trained soldier.

We stepped off the warm train at Brookwood and out into the cold January air. It was freezing out as we lugged our bags towards the parking lot, where we spotted a waiting mini-bus.

There were lads of a similar age to us hanging around it as we approached; some smoking and going through the motions of keeping warm as they rubbed their hands together or by jumping up and down. The driver, who was dressed in Army fatigues, stood to the side of the van and kept glancing down at his clipboard, ticking off names. "Jackson!" he shouted. "Where's Jackson?" he boomed a second time, before turning to see a young ginger lad running towards him from the train platform.

It may have been worth pointing out to him that none of us actually knew who Jackson was, but I thought I'd let someone else mention it, which, of course, nobody did.

"Easton!" he boomed again.

A Scottish voice replied, "Here, Corporal!".

"Nye, *yes*, Corporal!" came the response. "Burton!"

"Yes, Corporal," I replied.

"Chesters!"

"Here, Corporal!" came the shout from George.

"Right, on the bus and let's go!" he said, placing his clipboard on the centre console. "Time to visit the pleasure dome," he said out loud, turning left, heading out of the station and onto the main road.

There was complete silence from the back as the seven of us sat with a feeling of the unknown sweeping across us all. We were heading to the famed and feared Guards Depot.

MILITARY CHECKPOINT AHEAD in big bold letters was the sign I saw that told me we were arriving.

The drive had seemed to drag on for miles when, in fact, it had only taken five or so minutes from the train station to Pirbright Camp. We pulled over to the right before the checkpoint and were told to get our gear and report to the Guard Room, which was off to the side of the main gate. I scanned my surroundings as briefly as I could; it looked almost like a prison camp, what with the high fences and barbed wire that ran along the top of them. Two armed sentries in combat clothing casually stood guard at the main gate and chatted with one another, looking us all up and down. I'm sure I wasn't the only one to wish we could be fast-tracked and in their position as trained soldiers, but no; even then I'd realized there would be a lot of pain to get through first.

Closed circuit television cameras positioned at the end of the fence line and on high poles were scanning the area, while we watched a platoon of recruits in training being bounced around the parade square just up from the guard room. The place looked grim and miserable, but it would hopefully be my home for the next forty-three weeks. If it wasn't, that could only mean one thing: that I'd have failed—and I couldn't allow that. I wanted to be there, and it was something I'd signed up for. It wasn't the first or last time that I reminded myself that nobody had forced me to be there—nobody other than myself. I grabbed my bag and again looked over at the two soldiers manning the main gate. "I will not leave until I succeed," I said to myself as I turned to walk to the guard room, my big heavy bag over my shoulder. It was Day One and I had three hundred to go, but I felt complete confidence that I'd get the job done.

Here's the deal. What worked for me was that I was already dialed in to succeeding before I even began basic training. I hadn't even arrived at my accommodation block and I had no idea of the challenges that would present themselves, or even how difficult basic training would be, so you might wonder why I was so confident that I'd succeed in one the world's most challenging and demanding military training courses. The answer is simple.

Doubt. It was the doubt that was directed at me from some of those at home. It was the bets made against me and my ability to succeed and the voices of those who thought I wouldn't last five minutes—and family can be included in that, too. "He'll be back before you know it," was one comment I'd overheard. It was that doubt that I used to switch from one mindset with home comforts, a cozy bed and three good meals a day—a comfort zone, basically—to another that couldn't be more opposite in my goal of becoming a highly trained and professional soldier.

I'd bounced around different homes as a kid—my mum's, my dad's, my nana's and my aunties'. It had become a bit of a round robin-type situation. I'd had little success at school, and my mates just wanted to steal cars or be out and about on the streets at night; drinking, taking drugs, causing havoc. I'd left to make something of myself.

Doubt? Fuck off! All of those doubters were my biggest motivation when I boarded that train in Darlington. Maybe if I'd have stayed in that comfort zone I'd have been sent away to a young offenders' home, just like so many others of a similar age from my hometown. That's what happens when people doubt you, which was most definitely the case when I left home. It was that doubt that enabled me to attack everything with sheer determination, utilizing everything put in front of me from the point I arrived at Pirbright Camp, with each day pushing me more and more to position myself as far as possible from the doubters' predictions. I can hand-on-heart say, I really didn't care how hard it would be because I was ready for it. You keep doubting and I'll keep upping my game—*that* was my attitude, and I made sure I drilled it into myself always.

Don't confuse that with me feeling like I had to prove myself to others as I'm a firm believer that nobody should have to do that. But you can take people's negativity, whether directly or indirectly geared towards you, and turn it into something positive to motivate yourself. That's what I did. I was simply proving things to myself in that I knew I had something in me when I first thought of going in the Army, way before anyone knew that I was joining. I just used that negativity and turned it into positivity to push myself to succeed in my goal of becoming a soldier. Quite simply, failure just wasn't an option.

I joined the other recruits at the Guard Room and gave my name to the soldier who sat behind the window before being screamed at by some fussy Corporal in the background for not standing to attention. The Regimental Police Sergeant then stepped outside and, clearly unimpressed by our arrival, went on to make an unnecessary spectacle. He yelled and screamed like a lunatic over what seemed like nothing. *They don't hang about here*, I thought. We were quickly hustled to what was going to be our accommodation block for the next eleven months, and as we arrived, we found that other recruits who were part of our intake were already there. I figured that most of them would be from the South of England and, with a closer commute, would have arrived earlier on in the morning. For people like me coming from the north, as well as those from Scotland and Wales, we had turned up late-morning, as per our joining instructions.

I spotted a free bed space over in the corner and laid claim to it by putting my bags down on the floor next to the bed. It wasn't made up nor did I see any nice fluffy pillows or a cozy duvet; instead, there were two crisp white sheets sitting on top of a thin furry-looking blanket, with a single pillow laid at the head of an uncomfortable looking green mattress. I had a suspicion that we wouldn't be spending too much time in our beds over the coming months, and what time we would get would most likely be interrupted during the nights. There was a small bed space locker, as well as a single tall one in each person's domain, with a small light above each bed. We'd be expected to keep our area immaculately clean at all times, with shared responsibility for the communal areas.

In total, we had fifty-four recruits as part of the January intake, and we were all divided across two floors of the accommodation block. I glanced around some of the bed spaces and found that many of the lads were doing the same thing; unpacking, placing little pictures of their loved ones somewhere visible, and putting away their personal items in the small bedside lockers. There were small groups talking to one another, doing that whole getting-to-know-each-other thing, their eyes wandering and weighing up the competition.

I sensed that the mindset with some of them was that this would be a contest, but I knew that the smartest approach would be to make sure that the only battle for me would be with myself. On the train down, I'd decided not to get into the whole 'I'm here to make friends' routine. I knew the best strategy was to avoid the loud mouths, and there were a number of them who were vying for first place in that department. If they kept up that gobshite approach, they'd only flag themselves to the instructors for negative reasons—and I certainly didn't want any part of that. My plan was to isolate myself, to be the grey man; quiet, unnoticed, and focused only on what was important: passing basic training.

There were others sat on their beds who seemed to be taking in the shock of being away from home. I wasn't sure how long they'd last, looking at a few of them. I sensed they were about to have a breakdown, and all they were doing was unpacking their gear at that point. I couldn't help thinking: *but it's only Day One.* I felt for them in a way, but basic training was designed to not just turn us into men, but highly trained soldiers with the ability to kill in a split second. I knew—there wouldn't be any molly coddling around the place.

My thoughts were validated when the Chief Instructor entered the block and gathered everyone together. "You aren't here to make friends, and we aren't here to put our arms around you and tell you how special you are," he said, looking around at the wide-eyed bunch of young lads, including me. Towards the end of his speech, he introduced his instructors and then ended with one notable and sharp statement, "You all wanted to be here. We didn't ask you to be. If you want it, you'll find a way. If you don't, you'll find an excuse. Knuckle down and either fit in or fuck off."

We all went back to our bed spaces to finish sorting our gear out, trying as best as we could to prepare ourselves for the unknown.

Despite wanting to be the grey man, it was also just as important to build up a bit of a rapport with the rest of the recruits. We'd be relying heavily on each other and no doubt going through a hell of a lot of emotions and pain—those of us who would stick it out, anyway. The minute you stand out for being too quiet or not mixing with others in such an environment, that's when you could find yourself experiencing issues down the road, both with other recruits and the instructors. Egos and bullshit would soon be found out by everyone, just like they would be in any line of work. You need to find the right balance of slotting in and not standing out through being full of yourself, over-confident, too quiet or too gobby.

If you work in a company or corporate environment, you'll know how important teamwork is if you and the company are to succeed. You may all be working well to reach your department goals and then a new hire is brought in to work as part of your team. That new hire has a responsibility to be job-productive and to build positive relationships with everyone, but you also all have a responsibility to make them feel welcome and to get them up to speed on work-related projects. After all, everybody is new once, and being made to feel welcome is something that helps greatly. It's all part of the company on-boarding process; getting up to speed to get the job done. If done right, unity and results continue to grow for the benefit of the department and company. But if it's not done right—whether that's because the new hire can't settle, is too quiet or too gobby, is an under-achiever, thinks they know it all, or simply isn't liked—then animosity will set in, which, in no uncertain terms, means their cards are marked.

It's the same in the military: you've got to integrate and rely on one another if you are to achieve success, with teamwork a huge, critical aspect of that.

I knew instinctively: you can only get away with being a lone wolf for so long before your cards are marked. It's okay to be the very best you can be, but you need to do so by being a team player as well.

The first few days after arriving were spent with attending lectures on Army life, the principles and traditions, taking basic fitness tests, having our medicals done, as well as getting ourselves acquainted with the large camp. We had to know where the gym was located, the education wing, drill squares, cookhouse, assault courses, as well as the many live fire ranges. If any of us thought it would be a nice and easy first few days, we were wrong. Given the massive size of the camp, it only gave the instructors more space to bounce us around.

There were plenty of other accommodation blocks that housed a number of separate intakes, most of whom were well ahead of us in terms of training advancement. We were mesmerized as we watched the recruits march around, all in-sync, looking sharp, while us lot would fall in line like a rabble of shit, told to us by the instructors at every opportunity. Often, we'd hear a scream of "Don't look at them, you horrible fuckers!", which would come from the instructor marching behind his platoon. We could never help ourselves from sneaking another look, though. The idea, although never officially told, was for the instructors to beat us down as far as they could, both physically and mentally. Then, slowly but surely, over the course of our training, we'd be built back up as trained soldiers. That was the hope for most of us, anyway.

Only three days into our arrival at the Guards Depot, developments in Iraq were heightening, and in the little spare time we had during the evenings, we were all glued to the television screens in the "NAAFI"—a place we could sometimes go to relax in the evening, albeit only for a short amount of time. Initially, a massive air assault descended upon Iraq on January 17, 1991. We watched with wide eyes as it all unfolded on the screens before us, with some 110,000 individual allied missions flown between then and February 24. Under the control of the American General, Norman Schwarzkopf, United States and Allied forces, then began what was to be known around the world as "Operation Desert Storm", with more than two hundred thousand troops attacking Iraqi Forces in Kuwait—which Iraq had invaded—as well as throughout Iraq itself. This was, without doubt something in which we were all interested—well, most of us anyway—and it added an extra buzz to everything we were doing and learning in training.

The instructors milked it for all it was worth, too. The following afternoon, they came into the block, gathered us all together, and told us that our training was to be sped up as we would be deploying to the war zone. We all looked at each other like goons at the thought of skipping what was fast becoming grueling training in order to potentially head to war. Most of us would have swapped it right there and then, and some of the lads immediately shot over to the NAAFI to call their girlfriends and families to let them know they were going to be heroes and take on Saddam Hussein. We'd only just learned how to tie our boots properly, and some of us were getting a bit suspicious, proven so the following morning when we mustered for a drill lesson to be told that it had been a load of crap. The relief from some was clear.

We were soon well into our training and starting to understand the fieldcraft skills of the professional soldier. It was enjoyable but hard work, too. The days were long, and the sleep was little, but it was required in order to get us to fully understand the basic principles. We couldn't progress until we had down what we were being taught, and so we'd run through something and then run it again and again until the instructors knew we understood it. Army basic training is the framework upon which all-regular Infantry training is based, and it equips all trainees with the Infantry Special to Arms skills needed to operate in a rifle platoon.

Upon completion of basic training and for those that "passed out"—the term given to the completion of basic training—we would possess the fitness, knowledge and skills allowing us to join an Infantry Battalion ready to deploy on operations anywhere in the world, but that seemed a long way off for all of us.

It was difficult to establish any type of routine in the early weeks. There were, of course, the usual and expected stress tests from instructors, which were difficult to adjust to initially. Getting woken up at three in the morning for physical training or getting our lockers trashed all over the floor seemed to be a common occurrence—and, I can imagine, a whole load of fun for those carrying it out. All it was doing was pissing us off, but that was the general idea; test us and push us to our limits when we were tired to see who would snap. Some did and, as expected, they were soon gone.

We were also getting constantly "beasted", and no matter our performance, it would come at some point through the day or night, quite often multiple times. We'd be told to muster outside, only to be bounced around in double-quick time, back and forth, until we were exhausted. An alternative would witness us being dragged out on a long run before being made to crawl through muddy bogs in the pouring rain. It was all designed with one clear objective in mind: to grind us down quickly. It worked well. It was annoying, yes, but it was teaching us discipline. After all, if you could put up with this shit, you could tolerate most things once you got used to them, but it would take some time.

We were also becoming way too familiar with "the sand hill" located at the top end of the camp, near the forest plateaus. *What is it?* you might wonder. The clue's in the name, and it was a real killer. So much so that, halfway through our training, the Camp Commandant placed it out of bounds, with all instructors issued with warning orders not to have us face it. Unfortunately, however, we would have plenty of encounters with it before that happened.

The sand hill was a steep hill made up of soft sand, offering nothing but excruciating pain for those running up and down it. When you had to do it two or three times, complete with a heavy backpack pulling on your shoulders, it was the most unpleasant thing you can imagine. Once was always enough, but when the shout came that the last man would do it again, you had an incentive to beast yourself up and down it. Each time, we'd be marching back from the nearby forest plateau from doing fieldcraft or returning from one of the ranges, and then we'd hear a shout of "Get it together or it's the sand hill!" Our marching always seemed to improve when we were in close proximity.

Throughout the year, we'd all noticed a steady rise in our fitness, mainly thanks to those lovely beastings on the hill, but also through the number of combat fitness tests we'd been doing. They were more commonly known as a CFT. Once I got a couple of these out of the way, I actually loved them, and although we'd get one every few weeks or so, I felt myself improving each time. The CFT is designed to assess soldiers' lower and upper body strength and endurance and involves a fast-paced march in full combat gear, including personal weapon, across rough terrain and roads. The exact weight of the equipment carried depended on the type of unit; for the Infantry, however, it was 25kg, and all whilst covering a distance of eight miles in less than two hours. I was learning to push myself beyond what seemed to be possible and started to look forward to each one, but they weren't to be taken lightly. Weather, health, the terrain, and who was running it were all important factors in determining how well you did.

As the months went on, we were adjusting to life as trainee soldiers, but there were times when some things incorporated as part of our training simply went way too far, and although a lot of it was designed to instill discipline and accordingly aid our fitness, we could have done without some of it. Many of us in the platoon all had the same mindset and we'd deal with it collectively, but there were others who were not doing so well, both as a result of their fitness levels and with not being able to handle the amount of "beastings" we were taking. Quite often, at the end of a tough day, we'd hear of someone throwing in the towel for whatever reason.

I always found that tough, as that particular individual might have aspired to be a soldier but just couldn't handle it. We aren't all cut out for certain things in life, but if it's something you've dreamt of and are passionate about, surely, you've got to give it all you've got as you might only ever get one chance. Obviously, if you're unhappy in something and need to move on to better yourself, then that's what you must do, which some of the recruits in our platoon decided upon, but don't do that if it's something you've longed for and what you've set your heart on succeeding in, even if there are challenges that truly test you. Yes, we were going through a grueling training course, but over the years since then I've met a number of people who have given up too easily, in my opinion, in a job they'd always wanted to do. With the right mindset, anyone can overcome challenges, both physical and mental, as me and others were doing throughout our training.

We may have struggled in certain things and we may have been close to tears on many occasions, but by God we were going to stick it out because we wanted to succeed as soldiers. People from all walks of life and careers have tough days, but if you recalibrate your mindset and go again the next day, keeping in mind a new goal and adopting a fresh attitude, you're winning, you're progressing. Once you let things get to you, that can eat away at your thought process and sour both your confidence and ability. You might think it's easier said than done, but if you train your mind to deal with and overcome the tough days, you become stronger as an individual and find yourself adapting better to dealing with the shit. Physically tough, you can train; mentally tough, you can learn. If you believe in it, then go for it. Yes, it can still be tough, but you are better preparing yourself to take things on the chin whilst still making forward progress. Remember, you wanted it, so go out there and make it work for you.

Between January and December of that year, I had a tough day every single day. It was horrible, miserable and challenging, but yet, it was so rewarding because I put my all into it. I got through it not because I was the most physically fit guy but because I quickly learnt to have the mindset required in order to allow me to succeed, to keep pushing me through the tough moments. I was dialed into succeeding, and every day I woke at some stupid hour and said, "I'm winning today, let's have it". I was tired, aching, full of cuts most of the time, and I was pissed off. I could have taken the easy option and quit—others did, so why not me—but resilience and the will to become a soldier were my main factors. Of course, both were driven by that doubt from others that I talked about earlier.

"If you want it, you'll find a way. If you don't, you'll find an excuse," the Chief Instructor said on that very first day. I let that resonate with me every single day going forward.

Basic training was no doubt hard, but I'd grown to become extremely fit and, as much as the instructors were trying to pick the pace up when we were out running around, a few of us were matching them. Soon enough, though, we were pulled in to see the platoon staff and told that they wanted to see us helping others within the group as they thought we weren't team players. It wasn't that we were doing anything wrong; they just wanted to see if we had any leadership skills. It was never easy seeing other people struggle, but often the emphasis had been more on individual effort than a team one, and this had been drilled into us in sometimes confusing ways—"Help him out!" and then "Leave him alone!" were frequent shouts.

I went through basic training at a time when the Army hadn't taken a more relaxed approach to recruit training. It was basically no holds barred and, looking back, I'd have preferred it that way. If you couldn't get over a wall on the assault course, you weren't told to take a seat and have a cup of tea, but you weren't beaten up either. Yes, there were a few slaps and punches dished out if you screwed up or gobbed off, but I felt that it was a fine mix of constructive punishment.

Standing in front of your locker and feeling a right fist pummel your chest for the stupidest of things was a common occurrence as it was out in the field. It was par for the course. It wouldn't happen now as times, people, and policies have changed—you'd be straight on the front page of the Daily Mail being exposed as a bully, your Army career over and with a threat of a prison stretch, not to mention a lawyer chasing you down as their client would be traumatized, no doubt.

There is no need for bullies, but we were being trained to be professional soldiers—people who may need to kill and, most likely, in a split second, too. It wasn't a game and we weren't training to be diplomats. We knew what we'd signed up for.

As I said, however, some things would often get out of hand. This would be the case when some of the instructors went way beyond their boundaries.

One such incident took place when we were away on an exercise and, having had very minimal sleep the night before, our platoon was lining up for some morning scoff, which was to be served to us by the instructors. As we edged closer to receiving our food, one of them would ask "Hard-boiled or scrambled?", referring to how we wanted our eggs, of course. I replied "scrambled", and so the instructor grabbed the hard-boiled egg, wrapped in its shell, and crushed it with his hand before putting it in my mess tin, which was layered with baked beans on the bottom. I couldn't eat it so I threw the mess tin to the ground, told him to forget it, and walked off. It was a shame they were unimpressed by my actions.

I took a gulp of water from my pouch knowing that I'd be needing some in me before the impending "beasting" that I knew would soon follow.

It's okay having a laugh, but food plays a big role in basic training and Army life, and the instructors knew that well before they wasted people's rations. We'd been up most of the night, were freezing cold and wet, and had not had any hot food in us. None of us thought it was funny, especially as you operate at a much lesser level in those conditions. It had been the wrong attitude for me to take, but if they were looking for me to snap then it worked, and I gladly accepted the beasting that followed.

I was later spoken to about my poor reaction by the Platoon Commander, who assured me that, if I hadn't been a good recruit with a sound training record, they'd be sending me back to a remedial platoon—more commonly known as "back squadded"— which could put me back a number of weeks or even months. I could have done without that, but I didn't stand there and beg him to not do it, either. If it had happened, I'd have dealt with it and got my head into it, but thankfully I stayed where I was. My attitude may have been wrong, but I fully stood by the "fuck you" attitude I'd taken when throwing my mess tin to the ground. Could I have handled it differently? Yes, of course, but I handled it in the manner my initial instinct had suggested.

That incident was not an isolated one, however.

Towards the end of our training, we were on our final exercise at the Stanford Training Area, commonly known within the military as The Stanford Battle Area, out near Thetford in Norfolk. It's used as a British Army training area and is approximately 30,000 acres in size. It provides an exceptional variety of terrain for training, but it was during this exercise when another bit of so-called fun from the instructors went way too far. We'd been training hard during the morning before taking a break in a forest area when one of the instructors—who, notably, was a keen golfer—decided to show off his skills to a number of us and tee a ball with a three wood. No problem with that, in itself, but he asked one of the lads to lie down on his back with the tee sticking out of his mouth.

We thought he was joking at first but, as he lined up his club and pulled it back, we soon realized he wasn't. There was a *whoosh* sound and a scream from Gary soon followed. I didn't see the actual strike as I'd turned away, but our attention was immediately focused on Gary, who was rolling around on the ground. He was in extreme pain and needed to go to hospital. We could tell that the instructor involved, as well as the others standing around, knew the severity of the situation. It hadn't been intentional—in fact, the instructor had a good relationship with Gary—but nonetheless, this serves as an example of them trying to be clever. This time, however, it backfired big time.

Given that I'd been the recruit closest to Gary when he was lying down, over the hours to follow, I was kept quiet with the nice treatment; deep down, however, I was fuming. Gary was taken to hospital and, a couple of days later, I spoke to him when he came out. He said it was fine and that he wasn't going to take any action, which we'd expected him to say. It was only "fine", however, because the instructors had spent time with him at the hospital, kissing his backside and getting him onside. Gary was left with a terrible scar running out from the corner of his mouth to his cheekbone. A number of years later, when I bumped into him in Northern Ireland, that scar was still clearly visible.

By the time we approached our passing out parade in December, the number of recruits in our platoon had reduced dramatically from when we'd started earlier on in the year. Starting out with fifty-four back in January, we found ourselves down to twenty-four with just two weeks to go before passing out in front of our families, marking the end of basic training. The number of those that passed out on the day itself totaled eighteen—quite a significant drop over the duration—but there were plenty of reasons for that, and I'm sure the instructors made the right decisions with those it affected. Some were placed into a remedial platoon, whereas others gave up on pursing an Army career altogether, deciding it just wasn't for them.

Was it hard? You bet it was. It was the hardest thing I've ever had to do over a long period of time. I was sixteen years old when I started basic training; seventeen when I passed out. It was brutally gut-wrenching more times than not. I'd experienced aches in my body I thought I'd never recover from, and there were times, despite being fit, where I thought I might not make the end of a run. It was psychologically and physically hard for me to be put through the stresses and strains I had encountered, but I made it through.

Did I ever think of quitting? Not once. It wasn't in my mindset, and it was that mental strength and sheer determination that carried me through the toughest challenges I faced. I was also driven by the doubt from others—their voices resounding in my head from the very beginning. That doubt enabled me to become mentally strong with a mindset of succeeding. You can imagine the sense of fulfilment when I passed out, but I also knew that the real hard work would begin after the holidays.

CHANGE:
ADAPTING AND OVERCOMING

IT'S NEVER EASY GOING from one way of life to another but going from school to being a professional soldier is as big a culture shock as one can make. I needed to adapt to that change as quickly as I could when joining my Battalion. Over the years, I've met a number of people who have expressed their fears when it comes to making or adapting to change, but I've seen the majority come out the other side with a huge degree of confidence and satisfaction, and usually only because they put their mind to it.

It may not necessarily be a new career you are facing that encompasses challenges; rather, it could be anything at all with which you are completely unfamiliar, but you won't settle unless you put 110% into adapting. Not being able to settle into something means you aren't productive, and not being productive means a waste of an opportunity. To a company or a fighting force, such as that which I joined, if you aren't productive, what exactly is the point of you even being there? There is, of course, that new beginning period where you are learning everything you need to know, but some things take a lot longer than others, and so you need to have patience. If you have the right mindset, show enthusiasm, and have a positive attitude, your settling-in period will come a lot sooner than you might expect. *That*'s what I needed to follow. However, it takes some time to adapt—and I was no exception. In order to achieve my goal, I worked on it every day.

When you leave school, a path for many is going to college. I'd chosen not to do that, instead opting for a brutal year-long training course that prepared me for my new life in an Infantry Battalion, where I'd subsequently be enrolled in an alternative form of further education—done differently, of course.

Basic training had been hard work physically, but now the serious side of soldiering would begin. It was sink or swim time. Fit in or fuck off was the mantra, yet again.

I'd had a couple of weeks off for Christmas and took in a couple of Boro games. My aches and pains of the previous twelve months had gone, and I was ready to go to work. I was a trained soldier on paper, but I was a 'new draft' and, at seventeen years old, still had much to learn. On the morning of January 4, 1992, I left home and made my way back to London, ready to join up with the 2nd Battalion Coldstream Guards, who were based at Chelsea Barracks, working primarily in a ceremonial role.

The 1st Battalion were based in Germany and were a mechanized unit, meaning they were doing a lot of work with training and exercises. I was glad to be remaining in England and start Army life in a more familiar environment. I was somewhat excited, although without doubt apprehensive, as I walked through the gates and made my way over to the guardroom.

'Corporal,' I said to the guy in the window, 'I'm reporting to Number One Company.' He told me where I needed to go. I was the only 'new draft' joining the company. George, who had passed out with me, went off to another company but would also be based at Chelsea Barracks.

The company clerk gave me a load of paperwork I needed to complete and told me where I'd find my accommodation; upstairs, where I'd meet the members of my new platoon.

Over the next couple of weeks, I settled into Battalion life and started to do a bit of drill, which I'd never been keen on.

Nonetheless, as a member of the Coldstream Guards, it was a big deal, what with them being part of the Queen's Guard and participating in the Trooping of the Color, which celebrates the Queen's birthday. I'd been issued with my bearskin and tunic, the attire worn for such occasions, and, having tried it on, I realized I looked like a jazzed-up matchstick. I felt uncomfortable with it. I was soon off on my first guard duty at Buckingham Palace but hated the thing; being all glammed up like that, complete with my shiny boots and ceremonial uniform, really didn't appeal to me, although the attention we received from tourists was enjoyable.

For me, there was something about the ceremonial work that left me feeling far from at ease. Others thrived on it. Over the next couple of months, however, I got a few more under my belt—at Windsor Castle, St James's Palace, and the Tower of London—and I actually started to feel okay with it. All I'd needed was that patience I was so lacking, but it wouldn't be long before the enjoyment I was starting to feel had me back to disliking it.

Prior to one of these guard duties, I was part of the 'new guard' that was being inspected by the Adjutant on the parade square of Wellington Barracks. Once the inspection was over with, we'd then march over to Buckingham Palace's forecourt and do a Changing of the Guard in front of the hundreds there watching.

This time, however, they'd be doing it with a man less.

I ended up being locked up by the Adjutant for poor turnout. Captain Tower—I'll never forget his name—looked my uniform up and down, said I looked like a bag of shit, and had me marched off to the guardroom in double-quick time. I figured that every new member of the Battalion went through this, but it reignited my lack of enthusiasm for ceremonial duties. In-between being on guard, I'd be performing various platoon and company training, as well as familiarizing myself with the different weapons used by the Battalion. It was all good stuff, but I was still far from settled, which was showing.

I was becoming familiar with the Tower of London but, on April 10, 2002, my guard duty would be one I'd never forget.

I was resting in the guardroom with a few of the other lads, watching television before making myself a brew and readying for my patrol. My 'stag', the term used for our duty shifts, was going out at eight, and we had the responsibility of patrolling the grounds of the Tower, the famous Royal landmark and home of the Crown Jewels.

Ceremonial uniform was replaced by combat fatigues for the night hours, which was a lot more welcome, but with the first hour passing incident-free, the second hour would be very different.

It was 9.20PM, and as I patrolled along the back of the Tower grounds, skirting the perimeter wall, in a split-second and out of the corner of my eye, I became more alert when a number of the streetlights suddenly went out. Within a few seconds of that, there was an almighty *boom*! I ducked down in shock at the ferocious bang. It had been a deafening, panic-inducing noise. Fear immediately set in, and my teammates were running in and out of the guardroom, picking up ammunition in case the situation warranted it. In those days, British troops protecting Royal residences never carried ammunition in their magazines, despite the ongoing threat from the Irish Republican Army. Some of the guards were sleeping when the explosion occurred, but they soon awoke, no doubt in the same state of panic as their teammates. Myself and those close by me all immediately assumed it was a bomb. The explosion told us, however, that it could also have been gas-related. Nonetheless, with the IRA threat active across mainland Britain, a gas explosion seemed unlikely.

Practically all the streetlights were now out following the explosion; this meant the area was mostly dark throughout, with torchlights giving away the position of my colleagues. Some of the residents who lived in the Tower grounds soon came out to investigate the explosion.

"Stay inside!" came the shout from Jimmy as he pulled his weapon into his shoulder. Suddenly, an alert came over the radio: "Two males running near the East Gate."

We responded immediately, thinking this was it and we were going to get the bad guys. It turned out to be a false alarm. As I looked out across the moat, I was able to get a visual on the Baltic Exchange across the way. There were smoke and flames billowing and the noise of car alarms in the surrounding area.

We soon learned that the explosion had indeed been a bomb and that it was the work of the IRA. It had been the day after the General Election, which witnessed the re-election of John Major of the Conservative Party as Prime Minister. The one-ton bomb had been concealed in a large white truck and consisted of a fertilizer device wrapped with a detonation cord made from 100lb of semtex. The bomb killed three people, injured ninety-one others, and caused significant loss; destroying the Baltic Exchange building and severely damaging surrounding ones. In the coming days, it was estimated that the bomb had caused £800 million worth of damage—£200 million more than the total damage caused by the 10,000 explosions that had occurred during the troubles in Northern Ireland up until that point.

It then became widely known that the IRA had given a telephone warning twenty minutes before the explosion, stating that there was a bomb inside a white Ford transit van, positioned outside the Stock Exchange. These telephone warnings from the IRA were common at the time. The components were developed in South Armagh, shipped from Ireland, and assembled in England. The attack was planned for months and marked a dangerous advance to the British of the IRA's explosives manufacture. It was described as the most powerful bomb to hit London since the Luftwaffe raids of World War II.

A few hours later, at 1:10AM, another similarly large bomb went off in Staples Corner in North London, also causing major damage. Almost a year later, on April 23, 1993, there would also be another bombing in the area at Bishopsgate. Once again, the financial cost was severe, with both of these incidents contributing to the formation of the "Ring of Steel" in the city, protecting it from further terrorism in the future.

It had been a terrifying experience. I knew the IRA were very active with their attacks on various sites on the mainland, in addition to government and military targets, but this had been my first experience of it.

It's easy to show weakness when fear strikes, but this is what we'd trained for, and although I was a young soldier, my instinct told me that it had been a bomb, and when it exploded, it had scared the shit out of me. Army training prepares you for a lot of various scenarios with incidents like this being one of them. In reality, however, it's difficult to train for such an experience, and it can actually be quite traumatizing. Thankfully, I'd been some distance away from the impact zone when it exploded, but, still: when you're in the vicinity of such a large bomb, it's not something you ever want to experience again.

In July, my company would be heading away on exercise to Kenya and, in mind of this, had been rolling out some build-up training beforehand. We had all our inoculations and kit issued for the desert and jungle training, and I was looking forward to it as it would give me a good opportunity to get some solid training in. Prior to going, I'd been moved over to another platoon where most of the other lads were from Middlesbrough. The Platoon Sergeant was also from the Boro, and I was happy to make the transition across. Sergeant Stu Beattie seemed a really down-to-Earth fella, and I was looking forward to training with my new platoon.

The advance party had been at the camp a couple of weeks setting everything up, and so we didn't have much to do when we arrived. We unloaded our stores equipment and did a bit of camp familiarization before having a beer around the campfire. We were set up on a plot of land on the edge of the town of Nanyuki. The camp itself had fencing constructed to keep the locals out while we were accommodated in big Army tents. To our east, there was a stunning view of Mount Kenya, to which we awoke the next morning. We'd be working a round robin over the next five weeks, each of us partaking in range work, with jungle and desert training the main focus. We'd also be carrying out plenty of weapons training, going through medical lessons, map-reading and basically getting drunk every night in town when we weren't away in the field.

My platoon would be doing the range week first, and so we loaded up the vehicles a couple of days in, ensuring plenty of ammo, water and rations, as well as mosquito repellent, before heading out to a place in the desert known as Archers Post, where we'd be based for the next week.

Throughout the training, we were run through various live fire scenarios before moving up to two-man and four-man attacks, which culminated in a platoon attack later on in the week. It was fun to do, and I felt I'd learned a lot from it. After our range week, we went straight into desert training; during this time, a great deal of emphasis was put on the fitness side, and as fit as I felt I was, it was extremely hard going, what with the hot weather. With temperatures reaching almost 49 degrees Celsius, we were loaded up with more than 100lbs of kit, which included mortar equipment. Getting water down our necks was imperative, especially as we'd had a couple of lads go down with dehydration.

One day, we were out patrolling through a desert wadi and the sun was beating down on us. I suddenly heard a *thud* and turned around to see a member of the platoon had dropped to the ground and wasn't moving. If it hadn't been for quick-thinking people, he may not have made it. It was clear he was suffering from severe dehydration. I was told his heart had stopped—such was the seriousness of the situation. A helicopter was called in to take him away to hospital and, thankfully, he was back on his feet within a few days. Following that incident, we would start training before first light and then take a break for a few hours in the day when the heat was at its peak, resuming again when it cooled later on in the day.

Back at the camp in Nanyuki, we found ourselves with plenty of time to socialize in town and make the most of the local tiger beer. The bar owners loved us. We found a decent little place that did a good omelet and fries, which made a wonderful change from the boil-in-the-bag rations we'd been living off in the field. We were all doubtful about the cleanliness of the kitchen of our new-found delight, but we ate the food as if it had been cooked by a Michelin Star chef. The people were friendly, and many of them would often greet us with "Jambo, my friend," with *jambo* Swahili for *hello*. We'd be out and about giving it, "Jambo! Jambo!", thinking we were completely tuned in with the locals. It was good to mix and make friends with them, but we were to fuck that up not long into the trip.

At the camp, we found ourselves taking things a bit too far with some of the locals, who would loiter on the other side of the perimeter fence, hoping to get some freebies. We had what were known as hexi blocks, which help sustain a small fire, and someone thought it would be fun to coat them in chocolate, wrap them up in small plastic wrappers, and throw them over the fence. The locals would scramble to grab them each time one was lobbed over, and we'd watch as the winner opened it up and took a bite out of it. We'd be pissing ourselves with laughter as they realized it was nothing but a chocolate-covered hard, white block. I was caught up in the crowd with taking part, but it was bang out of order looking back at it. As young lads, we could be completely naïve with winning over hearts and minds.

The jungle phase was my first chance to sample jungle warfare training, and it was a real eye-opener. We were flown in by helicopters to a designated area, out by a big river that had been cleared by the three SAS instructors who'd be teaching us. The team was led by Charlie, who was very experienced and who came with many years of jungle operations and training behind him, so we were told. We knew we'd get some excellent training in.

Jungle training can be very difficult, and there were times where we all struggled with it—not only the fitness side of patrolling and dealing with the terrain, but also the obstacles that are, by nature, in the way; the humidity, bugs, wet clothing and sleepless nights. It takes some time to adjust under the canopy. The jungle is one of the few environments where military forces cannot fully bring their sophisticated technology to bear upon an enemy; whether systems such as laser-targeting, global positioning, night vision or communications. Some do not function at all or do so at a much-degraded performance level, and so we were forced to rely more readily on improving our soldiering skills and taking in some good training. Without question, it was very challenging but also very rewarding.

Back in London, following our trip to Kenya, we prepared to head straight into Northern Ireland training, ready for an October tour. I was really looking forward to it. This would offer me the opportunity to do some different training for a place where peace was far from forthcoming. Northern Ireland had been troublesome for years, especially with British troops on the ground. There had been many deaths, not only on the military side but also on either side of the Catholic and Protestant divide. The Catholics didn't want the British there, and what started out as rioting in the late-sixties had subsequently built-up to attacks on one another before the British Army was then sent over to have a presence on the ground. The IRA then became prominent, with the Army regularly targeted and attacked. Tensions were high and we were told that the threat was very real. We didn't doubt it for a second.

In preparation, we carried out a lot of range work and sat in on a number of lectures on the law about what we could and couldn't do. We conducted patrol exercises across various parts of Salisbury Plain before heading to the Northern Ireland training facility in Lydd and Hythe on the south coast of England to further our training. There, we were able to run different scenarios that we might face in the mock town that had been built especially for the

British Army units deploying over the water. It offered us real-world training with other members of the Army, who made up an opposition force and who lived in the houses during our training period. They played the role of members of the IRA, as well as the general public, and would realiztically put up resistance to our presence there. It was excellent training and it prepared us well for our tour.

Two weeks after the end of our build-up training, my company left RAF Brize Norton on a military C130 transport plane for the short flight over to RAF Aldergrove, just outside of Belfast. We were then transferred by helicopters into the small patrol base in the centre of Cookstown—a town in County Tyrone with a population of almost 22,000 people. From our pre-deployment briefings, we knew there was a strong IRA presence residing in the region, most notably in the estate that ran behind the patrol base. The IRA was still very much active and had already carried out five major bombings on mainland Britain throughout that year, one of which being at the Baltic Exchange back in April.

For the next six months, we would face real danger on a daily basis in a town that was home to a number of high-ranking IRA members and sympathizers. The security force bases over the water were designed to counter against attacks from the IRA, but, of course, they also constituted targets. They regularly came under attack from rifle fire, mortars, rockets, grenades and bombs. From the outside, our base looked reasonably secure; inside, however, there were constant reminders that an attack could come at any time, and although the perimeter fence was high, we didn't take it for granted that we were safe from attack on the inside. The base would be home to a number of patrol teams, as well as intelligence and logistics personnel.

There were four watchtowers or "sangers" where there would always be a duty team manning each one 24/7. Each sanger provided a view of the outside world, strategically positioned to monitor any incoming attack or to watch the movements of a known "player"—the term used for an IRA individual.

Our tour of duty would see us rotating through various cycles that would consist of two weeks of urban and rural patrols: one week of guard duty at the base, and one week of being the "Quick Reaction Force", also known as "QRF", where we would be responsible for responding in support of any incidents in our "Area of Responsibility" or "AOR". There were no days off, as such, as the environment wouldn't allow for it, but if we weren't on guard, out patrolling or sleeping, we could then play five-a-side football on the helipad, though we'd often have to grab the ball and move off to the side when a helicopter came in to pick-up or drop-off a patrol team.

We weren't allowed off-base—no British Forces were permitted throughout the province due to the threat. The only ones who could be out were either the Northern Irish part-time soldiers or the British covert intelligence and SAS teams. I had an enormous amount of respect for the local part-time men and women who would have to drive into the base on a daily basis. At the end of the day, they would then head home to their families, not knowing if they were being followed, or had surveillance on them by the IRA, quite possibly to be used as a hit against them at a later date. They would always carry at least a pistol and were allowed to do so in plain clothes, going to and from work, but it remained an enormous risk—and one they were required to take on a daily basis.

My first operational tour passed off relatively quietly, although during one Friday night patrol in one of the estates, a huge fight erupted between our team and a few of the local youths. A helicopter was called in to support us, and the QRF from the base in the nearby town of Dungannon were soon overhead, providing top cover. Most of the active IRA members kept out of things like this as it would bring too much attention to them and instead sent out the young lads as initiation to start a fight with us. They knew we couldn't open fire on them for just starting a fight, not unless they had weapons too, but it kept us on our toes.

It had been an enjoyable experience, but six months was a long time in a small base like that, and although we were going out on patrol, which offered us some form of escape from the confines of the tall perimeter fencing, we'd be back after a matter of hours or a night out on the ground. The highlight was going out and doing some real soldiering, as well as being flung around inside the helicopters, heading to a drop-off location somewhere out in the countryside. Both the RAF and Army pilots really know how to fly, and it always added a bit of fun to our patrols.

Back in London, we soon settled back into somewhat of a normal life for the next six months, with training and ceremonial duties high on the agenda. Towards the end of the year, however, and as a result of defense cutbacks, we were told that our Battalion was to be placed into suspended animation, meaning it was getting scrapped. A newly formed company would maintain the Colors of the Battalion and would be stationed in London with the primary role of carrying out ceremonial duties. All of us were asked what we'd like to do: either stay with the newly formed "Number 7 Company" or go out to Germany and join the 1st Battalion. There was no way I was staying put in order to do ceremonial duties, and so I put my name down for Germany straight away, and with it soon approved, I was told I'd be reporting to the Battalion in Munster following the Christmas break. My departure, however, would be delayed a little when I found out that volunteers were needed to go back over to Northern Ireland for a three-month stint at the end of January. As before, it was a fairly quiet time, but it was good to get out there again.

I finally left for Munster at the beginning of March, though, as soon as I arrived, I thought it was a pretty dull and uninteresting place. Even some of the 1st Battalion lads I met upon arrival were saying the same. The 1st Battalion was a mechanized unit, which meant they had the luxury of using tanks and armored personnel carriers. I say *luxury* but it was far from it. When I arrived, the core of the Battalion had been out in Bosnia for the past four months, and had two remaining before returning to Munster. There was a skeleton crew of around eighty left behind to carry out guard duty, also known as rear party, but there was a lot of time for them to chill out, play football, drink, play football again, and drink some more—and that's what I walked into and joined in with.

We were based at Oxford Barracks. It was an old camp that had been used during World War II to house German soldiers. It was built in 1936 and there were all sorts of tunnels beneath it. You could tell it had a lot of history. There was even a brass German eagle positioned on the wall of the main building, which wasn't allowed to be taken down, but it did have to be covered up. Before the Battalion had left for Bosnia, the Commanding Officer had approved a new football field made of the finest artificial grass, meaning most of our downtime for those that had remained behind was spent having a kick about. The guard duties weren't too frequent, and unless you were on duty during the weekend, we were off; most of us hitting the town, and sampling one or two of the local stein lagers.

Life in Germany was very plain, as far as I was concerned. There didn't seem much to do besides work the week and hit the town at the weekend, though we would often hit it during the week, too. There would be the odd weekend fight with members of the Kings Royal Hussars, who were also based in Munster. The Germans could never understand why, with us all being British, and neither could I. There were plenty of things to do around the city, but with a bunch of young lads together, the outcome was the same most weekends: drink, party, women.

The city had a population of around 270,000 people with an estimated 48,500 of those students, and it had a great amount of history. If I had a long weekend or a week off, I'd occasionally drive back over to England and take in a Boro game; looking back, however, I wish I'd have taken in more of the area as it would have been a damn sight less depressing! It wasn't long before I was keen to get away from Germany altogether, though, and having arrived straight from Northern Ireland only two months earlier, I was eager for more operational work.

One night, whilst sitting with Chalky in a bar in Munster, enjoying a few beers, we came up with the ridiculous idea of driving to France and joining the French Foreign Legion. Our thinking was that France must be nicer than Germany, and it seemed perfectly logical to us with a few pints running through our blood. We even packed the car up the following morning and planned the drive! I can't remember exactly why we backed out at the last minute, but it was just that: the very last minute. In hindsight, it was best that we did—for Queen and Country and all that—though it's amazing what young lads come up with after a few pints together!

As often as I could get away with it, I kept bugging the Ops Officer to see if there were any spots available to join up with the Battalion for the remainder of their time in Bosnia. I was glad the opportunity didn't arise, though, as they had such a short time remaining. Nonetheless, in early June, my request to go out there would be answered in spectacular fashion.

OPPORTUNITY:
WHEN IT COMES, GRASP IT

I THOUGHT MY CHANCES of going out on another operational tour were fading whilst in Germany, even though I hadn't been there long. The Battalion had just returned from their tour, and I watched in envy as they had a big parade with the troops receiving their United Nations medals. I felt as though I'd missed out. They'd all be heading away for a bit of leave before returning to Munster and into a busy schedule, once again as a mechanized unit. I'd been selected for the Army and Infantry football squads during the time I'd been in Germany and had flown back to England a couple of times, which was a great honor, but I wanted to be away on operations again.

I'd enjoyed my first couple of tours in Northern Ireland as it had meant something—up against it all and facing the threat of the IRA—and I hoped another chance would soon arise. I was in my room packing my gear as I was due to fly back to Aldershot the next day for a weekend game, and I was looking forward to it. One of the lads came in and told me that the Adjutant wanted to see me. My first reaction was, "What have I done now?" The truth was I hadn't done anything, but it wasn't everyday he would ask to see you. I headed straight down to his office, though I wasn't exactly dressed for the occasion, what with my Army football tracksuit on. I apologized for my appearance as I knocked on his door.

I was half-expecting bad news but, thankfully, that wasn't the case. He came straight to the point, informing me of a requirement for one person to deploy to Bosnia within the week to work with General Sir Michael Rose. I'd heard of General Rose as he'd also been in the Coldstream Guards, and I knew he had a fantastic reputation as the former Commanding Officer of the SAS, as well as having held the position of Director of British Special Forces. He had also been the SAS Commander of both the highly publicized Iranian Embassy siege in London in 1980, in addition to the Falklands War in 1982. In short, this was someone you wanted to work for. Rose was a highly respected British Army General who had gained a lot of respect throughout his career. His role in Bosnia, as the United Nations Military Commander, had the world's eyes on him, and it was a position he had held for the previous five months. My role would be to go out as the Generals "batman", meaning I would oversee everything he would need on a logistical level and accordingly manage his residency domestic staff—all local Sarajevans who had been vetted to work in his residency. The job would entail being part of the Generals team in Sarajevo, right in the heart of the war zone.

I was told to take the remainder of the day to think it over but that a decision needed to be made quickly as the General was currently in the United Kingdom on leave. I was also told that they wanted someone in place for when he returned to Bosnia. My decision was made before I even left the Adjutant's office: I was that keen to get it rubber-stamped right then and there that he couldn't get me out. To hell with the football, I was off to a war zone! Little did I know at the time, however, what the true horrors of war felt like, and of the memories it would leave me with. Nonetheless, I had been presented with a chance and I would have been foolish to pass on it. It was my confidence in doing that which enabled me to take every opportunity that came my way in the future. I knew I had to grasp it with both hands.

I packed up everything that I wouldn't be taking and took the big box to the company stores for safekeeping. That night, I headed into town with some of the lads for a few drinks, but my mind was firmly on getting out to Bosnia. My excitement was high. I touched down at RAF Lyneham in England the following afternoon and spent a night there as I wasn't scheduled to depart until the following morning. After a quick wash, I then took a walk over to the bar on-camp and sunk a few beers, wondering what might lie ahead. A sense of excitement hit me then: I was about to embark on a new adventure—and one I'd not experienced before. It wasn't going to be easy, and I knew it would be a bad place what with war going on all over the country, but I was a young, keen lad and couldn't wait to get there. I went to sleep around eleven, knowing I was about to enter a whole new world the next day.

The next morning, I left on a Hercules C130 transport plane, traveling to the city of Split in Croatia. It seemed that all Royal Air Force flights left at some stupid hour—this one left at 6AM. As the engines became louder and louder, we thrust forward down the runway and headed for Split, climbing our way through the scattered clouds. I could make out the M4 motorway, even though it was still dark out as we passed over Reading, before banking right towards the southeast and out over Dover before crossing the English Channel. We hadn't even reached cruising altitude when most of the other troops on the flight unfurled their sleeping bags and climbed into them. I was wide awake, so I read the paper and listened to some music.

On arrival into Split, I was met by a handler who would be assisting me with my transfer over to Sarajevo; however, due to the hostilities between the warring factions in Bosnia on this particular day, he informed me that there would be no helicopter flights into or out of Sarajevo; this meant I would need to stay at Divulje Barracks in Split for the night; it was situated on the coast of the Adriatic and housed international United Nations troops, as well as a number of British units. It was also the rear headquarters for logistics and operations in the war zone and acted as a transit base for those going to and from Bosnia. I found that there were too many people there for my liking, though it was probably a good place to be based right on the coast and with some quaint villages and towns nearby.

I ended up grabbing a bed in the Sergeant's mess, though I wasn't sure how I got away with that as I wasn't a Sergeant, and then went and found one of the bars on camp with a couple of lads I knew who I'd already ran into, one of which was a Sergeant Major from Middlesbrough. No matter where you go in the world you can pretty much guarantee you'll always meet someone from "The Boro". Unless you're from there, it's hard to understand. They just pop up everywhere, I've found!

The following morning, I woke with a bad head, and as I was having a wash, my handler found me and informed me that he was going to try to get me into Sarajevo on a Norwegian military helicopter that was scheduled that morning. I would need to be at the helicopter pad in a couple of hours, and so I squared my kit away in the hope that I'd get the green light to fly. I went and grabbed a brew and something to eat before making my way to where the helicopters were based. Twenty minutes later, I was on my way as we lifted off the pad and climbed towards the mountain range in the distance. *This is it*, I remember thinking.

As we made a tactical approach towards Sarajevo International Airport, I was surprised as to how grim the surrounding area looked. I remember smoke billowing out from different areas below, with overturned cars and houses without windows clearly visible from the air. Occasionally, I would spot the soon-to-be-familiar white United Nations vehicles patrolling around. It looked exactly as it was supposed to look—exactly like a war zone.

I'd walked no further than ten feet from the helicopter when the locals let me know exactly where I was. *Du dum, du dum, du dum!* A burst of dull thuds from a heavy caliber machine gun had suddenly erupted into life from the hills in the distance—and it sounded worryingly close. I was told they were firing on a Serb position dug in on the side of a mountain. I knew I'd be experiencing much more of this over the coming months—how much, though, I had no idea, but I was aware that daily delights and comforts would be few and far between.

When I landed, a driver had come from the General's residency to meet me, and as we drove a short distance from the airport, we were stopped at a Serb checkpoint known as Sierra Four. After a few minutes of checking our credentials and having a good nose around, we were on our way up through the city. Along the way, we passed wrecked tanks and shattered buildings. It was very surreal seeing the remains of battle, knowing all too well that this battle was still very much active, while only two days earlier I had been enjoying a pint in a quaint countryside pub in England. It was bizarre to say the least. I was reminded of where I was by the sound of rounds popping off again, this time as we screamed through "Sniper Alley", which was on the main drag through the city. At the end, we hung a left before the Bosnian Parliament and headed up towards the residency.

With the General back from leave the previous evening, I learned he was currently out on the ground attending meetings and wouldn't be back until later that day. Out with him were most of the people I would be working with on a daily basis. I familiarized myself with the residency, which was located next to the American Embassy on one of the main streets to the north-east of the town, five minutes from the Parliament building. The bottom of it was given over to a reception area, a large dining room and a kitchen, whilst the first floor contained the Generals office and bedroom, as well as the office of the senior United Nations Delegate from Russia, Viktor Andreyev. Viktor was a typical vodka-swilling KGB General, but I would soon learn that he worked closely with General Rose and was an extremely important and influential figure to the peace accord between the warring factions throughout Bosnia.

The outer office comprised of a large room shared by the General and Victor's staff, with a total of around eight people. On our side of the house was the Generals Military Assistant (MA), his Aide-de-Camp (ADC), as well as Jean from the Royal Navy, who was the assistant. A second door opened to the outside, leading to a wooden landing which, in turn, connected to risen wooden duckboards. Running the length of the top row of cabins, there were a number of small offices that housed cells for flight operations, foreign liaison officers, signals personnel as well as a small team of British Special Forces. I was told the residency was the former Delegates Club of Sarajevo. It was built around bugs, electronic type, and was swept regularly, though that didn't make any difference, apparently. Everyone was listening into what was going on in the General's office as well as the outer office. I found that there were even times when a laser was bounced off the windows, picking up every tiny vibration.

Then there were the electronic people that were based in an annex in the grounds of the residency—American NATO individuals who were hidden away. They had a forest of antennas and boxes. I'd get used to seeing them when we went over to the annex across the way; they weren't for show but were up to something. Captain "Mike Stanley", the General's translator and fixer, wrote the following in a book, "Trusted Mole", which he later published following our time in Bosnia.

"They were busy sweeping up every little bit of information to come out of the residency. Later when General Rupert Smith took over from General Rose, one of his American communications guys attached to his protection team wasn't even U.S. Army; he was from the CIA dressed up as a soldier. By all accounts he couldn't carry it off very well, couldn't answer simple questions about where he'd been or what courses he'd done. While General Rose was still in charge he knew it was going on, but he used it as a double-edged weapon to his advantage, he could say what he wanted on the phone, lie about anything, whoever was listening wouldn't know what was true and what was not."

Trusted Mole
Milos Stankovic
Harper Collins Publishers, 2000

After meeting and familiarizing myself with the various people who were around, I returned to my room to finish unpacking. As I was doing so, I suddenly heard the sound of vehicles pull into the driveway. Stepping out onto the balcony to take a look, I saw a convoy of two Range Rovers and a Land Rover had pulled into the driveway. The General had arrived. I wanted to give it a little time before going downstairs—I didn't want to look out of place to him or to his close protection guys, a small team of scruffy looking soldiers who had a real look of seriousness about them. They took up position around the vehicles as the General stepped out. It looked every bit the part of a high-level close-protection operation, and it was impressive to watch. It was the first time I had seen General Rose in person. He was a tall man and was impressively dressed in his crisp set of combats.

The first person I met was Mac, from the Parachute Regiment. He was the driver and close protection to Viktor Andreyev. He seemed like a solid guy. Then I met Mick, who was from Sunderland and on the General's close protection team. He was a member of the SAS 264 Signals Squadron. I found out over the coming months that Mick was a great guy who maintained exceptional fitness and was someone with whom I would ultimately forge a sound relationship. Frank had a lot of military protection experience from Northern Ireland to Beirut. Prior to deploying to Sarajevo, he'd spent three years as an instructor at Longmoor, the home of the Royal Military Police close protection training wing. Frank had an eight-month tour in Khartoum protecting the British Ambassador under his belt and had a lot of protection experience. Unfortunately, I wouldn't get to spend much time with him, however, as he'd be moving on to another position overseas within the coming weeks and would be replaced by Clive.

There were also Jim and Mongo, two American Special Forces communications guys. A rarity that US soldiers would be on a British General's close protection team; however, their main role was to provide secure communications back and forth between

General Rose and the US Command; the Commander of the 5th Fleet in the Adriatic, which was commanded by Admiral Leighton Smith, the US Army Commander General Wesley Clark, and up to the President of the United States.

Finally, there was Goose, the team leader. He was a monster of a man who had spent most of his military career in the Special Forces. I soon found that Goose had little thought for his own safety; his priority was the "boss", and God help anyone that posed a threat to him. He met any obstacle or threat to life with extreme force. I learned that, on one occasion, Goose was sitting in a bar in Sarajevo with one of the bodyguards of the Serb Military Commander, General Mladic. Goose was getting to know him and gleaning information when another Serb soldier challenged him to an arm wrestle contest in the bar. Mladic's bodyguard whispered to Goose that he should let the Serb soldier win as, just the day before, this particular soldier had killed someone who had beaten him at arm wrestling. Just as he was about to let the guy win, Goose suddenly changed his mind and slammed the guy's arm down on the table. The angry soldier left abruptly and returned soon after with his rifle, walked over to the table where Goose was still sitting, only to put his rifle down and shake Goose by the hand. When General Rose found out about this, he asked him what he would have done if the soldier had tried to shoot him, to which he replied, "Don't worry, Boss, I had him covered with my pistol under the table from the moment he walked back in".

There was a renegade Croat roaming around Bosnia called "Vlasko", who was working as a mercenary for the Serbs and who, later on in the tour, confronted our convoy. Vlasko was a notorious killer. He had a long black beard, wore a necklace of human teeth, and drove a black Toyota Land Cruiser with a child's skull on the bonnet. The week before, he had threatened to kill a United Nations Brigadier. As we left the Serb Headquarters near Ilijas, he was waiting, surrounded by his heavily armed, black-suited henchmen. The General walked by without comment, but Goose stopped in front of Vlasko, and stood for some time staring down at him. Vlasko suddenly turned around and climbed into his vehicle and drove away.

Goose had heard that Vlasko had been boasting that he was going to kill the General's bodyguard. It appeared that, on meeting him face-to-face, he changed his mind. When Mick later read this chapter, he reminded me of another time the team ran into Vlasko, who was closing in on our vehicles from behind. They were getting closer and closer until Mongo pulled his weapon up and aimed his sights on the driver from the hatch in the Land Rover that followed the General's car everywhere. They soon backed off. Maybe they knew Mongo better than we thought. I would soon learn about each of their characters, but found immediately that, behind the dark menacing stares and big frames, this was an exceptional group of lads to work with.

I got around to meeting the remainder of the General's staff, which included Captain Jeremy "Baggers" Bagshaw. He was the General's Aide-de-Camp and had his work cut out organizing his busy military and social schedule. Lieutenant Colonel Simon Shadbolt was the Generals Military Assistant; he would be leaving soon, though, to take up a new position in the UK, and was set to be replaced by Lieutenant Colonel Jamie Daniell, who was from the Royal Green Jackets. I found them to be very approachable people and got on well with both.

Lieutenant Colonel Tim Spicer arrived on the team four weeks after my arrival and became the General's Press Liaison

Officer. He had a short fuse, but I found him to be a rather decent fella and we got on well. A veteran of the Falklands War, he was involved in a controversial incident in Northern Ireland in 1992, when soldiers of the Scots Guards, under the command of Spicer, shot and killed a Catholic civilian on the streets of Belfast. Believing their lives were at risk, Lieutenant Colonel Spicer stood by his men and, according to news reports, the IRA placed a bounty on his head. He was promptly removed from Northern Ireland by British Army Command in order to save him from possible assassination.

Captain "Mike Stanley", later promoted to the rank of Major while we were in Bosnia, was from the Parachute Regiment and was another with a short fuse. I got on well with him, though. I quickly learned that he had an enormous amount of pressure in his job. He would later be the victim of a double jeopardy, and his Serb language made him gold dust to the British Army. Mike worked as an interpreter and fixer to General Sir Michael Rose, and then later to his successor, General Sir Rupert Smith. Anticipating trouble from his role in Bosnia, the British Army gave him a cover name and referred to him as "Mike Stanley". They assumed it to be safer than his real name, Milos Stankovic.

Two other Brit-Serb soldiers were called "Abbott" and "Costello"; "Stanley" came from Stan Laurel. Once the Bosnian Muslims had worked out his origins, Stanley-Stankovic would be under a cloud of suspicion. One of their newspapers referred to him as a "trusted mole" of the Bosnian Serb authorities. Mike had been on the ground in Bosnia since 1992—a long time to spend in a place populated by the dead and whose hope had died. He had plenty of experience of it all—most of it unpleasant. He was christened with the nickname "The Schindler of Sarajevo" for his actions in helping to smuggle people out of the city. I'll get into a little detail about that, but more can be read about it in his excellent book, as mentioned above. Written in 1997 following his arrest on suspicion of treason, it wasn't what he needed after spending three years helping dismembered children out of armored personnel carriers and trying to persuade mass murderers to stop shelling them. I've read his book twice since I bought it a number of years ago and, upon first reading it, it gave me sleepless nights for the first time in years. It re-awakened some of the buried memories of the time spent in Bosnia and what was to become an astonishing period of my life.

We had a small team of British Special Forces who were also based out of the residency, and we would work and socialize with them on a daily basis. Led by Jamie, there was also Geordie, Bob and Martin. They were all veterans of the SAS and reported directly to the General on a number of matters throughout the region. The "Joint Commissioned Observer" team was formed after the General grew tired of the bullshit from the warring faction leaders in Bosnia. He wanted a trusted team working directly for him; one he could rely on and who could be his eyes in and around the war zone. Who better to be those people than members of the SAS? And so, the JCO cell was formed as a bit of a cover name and they cracked on with it. They weren't there to be seen. It was a very small team, and both the JCOs and the General's close protection team seemingly worked well together. With both teams, one led by Goose and the JCO team led by Jamie, I would be working with one of the most highly trained group of soldiers in the British Army.

I soon settled into my new environment, my role as the General's "batman" was a relatively easy task as the residency was staffed with locals that took care of everything he needed. My job would, however, change to encompass various things over the coming months, from driving the General and helping as part of the close protection team to making sure that all the staff in the residency were carrying out their daily tasks. It was an interesting job, and I found I had a great amount of freedom. I was soon enjoying it.

On occasions, we would head to Trogir—a historic harbor town on the Adriatic coast in Croatia. It's situated on a small island between the Croatian mainland and the island of Ciovo, which is twenty-seven kilometres west of Split. It was a place that offered the General a great haven to be outside of the war zone, but within minutes of the rear command at Divulje Barracks. It also offered us an opportunity, not so much to let our guard down but to work in a more relaxed environment; have a swim in the sea—something Goose made the most of. He was like a fish, and once he dived into the clear water, it wouldn't be long before he'd disappear into the distance.

A couple of months after my arrival in Sarajevo, a few of us had arranged a football game at the Olympic Stadium, which was not far the from the residency. Geordie and I had worked hard on making it happen, recruiting a mix of locals and military personnel. We faced the threat of snipers, who were constantly firing down from the surrounding blocks of flats, but we carried on regardless. With the score at 2–1 to the residency team, the game had to be abandoned as a result of an incident that had taken place outside of the city. We received word that a British UN convoy had been traveling down from Mount Igman, through the Serb stronghold, and had been ambushed. The next thing we knew, there were helicopters landing at the Olympic Stadium to offload the wounded and, as we soon found out, the dead.

We immediately helped the aircrew cross load the casualties to the waiting military ambulances who'd arrived a short time earlier. Two of the stretchers had lifeless bodies on them, one of whom was a British Soldier. Geordie and I were saddened, but above all, we were really fucking angry. We were there to help these people as part of the United Nations, yet horror like this was unfolding right in front of us. We all knew, however, that we were in a war zone, and the chances of losing your life, or at a minimum, witnessing others losing theirs, would be quite high. This particular convoy had been targeted—and that's what fucked us off. If people wanted to shoot the shit out of each other over whatever religious or political beliefs they had, then fine, but innocents shouldn't be dragged into it. But then again: it's war. There are no rules for the bad guys, as was again proven in Gorazde when one of the JCOs was killed. Corporal Fergus (Fergie) Rennie was in the SAS and he was shot by a sniper. His loss was a sad time for all who knew him.

Sometimes I found certain situations strange for me personally, but these were the things to which I was quickly adapting, and which were, as a result, helping me mature. I was a young soldier, but the people I was being exposed to—Presidents and Prime Ministers, Ambassadors and Generals, Personal Security Teams and Special Forces personnel—were teaching me a lot. There was also a lot of spying going on while we were there— sometimes against us, other times the other way around, and there were all sorts of agencies involved. The JCO team, as well as British and American intelligence agencies, MI5, MI6 and the CIA, were all active and giving out questionable reasons of who they were and what they were doing.

Then our team found itself a new member, Captain "Penny". She'd be joining us as a translator, though she couldn't carry it very well, which was obvious as soon as she turned up. Penny soon settled into the team, and we got on rather well, though, like I said, naïve I am not. It turned out that "Captain Penny" was actually "Agent Penny"; she was MI5 and sent by the British Government to our team to get her eyes on what was going on in Bosnia.

It made sense, but not because we were up to no good. Well, we *were* up to all sorts, but we thought it was for good reasons; however, there were no others closer to the action than us, and so she was planted in our environment. That's how cunning government agencies can be; sometimes even against their own people. That sort of thing is nothing new and has been going on for years, and it will continue to be that way for many years to come, too. The bottom line is, nobody really trusts each other.

Working with the General gave me the opportunity to meet some big-hitters, though not all were good guys. Top of the list was Radovan Karadzic. In his roles as Supreme Commander of the Bosnian Serb Armed Forces and President of the National Security Council of the Republika Srpska, Karadzic was accused of being responsible for more than 7,500 Muslim deaths. Under his command, Bosnian Serb Forces initiated the Siege of Sarajevo and carried out numerous massacres across Bosnia.

Tens of thousands of non-Serbs were killed; hundreds of thousands were driven from their homes; thousands more were imprisoned in concentration camps, where many died. Karadzic was later accused of ordering the "Srebrenica Massacre" in 1995, directing Bosnian Serb forces to "create an unbearable situation of total insecurity with no hope or further survival of life" in the United Nations safe area. In addition, he was accused of ordering that UN personnel be taken hostage between May and June of 1995, notably at a time when we had left Bosnia and General Rose had been replaced by a new man in charge, General Sir Rupert Smith, due to his tour coming to an end.

I first met Karadzic at the Hotel Panorama in Pale, a small town in the mountains eight miles south-east of Sarajevo. General Rose was to attend a meeting in the morning, and I'd be traveling out there with the team. We made our way through the hills, passing the Serb troops in their bunkers, dug in, and ready to fire off mortars at the Muslim positions down below. If the General ever saw this happen, he'd have the motorcade stop and jump out before firing a volley of profanities at those responsible, ordering them to stop at once. Mike would be doing the interpreting, of course.

We swept straight through the gates of the hotel as the Serb soldiers stood guard, waiting for their leader to arrive. Our vehicles were well known throughout the war zone, and although we were occasionally stopped, it was more of a nose around from the soldiers manning the checkpoints than anything more serious. Goose walked the General into the hotel, accompanied by Mike, while Clive, Mick, as well as Mongo, Jim and I, waited outside and sorted the vehicles out. Mick was on the radio to Jeremy back at the residency, letting him know of our position, a regular occurrence in case things went bad at any point, and also so he could monitor our movements.

We could hear police sirens in the distance, which we knew would be Karadzic and his crew arriving. Once they swept through the gates and up towards the circular driveway, we moved out of the way. We weren't so sure they'd avoid us. Goose had made his way over to us, and we stood chatting as the motorcade pulled in.

We watched as everyone hurried around the cars—soldiers, police, as well as Karadzic's security guys, one of which was a monster in size. We didn't expect any problems: the people meeting in the hotel would be discussing the matters of the war, and only if something occurred in the room would there be an issue. Not only that but, as with most meetings, Goose would be right outside the meeting room. The rest of the team would get the vehicles sorted and would then be standing by outside for each of the places we visited to ensure a safe exit. It was a military close protection detail, and I was learning a lot from being a part of it. It was both interesting and exciting.

Occasionally, however, things didn't go to plan. We were shot at a number of times, possibly from the Serbs. Other times, it was most likely by the Muslims and even rebel forces or mercenaries. It would never be from close range, just always from a good distance, though everyone would blame each other for it. We got used to the game. What better way to drop one side in the shit than to fire on the top man and then blame the other? On other occasions, we would get to a checkpoint only to be held for some time before a message would come from the local Serb or Muslim Commander that we couldn't pass. General Rose was the United Nations Military Commander on the ground, though this didn't stop them from trying to mess him around. It would often lead to a nasty verbal exchange.

I quickly learned the drill and became part of a team that would not hesitate when it came to mitigating any risk that might be posed to the General or indeed to ourselves. Most times, if Mike was around, he would deal with it: he spoke the language and so we'd watch from a distance as he got into verbal disagreements with the soldiers. It was hilarious. If nothing was moving forward after that, then a phone call would be made to the Bosnians or the Serbs, and, after a short delay, we'd be on our way. Other times, even with the hint of being slowed down by one of the guards, we'd just carry on and run the checkpoint. If they were stupid enough to have opened fire on us, then the team were always ready to respond, but we weren't there for that. It wasn't our mission. We had some close moments, though, and Frank wrote about one serious incident that took place.

"We became involved in a fire fight just beneath the Holiday Inn where a sniper shot an old lady. Having dropped the boss off at the airport on his way to Zagreb, we all drove back to the residency along sniper alley. Incoming fire started and the old lady dropped to the ground. By prior agreement and well-rehearsed drills, we positioned our vehicles into a triangle around the fallen body and, following a rudimentary fire control order, the outgoing rounds commenced. Goose started dispensing his armor piercing rounds from his 7.76mm H&K G3 towards a well-known sniper lair across the valley. The team were having a whale of a time supporting Goose with suppressing fire and pinpointing potential secondary targets; essentially, we had outgoing fire directed at near 270 degrees of the compass.

Meanwhile, I was busy rendering first aid to the 'bag of clothes' that was now slumped lifeless on the pavement—it didn't look good as we couldn't find either an entry or exit wound. My attempts to save her life were temporarily halted when Goose instructed me to get his H&K MP5 A3 (a 9mm calibre short distance but rapid-fire automatic machine gun) from the back of the Range Rover so he could continue the fire fight.

After what seemed to be a lifetime, we lifted the old woman in the back of the Land Rover, rallied the troops and then set off, at pace, toward the local hospital. Not wishing to attract too much unwanted attention and still suffering the ear-splitting effects of a violent contact, we chose not to accompany the lady into the inner sanctums of what was an extremely busy hospital and instead handed her over to white coated medics who appeared to have not slept for a good few days. Unfortunately, we later discovered that the elderly lady passed away from her injuries. Another unnecessary victim of a brutal civil war.

On the return to the team room located on the third floor of the residency, and after preparing the vehicles for our next trip— which involved pulling out the front wing of the Range Rover following a slight coming together during the immediate response to incoming fire—we commenced the 'hot-debrief'. The aim is to review the incident to see if we could learn lessons that might help us be more effective should we find ourselves in a similar incident in the near future. Having shared the personal recollections of the event, and marvelled at just how many different accounts we had, it was time to account for the expended ammunition and check that no injuries were sustained.

It's important to remember that, at the time of this incident, and despite the Gulf War in 1991, it was uncommon for British soldiers to be involved in street shootouts. As each team member called out the rounds fired, I was becoming extremely agitated as I knew what I was about to say. 125, 84, 39, 96... an enquiry was aimed my way.

'Frank, how many rounds did you fire?'

'Zero!'

'What?'

'Zero,' I repeated.

'Fuck off, you can't be serious!'

'I fired zero rounds, lads!' This was because I was the one in the middle giving immediate first-aid and recovering the casualty to a safe place. This partially reduced the ribbing and jovial banter aimed at the only Military Policemen in the team but this soon became a full onslaught when we discovered that my medical ability was on a par with my marksmanship skills, both of which drew a blank."

Serbian General, Ratko Mladic, would often try to make it increasingly difficult for General Rose and his team by restricting our movements throughout the region. Returning from a visit to a Canadian troop position in August, we were ambushed by a Serb paramilitary force armed with anti-tank weapons and machine guns. The General told Goose to stop the car immediately. As the vehicle came to a halt, he got out and demanded an explanation from the local Serb Commander, who told General Rose that he and his team were illegally on Bosnian Serb territory and were therefore under arrest.

"Preposterous, you buffoon!" was the reply, with the General further stating that, as the United Nations Protection Force Commander, he was entitled to go anywhere he wanted.

The Serb said that one of his soldiers recognized Mike as being a Muslim taxi driver from Visoko and that he was a spy. Mike was furious with this and replied that he was as good a Serb as anybody, proving it by showing them photos of his grandfather dressed in Royalist Serb uniform. While all of this was going on, and such was the deteriorating situation, our team slowly got into fire positions. Colonel Gordon Rudd, from the US Army, who was out with General Rose that day, thought it so risky that he was heard cocking his weapon, though everyone else, on the other hand, already had one in the chamber, ready to fire.

The Serbs responded by taking up fire positions in the ditches on each side of the road. General Rose, ignoring this, told the Serb Commander that he was soon going to be seeing General Mladic and would be reporting him for his discourtesy, which seemed to eventually encourage him to back down. I'm sure the fact that he could also see that the team was ready for action played a part, too, however. General Rose was a brave man and wouldn't back down in this situation and many others throughout his time in Bosnia, but all it would have taken was a nervous Serbian soldier to accidently pull the trigger and there would have been dead bodies all over that road.

On September 18th, another incident occurred. We had been out most of the day with the General who, along with Viktor Andreyev, the senior Russian UN Delegate, had been up to Pale for meetings with the Serbs. We returned to the residency late in the afternoon, and the General was in his office, reading up on some paperwork while the remainder of the team were pottering around, doing their own thing. Despite the General recently negotiating a cease-fire with the Serbs, they suddenly attacked out of the city; baiting the Muslim forces in the area. We heard the start of it all from the residency, and the building started to shake.

I was doing a workout with Goose and Mac upstairs when we heard an enormous amount of firing and explosions going off in the distance. Although we were used to hearing these on a daily basis, they didn't compare to the volume that we were hearing now. We immediately stopped our workout and prepared for the worst. This seemed to be the biggest attack on the city we had ever experienced.

When the General made the decision to head out to where the attack was taking place, Tim Spicer was busy on the phone dealing with the reports of it. General Rose, however, didn't want to wait, and so he left immediately with Jamie Daniell and the team. Tim would have to play catch-up, so I stayed behind and readied one of the vehicles. When he finished his business, we left at speed to catch up with the others. We were both armed with a pistol and an MP5 each, and as we sped out of the main gate through the streets of Sarajevo, we noticed people with fear clear on their faces; hiding in doorways, not daring to move out into the open.

When we reached the top of the winding road near the castle, however, we came under fire from a Serb position to our right, located in the distance. We had a good view of the area but we were nonetheless unable to reach the team from our current position and, with the narrow road, it was difficult to do a quick turnaround. We got out of the vehicle to return fire and get into some cover. Rounds were pinging off the car and whooshing past us, with shrapnel flying around. I've no idea how either of us weren't hit, but I was expecting one or both of us to go down, such was the seriousness of the attack.

We didn't have a visual on the General and the rest of the team, but what we did know was that they were close as we were on the radio speaking with one another. Eventually, we had a break in the firing; this allowed us to get back in the vehicle and drive further down the hill. Once we reached the turn, we were then able to pull into the Cymbeline position and meet up with the others who we had spotted crouched down behind a wall. We could see the Bosnian Infantry in the distance, notably on the side of a hill, mounting a large-scale offensive against the Serbs, who were responding with heavy machine guns and rocket launchers. It was quite a sight. The noise was deafening, and our position was being hit by fire from both sides. We were all now crouching down, monitoring the fighting and popping our heads up occasionally because, apparently, that's exactly what you're supposed to do when there are rounds flying inches above you!

Mick had been stood behind what he thought was a wall, with rounds whizzing around all of us. The General tapped him on the shoulder and suggested he move back as he was only sheltering behind some hessian material. A saved-by-the-boss scenario, if ever there was one! There wasn't any fear, and I knew that applied to all of us. It was simply a case of our training kicking in and us reacting in a calm manner. If you start panicking in a situation like that, you really are rolling the dice because you aren't thinking or acting straight. It's hard to describe the feeling of being immersed in such a situation, but the adrenaline within us just burst to life. More importantly, though, so too did our military skills, highlighting the importance of training for such an environment. If any of us had switched off here, even for a few seconds, it could have proven to be fatal.

When the attack was over with, we headed straight back to the residency where it was business as usual, though the General worked with his team on drafting letters to the military leaders of both sides threatening NATO air strikes if the fighting continued. They all knew from experience that this General would not hesitate in dropping a bomb on them, though I don't think he was far from calling in an airstrike on both sides when the attack was ongoing. It had certainly been warranted as it had spiraled out of control. Without question, something needed to be done.

General Rose was a fit man and had a thing about running. At fifty-four years old, I was impressed with his stubbornness and tenacity when it came to running. Of course, it was also good for him to be seen out and about by the people of Sarajevo, and it was the General's way of telling them that everything is going to be okay. At least twice a week, we'd be off on a run when his schedule permitted, and I remember the first time I went out with him. We shot off at a rapid pace, out of the residency, and as I looked back, I spotted Mike on the stairs, laughing, as he stood with a coffee in one hand and a cigarette in the other. He'd no doubt given a great excuse to get out of it—probably some duff meeting he'd need to attend somewhere. We hung a left towards the old Zetra Olympic football stadium and out towards the edge of town towards a steep hill called Hum. I'd been told that the General had a thing about fitness, and so I was glad I was up to speed with my running, but even so, I found it hard going.

Clive was driving the backup Land Rover behind with Mongo and Jim while Mick, Goose and I ran with the General. As we headed up our first steady incline, we started to feel the heat. It was summer in Bosnia and that, mixed with the smell of cars spewing crap out of their exhausts, was making the run more difficult. It wasn't going to put anyone off, though.

We wound our way through the local communities and up the hills, and it wasn't long before we gained attention from the locals. There would also be plenty of chasing dogs, too, which one of us or the backing vehicle would have to deal with by scaring them off. Most of the locals seemed friendly and offered the odd wave, though they must have thought it strange to see six men running by in such heat. After a number of these runs, more of the locals would recognize us and, at times, the local children would run alongside us. It would only be for a hundred meters or so before they realized we weren't going to slow down for them and then they'd drop off. We didn't mind it, especially as it could deter a potential shoot on us, but then again this was Bosnia. If the Serb snipers in the hills overlooking the city could take a shot at these people running alongside us, then they would.

As the former Commanding Officer of the SAS, as well as Director of British Special Forces, the General maintained his fitness to a high level and, on our runs, I was surprised at the speed and distance we covered each time, with a minimum of six miles through hilly terrain. It felt great afterwards, but it had been rough going for the first few. The General didn't let up for anyone, and nor should he have done: if you were on a run with him, it meant you were fit. There were others that would occasionally turn up and join in with us, and we could tell they found it hard, too. I think, for many, it was an opportunity to get some good face time with the General, but if you didn't keep up with him, you'd pretty much just screwed yourself.

Later in the year and whilst running the same route, we were almost hit by sniper fire. It was late November. The evenings were getting darker earlier and there was a cold chill in the air. On that particular day, Mick, Goose, General Rose, Jeremy and I were running. In the Land Rover was Clive, Mongo and Jim. We headed out of the gates of the residency and took the left again towards Zetra football stadium. Once we came to the junction, we curved left onto the Alipasina Road, heading towards the Hotonj District. We were roughly two-and-a-half miles from the residency. To our front, approximately two hundred meters away, was one of the local schools; to our right were open fields, shadowed by the Betanija Foothills. The Land Rover closed in a little due to the open ground and was approximately five meters behind the running group. Suddenly, we heard a crack and then a thump. A round fired at you, assuming it misses, gives you a direction and range on the target by the "crack and thump".

To determine it, you would start a rapid count the minute you hear the "crack" and stop the instant you hear the "thump" of the muzzle. It really does sound like a "thump"—not a sharp sound—and then you convert time to distance. For practical purposes, if the "thump" arrives on top of the "crack" your opponent is within battle sight range—three hundred yards or less. If there is a distinct, albeit short interval between the "crack" and the arrival of the "thump", then they are five hundred or more yards away—the "more", in this case, being established by the rapid count. As soon as we heard it, we immediately knew what it was. We were all familiar with rounds going off, especially in this place.

The Land Rover suddenly came up on our right, giving the General cover from that side. I looked over to the area of the foothills and saw the flash from the firing point of the second shot. Amazingly, we kept running instead of getting in the Land Rover and heading out of the area. The General was stubborn like that, and it was a show of force. We were all fed up with the Serbs firing into the city at the local population. That was another time where I was expecting rounds going through my body at any moment. There was no point in returning fire as it was too far away, though we were all ready and eager to do so. The guys in the backing vehicle could have done, but they were doing what they were supposed to do and came up to cover the General. The firing point had been approximately eight-hundred meters at the bottom of the foothills in a small wooden hut. When we were out of the area and still running, Goose dropped back a little from the

General. I mentioned to him that I was sure I'd seen the firing point.

"Are you sure?" he asked. I was positive, absolutely positive I had.

Back at the residency, we stretched off as the General headed up the stairs to his office. Goose held a team meeting outside straight away to go over the incident. The initial response from everyone had been good and effective.

It was the decision of the boss to carry on but the Land Rover responding to cover him in such a quick manner had been key.

A few of us running were armed; Goose, Mick and I had pistols tucked into our tactical waist packs, but they'd have been no use unless it had been a close quarters attack. The rest of the lads in the Land Rover were fully armed, from phosphorus and smoke grenades to high-caliber automatic weapons, but they hadn't seen the firing point. They weren't about to just start shooting rounds off: we don't do that and, besides, they did exactly what they needed to do to cover the General.

Goose and a couple of the other lads from Hereford who were at the residency on another task would go out to take a closer look at the firing point later in the evening to see what they could find, and I learned I'd be going with them. Once the debrief had been finalized, it was back to normal straight away. I went and grabbed a shower after the run and headed downstairs for a brew with Adie, who was preparing dinner for everyone. As the sun was setting, Goose, Geordie, Martin and I loaded up the Range Rover and headed out. In the back was a Barrett .50 caliber sniper rifle. It seemed somebody might be in for a nasty surprise.

We drove for ten minutes to an area out of sight on the high ground near to where we had been fired upon. From there, the team was able to get a visual on the wooden hut in the distance.

We had to be discreet due to the nearby homes and the people walking around. The last thing we wanted to do was scare the locals, and it was one of the reasons we'd left it until the sun went down. But even so, it wasn't fully dark just yet, and so we waited.

We parked the Range Rover and got the long gun out of the back. There wasn't any intention of blowing the hut to bits: this was a reconnaissance job, and it would only be used to get the distance from our location to the target. If we noticed people milling around and carrying weapons, then that may be a different ball game, but even then, that alone wouldn't be sufficient grounds to act. At this moment in time, I was working with an SAS team to find out exactly if I was right with making the call about the firing point. But I knew I was.

It was both intriguing and exciting being out on the ground in this capacity. These fellas were the real deal and knew exactly what they were doing.

Having observed the hut and surrounding area for a while, utilizing night vision goggles, we were noticing movement. While the team noted what was going on, I'd been designated with watching out for any locals that might wander over to our position. Having spent around ninety minutes on the ground, we wrapped up the op and headed back to the residency. I was eager for more of this type of work as it had been exciting and different.

When we arrived back at the residency, the others were in the bar, so we freshened up and joined them. I was immediately struck by the fact that it wasn't discussed. The way these guys rolled was impressive.

Two days later, we were back out on another run with the General. Setting out on our route, we passed the same location where we had been fired upon, only this time there was no one there to take a shot at us. By continuing our runs, it was a clear indication that we weren't going to be intimidated by the Serbs or Muslims. The message was clear: try it on and there will be a response, with no fucking about.

A number of days after that incident, I was having a brew with one of the Army signals girls downstairs when Colonel Daniell found me. With a straight face he asked if I fancied going camping. I thought he was joking! We walked up to the outer office together to find the General pacing around with his fishing rod; I knew, then, that it wasn't a joke.

"Camping, Corporal Burton." Again, it wasn't a question but more of a statement from the General.

When he returned to his office, both Colonel Daniell and I just looked at each other with looks of astonishment, though when it came to General Rose, nothing came as much of a surprise. Quite where we were going to go camping would be interesting: we were in the middle of a war zone! I figured he must be mad as I headed off to find the rest of the lads.

"Fucking camping... Out here? Yeah, okay!" said Clive as he lay motionless on his bed, reading a book without so much as glancing up.

Goose looked at me with as straight a face as you can imagine. "Are you serious?" he asked.

"Yeah, I'm serious."

He went for a walk down to the office but soon returned, confirming I hadn't been winding them all up as he gave everyone the details of this mad venture, and so off everyone went to get their gear ready. Most people pack sandwiches for such a trip, but we were packing guns and ammunition. Some of the team had actually done this before with General Rose, and Frank noted the following during a previous trip out:

"The camping was great. On one fishing trip, both Goose and I became worried when a wedding party on the opposite bank celebrated by firing a volley of shots into the air. Our concerns were not based on the direct fire risk but more on the understanding that gravity will bring them back to earth at some stage, and it would be embarrassing to admit that we lost our principal based on incoming celebratory fire from a local wedding party."

Not only were we going fishing and camping but the General had picked out a lake on the map that was right on the BiH-Serb frontline near Zepce. When a number of others found out we were off camping, and after the initial astonishment had set in, they bombarded Colonel Daniell to see if they, too, could get in on the trip. It was a one-off experience that no one wanted to miss; they all knew that nobody does this in a war zone! *Welcome to the world of General Rose*, I had thought. We found it hilarious once we were ready to go, but initially we were like everyone else. Mike even wrote about the trip in his book "Trusted Mole".

" 'That's where we're going. Looks like a good stretch for trout!'

My heart sinks. It's right on the front line. And anyway, how can he tell what's going to be in a tiny strand of blue on a 1:100,000-scale map? Off we went and, two hours later, we turned off the main Zenica-Zepce drag and onto a minor road that led some five kilometres to the supposed 'trout haven'. As we turned off, we hit a BiH checkpoint manned by soldiers who told us we couldn't go any further because of combat activities in that area. They were exercising or preparing for an attack on the Serbs and didn't want anyone snooping in the area, least of all the UN—and, even more so, least of all Rose! It was a fair one, really, but Rose wasn't having it and demanded to exercise his freedom of movement.

They refused and asked what business we had in the area and, when we told them, they didn't do anything but laugh before saying we were wasting our time. 'The rivers are too shallow and there are no fish.'

But Rose wouldn't have any of that either. 'Rubbish. Of course there are fish there! That's perfectly obvious!'

Eventually, the guards became so fed up that they told us to go into Zepce and get permission from the local Commander. If we could do that, they told us, then we could pass with an escort. So that's what we did.

Upon getting to the HQ in Zepce, I was sent in to haggle with the Commander. None of them went with me; they just sat in the vehicles, impatient to get on with fishing. Jamie Daniell in particular was sat getting stressed as the whole fishing plan was about to go down the tubes; it was already three in the afternoon and the General had yet to cast a fly.

At first, the Commander wouldn't hear of it. I was virtually on my knees begging him. Failure really wasn't worth contemplating, not where fishing was involved. Parasols, deck shoes and coffee grinders are one thing, but fishing's a different ball game altogether. The BiH Commander finally relented and so we got our military escort. We rattled down this track for five kilometres to the exact spot, and I was feeling quite pleased with myself. Out we hopped, with Rose striding down to the river, only to then take one look at it and say, 'That's no bloody good! Far too shallow. Let's find somewhere else!' The escorting soldiers smirked like mad. You couldn't even call it a river. You couldn't so much as get your toe wet!

Rose was wrong about the fish, but that wasn't the point.

He didn't care whether there were fish or not. He didn't want to be told he couldn't go down a track. He was just making his point and exercising his right to free movement. But that didn't help the MA who, by this point, was in panic and desperate to save what little was left of the day. We went for the safe option: to drive all the way back, virtually to Kiseljak, and then down the Fojnica Valley, through that town, and then straight up a steep wooded mountain track. This eventually escaped from the tree line and into a peak of high alpine grass and boulders. At the very top was a lake, a small tarn set in what looked like a little volcanic crater. Dotted around the lake were old wooden huts.

The mountain area was called Travnica Vrata and is one of the highest peaks in Bosnia, but with a lake. All very remote and otherworldly, and it was close to eight by the time we'd parked up. Rose didn't lose a moment and rushed off down to the water with his gear. Goose and I went with him and sat beside the lake, watching the General casting away. It was quite magical: wild horses champing in the bulrushes; smoke twisting from the wooden huts. The sun had gone but there was still a pinkish warmth to the dusk. After about ten minutes, a Croat soldier appeared and asked us who was fishing. When I told him, he immediately asked whether we'd stopped in Fojnica and asked permission from the Croat Commander to come up here. I just lied and said 'Yes'.

The soldier became curious and started asking about Rose's gear: 'What kind of bait is he using?' Instantly I replied, 'Wet fly,' because, by then, I'd bothered to find out and learn the fishing vocabulary. 'Wet fly, eh? No way is he going to catch anything with that!' said the soldier before ambling off.

Goose was sipping from a can of coke. When I voiced my concern at what the soldier had told me, he didn't even bother to look at me or lower the can, but said, in a tired but wise voice, 'It doesn't matter, Mike. He's never caught a thing out here. So long as he's made that first cast, he'll be happy.'

He was right. Goose knew the boss better than any of us.

In the evening, once the sun had gone down, we sat around the campfire eating German rations with the General, and he shared with us some interesting stories. We eventually crashed out in our sleeping bags in the open air, though throughout the night we had one man awake in two hour-shifts, just in case. Early the next morning, there was a bit more fishing. Jamie Daniell had brought his telescopic rod and was casting away on a rock until some jealous Croat caught him in his spot and then went on to sit in the woods throwing stones at the MA until Jamie was driven off. We then packed up and drove back to the mayhem of Sarajevo."

Our little camping trip turned out to be quite fun, actually—once we managed to find a decent spot, that is, though it had taken some time to do so. The little jaunt left us looking forward to the next one, though it wouldn't have surprised us if that would see us pitching up a tent somewhere on Sniper Alley!

With the weekend approaching, we were all looking forward to some time off. It had been extremely busy the last few weeks, and the next day would see the General flying back to the United Kingdom for a week's leave and to attend meetings at the Ministry of Defence in London. Mick needed to get home to take care of some family matters, as did Clive, while Goose had to go back with the General. Back on home soil, however, he'd have some time for himself. I decided to head over to Italy: one of the Squadron Leaders who ran the flight ops out of the residency grounds had arranged for me to fly over to Ancona on one of the relief flights.

The following morning, I woke early and went and grabbed some breakfast with Mick, who had been out for an early run. The night before, we were in the bar until late, and so he'd been out running the effects off before heading back home. They'd all be flying out later in the day after lunch, but I had to be at the airport at ten to catch the only flight out to Italy on a German C130 aircraft. I'd flown on the British version many times, and although noisy, it was much preferred in this environment over anything else. The C130 Hercules is a four-engine turboprop cargo aircraft and is the main tactical airlift for many military forces worldwide.

I would later go on to do my parachute course jumping out the back of the British version. The models were the same as other countries, with only the exterior design different in color, pattern and home nation information. Over forty models and variants of the Hercules serve with more than fifty nations. Capable of short take-offs and landings from unprepared runways, the C130 was originally designed as a troop, medical evacuation and cargo transport aircraft. The versatile airframe has found uses in a variety of other roles too, including as a gunship, airborne assault, search and rescue, scientific research, weather reconnaissance, aerial refueling as well as firefighting.

I sat in my uncomfortable seat and watched as the loadmaster checked that all the doors were closed.

A member of the flight crew then came over and handed me a bag of sandwiches and a bottle of beer, as well as a packed parachute. The sandwiches and beer would go down well, but I'd received no briefing as to what I should do with the parachute, so I simply placed it under my seat. *I'll give it a go if it comes down to it,* I thought, as I buckled up, ready for take-off. I didn't go on to take my parachute course until after my time in Bosnia, so I was totally lost with it, but apparently it was standard issue to anyone flying on the German C130s.

We took off and enjoyed a smooth exit out of Sarajevo, with the hills of the troublesome Mount Igman to our right allowing us to fly off peacefully for now.

It wasn't a long flight over to Ancona, and the German flight crew were very hospitable, so much so they even invited me up to the cockpit for most of the flight, as well as for the landing. I was met on the ground by one of the RAF drivers, who drove me up to the local port town of Senigallia on Italy's Adriatic coast, thirty kilometres north of Ancona. Arriving at the Palace Hotel by the beach, I found there were various flight crews and support staff staying there, though as soon as I walked in, I knew this wouldn't happen in the Army. The hotel was nice, and I was looking forward to grabbing some food as soon as I settled: as great as Adie's pasta was, I was now in pasta heaven.

I freshened up and watched a bit of television in my room before heading down to meet a couple of the Squadron Leaders in the bar who were over from Sarajevo. With them was their whole team and, being as it was Friday night, I sensed they were ready to hit the town. We ended up in a nightclub near the beach and I got talking to a Swedish girl. It was a cracking night, and I kept having beer bought for me—the RAF lads were sound. We returned to the hotel bar sometime after midnight to carry on the drinking and ended up taking over one of the large dinner tables. It was all getting a bit crazy with guys and girls all having a laugh and a singsong. One of the lads, who was an experienced pilot, jumped up on the table and danced along to the music with a couple of beers in his hand.

He was thoroughly enjoying himself, and rightly so, though I was told that he was scheduled to fly a C130 into Sarajevo in six hours' time. By all accounts, this was the way he was; he was said to be a legend with his flying in combat zones, though I was relieved to not be flying back with him.

The following morning, I headed out with a couple of the lads to visit a wine-tasting facility a couple of hours away before hitting the town again in the evening. The place was offering me a great escape from the bombs and bullets of Sarajevo. The next day, which was Sunday, I had a walk around town and did a little shopping, though I didn't get much as I figured I wouldn't be needing it back in Sarajevo when I returned in a few days' time— or at least I thought it would be in just a few days' time.

That afternoon, I was laying by the pool early in the afternoon, my new Swedish friend next to me, when I received a message from one of the Squadron Leaders, advising me that Jeremy, the General's ADC, had been frantically trying to reach me. The message was very clear: I needed to get back to Sarajevo immediately. By all accounts, the situation on the ground had deteriorated and the General would be making his way back from the UK. His leave had been cut short due to escalating fighting while air strikes from NATO aircraft were pounding Serb artillery positions. I learned that Goose, Clive and Mick had made their way back to RAF Brize Norton for the flight back with the General that day.

I wasn't aware of everything at this stage, but I could see from turning on the news that air strikes were going on by the Serbs, who had been constantly shelling Muslim positions. The United Nations, as well as NATO, therefore reacted accordingly, with the majority of the air strikes courtesy of aircraft coming in from the Allied Tactical Air Force (ATAF) in Vicenza, Italy. I managed to get hold of Jeremy back at the residency after an hour of trying to reach him; he told me I should try to get on the next flight from Ancona to Sarajevo or over to Split in Croatia. The General and the team couldn't fly back into the city due to the air strikes and the amount of firepower coming down on the airport from Serb positions in the hills, and so they were being diverted to Split.

The situation was restricting any aircraft attempting to fly in, so my best bet was to try for the same place. I spoke with one of the pilots—incidentally, the same one who'd been dancing on the tables. I thought if anyone could get me in, he could. He went away to see if they had any flights scheduled. While I waited, I grabbed a brew in the hotel restaurant with my friend after packing up my kit and changing back into my combat uniform. Watching the news again, I thought of how hard the General had worked to establish peace throughout Bosnia. He'd gone on leave thinking that things were improving, and so to learn of this must have been immensely disappointing to him and his ongoing efforts for peace between the warring parties.

The pilot found me in the bar forty-five minutes later and informed me that the situation was really bad.

"You're kidding me," came my response. "Our leave has been cut short, the bloke who runs the show can't even get in, bombs are falling all over the place, and you tell me the situation's *bad*?" We both laughed at his comment. He informed me, however, that there was a scheduled C130 drop into Sarajevo leaving Ancona the next morning, but it wasn't a guarantee that it would go if the situation stayed as it was or if it escalated. I hoped it would go: I was keen to get back, but there was of course a downside. *He*'d be flying it.

I'd be keeping a close eye on him in the bar that evening after his previous antics. I let Jeremy know that I'd be trying to get on that flight. He told me that even the General hadn't been able to land there and had now arrived in Split. If he couldn't get in, then I wasn't seeing much chance for myself considering I was way down the pecking order! Even the most highly experienced helicopter pilots based there, whom we used on a frequent basis, the British, Swedish and French, wouldn't fly into Sarajevo.

Everyone was going over all possible options for getting the General back in.

I was in the hotel lobby waiting to go out to the airport the next morning when I was told it wouldn't be happening. The situation had worsened overnight, and there was no way the RAF were risking one of its aircraft going in, which was understandable. I wasn't the sole reason it was going as it had been a scheduled supply run but, as far as the RAF were concerned, that could now wait—at least for another twenty-four hours.

My pilot friend told me that the British Navy's HMS Invincible was moored in the Adriatic Ocean—which notably acted as the springboard for RAF fighter planes taking off to carry out bombing missions in the Balkans—and that this could also be an option. I'd have to jump on one of the helicopters in Ancona out to the vessel, but I had no concerns about that if it meant getting to Sarajevo. Once there, I would then wait around for either a helicopter to Split or go directly into the hot zone, but that would no doubt be the more challenging scenario. I posed the option to Jeremy and he simply told me to do what I could.

Throughout the day, a number of other options were discussed, but I still wasn't getting anywhere, and I was still stuck in Ancona. There really wasn't anything else I could do other than be patient, but patience was never my strong point (as I'll cover later!). That afternoon, the General arrived into Sarajevo after a couple of the lads had driven the Range Rovers down to Split. It was a four-hour trip each way through the best part of hostile territory, and I found not being there very frustrating.

On the ground, the General was no fool and wasn't one to mess about—something which I greatly admired with him. Once, after a heavy-weapon exclusion zone had been created in and around Sarajevo, he was so angered to hear that a Bosnian Army tank had been spotted inside the zone that he immediately threatened to call a NATO air strike down on it. On another occasion, he made the same threat when he learned that the Bosnian Army Infantry were violating an earlier agreement to vacate a "demilitarized zone" on Mount Igman, just to the south-west of Sarajevo. I knew he would make yet another impact, and I was sure that many were glad that he was now back in the country, though many probably weren't, too.

That evening, I received another message from Jeremy that the General, who had now settled back into the residency, had been asking where I was—more specifically, "Where the hell is Corporal Burton?" I was quite flattered, actually: there he was, the big boss with all this drama and hostility going on around him and having to report to the British Prime Minister as well as the Secretary General of the United Nations, and he was worrying about me. Deep down, I knew that wasn't the case, but having got to know General Rose well over the past few months, I knew he would have wanted his entire team together in the warzone.

I woke early the next morning and got my kit together, went down for some breakfast, and waited for the transportation that would be taking me out to the airfield. After a quick chat with the flight crew when I got down there, I learned that everything was looking good: we were going to go for it, despite the continued fighting. I then made a final call to the residency. Jeremy was in a meeting, as was Colonel Daniell, but I got through to Jean in the office and asked her to arrange for some transport for when I arrived and to make sure the General knew I was on my way.

I smiled as I pictured him sat in the war room, surrounded by the world's top military leaders, only to be passed a note saying, "Sir, we have a breakthrough: Corporal Burton is inbound". I'm sure it would have made his day knowing I was finally on my way. However, a part of me was thinking that, after all the hassle of trying to get there, we'd get shot down somewhere over Bosnia before spending days on escape and evasion through the remote mountainous terrain.

We took off over the Adriatic and headed straight towards Croatia and then up for Sarajevo. Given that we'd be coming in under a high possibility of enemy fire, we'd be making what was known as a "Sarajevo Approach"; the aircraft aggressively jinked from side to side on final approach in order to confuse and evade a missile threat. It was heart-warming stuff, but it's a maneuver that will often be carried out by military aircraft in hostile territory. We turned onto final approach at a high altitude and, once level with the runway only a couple of miles out, the nose of the aircraft suddenly dropped towards the ground.

My stomach immediately turned over as the bulky aircraft, helped by the alarming impetus of gravity, went into an indecently steep dive, the plane pointing almost directly at the ground. The drone of the propellers increased in pitch as the air rushed past them, causing them to spin more quickly. The knot in my stomach rose up to my throat as I figured that the aircraft was surely going to crash. Then, at the very last moment—and it really was the very last moment—the pilot levelled out with the wheels perilously close to the ground whilst making a pass along the runway. It was outstanding flying, though how I didn't throw up or pass out I'll never know. There was, of course, a reason behind such madness, and that was the need to avoid enemy fire as best the pilots could. So, although it was unquestionably uncomfortable, it could have been a damn sight more so if we had been brought down by enemy fire—or, even worse, shot out of the sky.

For take-off, it's a reverse procedure with the aircraft going full throttle down the runway before climbing steeply into the air. Within seconds it would be two-thousand feet up and banking sharply away. Being in the cockpit for the landing was truly an experience I'll never forget but also one I didn't care to repeat in a hurry. I did, however, get to experience one of the take-offs at a later date, and it felt just as nerve-wracking as the landing. Looking back, though, it was a great experience. I felt that the pilots working out in Bosnia, especially the British, were out of this world, but I wasn't making that assumption based on this tour alone. From Northern Ireland to the jungles of Kenya, they were fearless and would not only go in when others wouldn't, but they'd fly as aggressively as they could in order to ensure the mission was completed successfully. They may well have stayed in the nicest of hotels and ate the best food but, for me, they thoroughly deserved such luxuries.

Upon landing in Sarajevo, and when my stomach had finally left my throat and repositioned itself where it belonged, I noticed Clive and Mongo on the tarmac waiting for me. They'd come down from the residency in one of the Range Rovers while the General was in a meeting, though it wasn't good news when I exited the aircraft.

"The old man is pissed at you," commented Clive as I walked towards him.

"Hey, it wasn't my fault I couldn't get back!" I responded.

This went back and forth for the best part of the journey back, while Mongo kept quiet save for the occasional laugh. After dumping my kit in my room, I walked down to the outer office, expecting an earful—but it never happened.

The first person I spotted was Jeremy. "Ah good, you made it back, Burt!"

Then Colonel Daniell: "Hi, Corporal Burton. Have a nice time?"

I considered this to be the calm before the storm; preparing me for the General. I didn't have much time to reply to either of them as he overheard them greeting me and popped his head around the door of his office. "Corporal Burton, run this afternoon." Again, it wasn't a question.

"Yes, Sir." And that was it. Clive had been on a wind-up, and it seemed I was right about the General just wanting his whole team to be with him. It was just like one big family except we didn't do bullshit in this one.

The following few days were spent running around all over the place. There were a few more people traveling with us due to the nature of the situation and the people the General was meeting with; Karadzic up in Pale representing the Serbs, then the Bosnian Muslim President Alija Izetbegovic, as well as various Military Commanders from the warring sides. The residency was a hive of activity, and we also received a visit from Yasushi Akashi, who was the "Under Secretary of the United Nations". As usual, he brought with him a fair-sized entourage. I was meeting a lot of people and it was benefiting me greatly, learning from everyone I interacted with.

Another regular visitor to the residency was a gentleman by the name of Sergio Vieira de Mello. Born in Rio de Janeiro, Brazil, in 1948, he came across as an extremely nice guy to everyone he met and spoke with. He was very polite and always impeccably dressed. As the Head of Civil Affairs of the United Nations Protection Force, he worked closely with General Rose and Victor Andreyev, and would always make a point of speaking to everyone when he visited. By all accounts, Sergio made a great impact on the change in Bosnia and worked closely in order to try to ensure peace for all sides. He took great pride in his work with the United Nations.

Later on in his career, he went on to become the United Nations High Commissioner for Human Rights and was mentioned in some circles as a suitable candidate for Secretary General. Unfortunately, Sergio was later killed in the Canal Hotel bombing in Iraq on August 19, 2003, along with twenty-one other members of his staff. He had been working as the Secretary General's Special Representative in Iraq. Although I wouldn't have classed him as a friend, I was shocked and saddened by his death, as were many others who had the pleasure to know him.

In early October, we continued to be busy out visiting the troops, taking regular runs with the General and hitting the Star Wars bar during the evenings. We also spent a few days at the villa that was available to him in Croatia. During one trip, the General was invited to a concert in Split, which Goose and I attended with him before returning to Sarajevo. The situation on the ground seemed to be worsening, however, with significant incidents occurring daily.

One day, we were at the BiH headquarters in Sarajevo where the General was attending a meeting. As usual, Goose was inside with him while the rest of us were outside. As the General and Goose exited and approached the vehicles, we heard someone from inside the building shouting about something, and so they shot off back inside to see what was happening. Mike followed to interpret what was being said. When they got back upstairs, they learned of an incident in town not far from us: a tram had been shot up and a number of people had reportedly been killed.

Within seconds, the General came out, and we raced off to the site; as we arrived, however, the waiting media tried to ambush the vehicle and get an interview from the General. Never mind the dead and wounded lying around; plenty could have used the help. Most of them must automatically become twats when they get their media badge or when handed a camera. I've been dealing with them for years since, and I wish I could say much has changed. Whether in a war zone environment or chasing celebrities around the streets of Beverly Hills, it can often be very challenging working around media personnel, and I've always found it strange that they almost always show up to an incident soon after it has occurred—sometimes even within seconds of it.

We drove around to the side out of view from all the cameras as the General surveyed the tram; it was full of bullet holes and there was blood everywhere.

Goose and Clive were shadowing the General, with Mike not far behind. It wasn't a pleasant sight at all, but it was something we'd somehow gotten used to. A big investigation took place after the event: although it was determined that the firing came from across the river on the Serb side, they denied it, but the General nonetheless concluded publicly that they were to blame.

One operation that was ongoing during our time in Sarajevo was somewhat critical and something of which only a small number of people were aware and involved in. During the day, we were in the public eye with the General, but as nightfall came, the team adopted a very different role: one that went on to save many people's lives, both Muslim and Serbs. I only talk about this now as the news of it was released a number of years ago, and Mike also wrote about it in his book.

Our small team regularly smuggled people out of Sarajevo. We simply drove them out; those who wanted to go and those who had no money or hope. Those going out would be hidden in our vehicles and be driven straight through the Serb checkpoints surrounding Sarajevo. If they had tried to do it themselves and were caught, they would have at least been arrested, if not assassinated.

Only a few people in the residency knew about this little arrangement and were involved in some way. Outside of that, it was never spoken about. Due to the nature of the operation and the consequences if we were caught, only the General, Victor Andreyev and other key personnel were aware of it. Other than that, there was only a handful of people that were aware. A lapse in concentration by anyone could see the whole operation blown—and with severe consequences, with a high probability of those caught being executed.

Mike became heavily involved when he took over from his predecessor, Nick, and put a lot of effort into the operation. These people were surely going to end up dead due to the terrible conditions if they didn't get out, so that's where it all began.

The numbers involved in carrying out each operation were kept to a minimum and, for it to succeed, a huge amount of planning and discretion was required. It was worth the risk to most of them so they could re-join their families or start a new life. There were kids and old people—those who were in real danger in Sarajevo. It really was a grim place during the war, what with the weather, the squalid living conditions without power, as well as the day-to-day threats, and so it gave them a chance to escape from the never-ending hell they faced.

But—and I do not say this lightly—even though they could hide under a blanket in the back of one of the Range Rovers or in the boot, out of view, the risks to them and to us if we were caught were absolutely huge. It was an unofficial operation; nobody would have laid claim to any knowledge of it. The General might have done had it come down to it, but the British Government would sure as hell have denied it—*if* they'd have known about it, that is. We might have rolled the dice when it came to smuggling people out, but we knew the risks involved. Whoever was doing "Schindler" that particular day or night would just need to get the package over to the other side and, from there, would then make their own way to wherever they were going. This offered them a lot more hope than what they were used to. No one made a note of how many were smuggled out; it just got done and then forgotten about.

The General had laid down the ground rules from the outset. He told Nick that only the helpless, displaced people separated from their families would be moved. The team would never do it on official demand from either side, nor would it be done for money from those wanting to escape. It went deeper than that and, as we spent more and more time in the place, we could feel the pain of those that needed to escape from this hell. It was help for people that really needed it. It was an unauthorized operation, and if we were caught, we'd be well and truly up shit creek without a paddle. There was absolutely no two ways about that, and we were all okay with it.

I know I speak on behalf of the team by saying that, to us, it was worth it. The following is a more detailed account of *Schindler's List* from Mike's book "Trusted Mole":

"'We run an operation and get people out of the city... just drive them out, those who want to go...those with no money and no hope...' The General knows, we tell him each time we're doing it.

He sees it in the humanitarian mandates and so long as we do it on an equitable basis, for those who are desperate, then it's okay.

Nick justified it. "Look, there are four ways out of this place. If you've got money, then you can buy your way out with the mafia who control the tunnel under the airport. Or you can bribe one of the more unscrupulous UN contingents that charge 1,000 Deutschmarks per head. If you've got no money you're pretty much fucked, and if you're still desperate you can take your chances and try and leg it over the line... it's usually fatal as the landmines or snipers get you... and then there's us, Schindlers List.'

The beneficiaries of Schindler's List were all carefully screened. All of them had to be verified and checked out as to whether they fell into the 'endangered to no-hopers' category. Despite the deteriorating security situation, we managed to forge ahead with the Schindler's List operation. If anything, the situation gave it more impetus and urgency. The thing developed into a slick, well-practised event, which minimized the risks to the beneficiaries. I wasn't interested in Schindler's List. I'd scared myself to death getting Una's folk's out with Matt Brey and didn't want to go through all that drama again. Besides, the situation had deteriorated; the Blue Routes were closed, and it was no longer a case of bundling folk willy-nilly into a vehicle and just driving them out.

With the closure of the Blue Routes the Muslims and Serbs had activated their checkpoints again and the risk of discovery was that much greater.

By 'risk', I mean it in a two-fold sense. The risk of beneficiaries being lifted at a Bosnian checkpoint was unthinkable—they'd probably be made to 'disappear'. The risk of compromise to General Rose was also huge and just not worth the hassle. The other thing was that although Nick told me that Rose was briefed every time one of these Schindler's went down, exactly who briefed him was still unknown to me.

I must have just flipped, blew a fuse, rang her back and snapped, 'Ok. Be ready in half an hour. And no suitcases, nothing except passports and documents!' Suitcases were a terrible hassle: they took up room and could be seen. Moreover, if anyone observed them getting into a UN vehicle with suitcases it would have been bloody obvious what was going on. When you think about it, what an unreasonable demand. These people were going to leave this city forever, to start a new life somewhere, and here I was telling them no suitcases.

I grabbed Goose and explained the problem. He'd known that something was afoot. I half expected him to refuse to help but he agreed at once and went off to get the vehicle started. Within twenty minutes we'd driven to where the Pandurevics lived. Ominously, their road was a dead end, while they themselves lived on the fourth floor of an apartment block. It didn't look good at all. It got even worse when they answered the door and started lugging out one suitcase after another. I was cursing and swearing under my breath. What if some nosy neighbour poked his head out of a flat and saw us lugging this lot down the stairs? We looked as though we were off on holiday. Just about everything went bar the kitchen sink. The husband was nervous as hell, pale and sweating. The little girl looked ill too.

I was fuming about the suitcases and really quite panicky, their nervousness infected me, mine them, and by the time we emerged onto the street we were a bundle of sweating, swearing nerves. Then disaster struck. Goose had turned the vehicle round ready for a quick getaway. As we struggled to stuff the cases and their owners into the vehicle a Bosnian policeman rounded the corner. He took one look at what was going on and, hackles up, marched straight up to Jasna. 'ID card!' he snapped. Stupidly she produced it and gave it to him. Goose looked horrified, his face a black mask of anger.

'Fuck!' he spat jumping into the driver's seat and gunning the engine. We'd botched it badly. There was no going back. 'Fuck this!' I was angry and scared. The policeman was starting to say something to Jasna. I didn't give him the chance and just pushed her into the vehicle and jumped in behind as Goose roared off. In the rear-view mirror we could see the policeman still holding the ID card and talking urgently into his radio. It couldn't have been worse. Caught red-handed. What could we do now? They couldn't go back there. They'd be arrested. If we went straight to the residency, we couldn't harbor these people forever. They'd probably plastered the vehicle's make and number plate all over the city. Basically, we'd screwed up the whole show. Goose was fuming. I was fuming. What to do? For want of nothing better we raced into the residency.

'Get 'em into the other vehicles,' someone hissed, Goose probably. Some of the other blokes were on hand and we stuffed the family and their gear into Victor Andreyev's pimp-mobile, a huge American GMC with black-tinted windows and violet, carpeted upholstery. With that and the snatch we tore out of the residency and sped west along Sniper Alley. There was an outside chance that, in different vehicles, we might just bluff our way through the BiH checkpoint at Stup if, and only if, they hadn't raised the chain. If we were stopped there, if they demanded to check the vehicles, the game would be up. I didn't even want to think what would happen then.

123

As we sped through the city we could see policemen eyeing every UN vehicle and reporting into their radios. They were alert and looking for us. The only thing they didn't know was which vehicle to look for.

Sweat was pouring down my face and soaking my shirt. Nobody said a word. The snatch raced through the barriers at the Setup checkpoint just as the guards came running out trying to grab the girder bollards, one tug of which would have raised the chain suspended between the two. We shot across the chain just as it started to rise. I don't think Goose had any intention of stopping anyway. We were through, just. A little further on, right under the flyover, was another BiH checkpoint but having no physical barrier they could do nothing except stare at us as we swept past. Those were the worst two. I don't think Jasna and her family realized that. They were probably flapping about the Serb one at Sierra 4 on the other side of the dash across no-man's-land. This really wasn't a problem. I knew the crew there and just got out and briefly chatted with them. Told them we we're off to a meeting at Lukavica for a meeting with Major Indjic. They didn't even bother to come close to the vehicle.

We were through the worst of it and got through the two French checkpoints at the airport and a final Serb one near Lukavica with no mishaps or drama. They were thanking us, but in reality, we'd so nearly got them all killed and at the same time all this stress is washing off you. Made you feel weak. At the time we didn't really register what we'd done. There was no feeling of having saved someone's life, just immense relief that we hadn't actually killed them. As far as I was concerned it was too risky to do again. Of course, we did loads more. Lots of blokes involved including our American communicators and a couple of

Canadians. I can't adequately explain why. I suppose we got hooked on it. It had a tangible result.

Someone's lives were being affected for the better. There's no point trying to justify Schindler's List: we don't have to do that, those of us who took part in it."

Following that close call, which started off "Schindler's List", each one was carried out with precision, where many others were able to escape from their hell through the team helping them. For them, it was their only hope; for us, it was something special in which we were involved, knowing we were giving those with no hope an opportunity to start again, to get away and to live better lives. To see the fear combined with excitement on their faces as they were bundled into the back of the vehicle before driving them out is something I am sure none of us will ever forget. What the team did should be looked at with great admiration because these people were in a really bad place and in a shit state, but if it were now, there would no doubt be a load of lawyers chasing down those involved.

Another trip to the villa in Trogir for meetings had been planned just a couple of weeks after our last trip there. Most times, as would be the case this weekend, I left a day before the General and jumped on one of the helicopters heading down to Divulje Barracks. I enjoyed doing this and advancing everything as I could fit in a little relaxing myself once I'd taken care of business. When I arrived, I signed for one of the United Nations cars from the transport team and drove over to see the Head Chef, who would be supplying all the food for the next few days before driving out to the villa. Having unloaded the car and put everything away, I then took a drive into the small fishing village of Trogir and did some shopping before returning to the villa a couple of hours later, where I lay on the beach.

The next morning, I drove out to the airport, having first stopped at Divulje to pick up another driver and vehicle. Goose would be driving that car so we would have two in total during the trip.

The only people coming down were the General, Goose, and Jim, one of the America Delta Force lads who was on our team. The remainder of the team would have a few days to relax back in Sarajevo while we were gone. The General would be attending meetings at Divulje Barracks, as well as entertaining a number of senior military and political figures who were visiting from the UK.

I enjoyed these visits, and it was quite a relaxing time there. The General liked to visit as much as he could, and we would usually come here once or twice a month. We knew when it was the right time to relax, and if the General had visitors at the villa, we'd be a little more discreet with our relaxation efforts—though if it was just him, then we'd be lazing around in shorts and T-shirts, but still remaining vigilant, despite the lower threat.

One visit in particular stood out, with Mike, Goose, Jim and I joining General Rose as we departed Sarajevo on a Sea King helicopter for the flight down to Split. Once there, we drove out to the villa to await the next morning's arrival of Lady Rose and their two sons. That evening, we were sitting outside a Trogir fish restaurant dressed in civilian clothing, and the General treated us to dinner. We were all looking forward to a week's R&R. Lady Rose and the boys had driven down from Germany in a new tax-free BMW and were met at the Austro-Slovenian border by Mick and

Clive; they were then escorted to Rijeka in Croatia and then onto the Split-bound ferry.

We were due to meet them at six the next morning. The Roses, Goose and Jim would then motor down the coast to Korcula and stay a week in Fitzroy Maclean's house. The General had known Fitzroy for a number of years as they had both served in the SAS together; there was some military experience between them. The rest of us could do what we wanted while the Roses holidayed: Mike went off to Bol on the island of Brac; Jeremy was off to Rome; Jamie Daniell stayed in Sarajevo to hold the fort; Mick and I went back to Hereford for a night, and then up to the north-east, while Clive stayed in Croatia as backup to Goose and Jim.

We spent most of November back in Sarajevo, with the General having a number of important meetings with the leadership from the warring factions before we all left for the UK on a bit of leave, the plan being to return to Sarajevo for Christmas. It was strange flying in over London; there were lights everywhere, which was a stark contrast from where we'd just come from. We turned left over Biggin Hill, and soon the aircraft banged down on the tarmac at Lyneham—no crazy dive from 18,000 feet here! If the truth be known, I found it rather disappointing. I had a night out in Hereford again and then headed north for a week. As with most visits back whilst having been out in Sarajevo, I felt that popping up in England straight from the war zone was a sharp culture shock, and I needed some time to adjust. Unfortunately, however, by the time I'd done so, I was heading back again.

I knew it was going to happen. I'd been in Middlesbrough for only a few days when it all went pear-shaped back in Sarajevo. I'd been monitoring the news whilst at home and, yet again, the situation on the ground was deteriorating. During my third day home, I was out and about visiting family when I received a call from my mum just after six in the evening.

The Ops desk at Joint Headquarters Wilton in the south of England had called the house trying to reach me. I had to get back to Sarajevo.

Here we go again, I thought, with memories fresh from my time in Italy. I needed to be at RAF Brize Norton by six the next morning in order to meet up with the General and fly back with him to the war zone. Getting there would be a complete pain, and it took me a few hours to even get a rental car arranged.

I knew, however, that the General would want his whole team with him, and so I made sure I got everything squared away. I wasn't going to miss out on whatever the team was involved in again.

It was gone ten in the evening by the time I pulled out onto the A19 and started my journey to Brize. I drove through the night with just a couple of stops off along the way for a coffee, finally arriving at three in the morning. This was made easier by being able to drop the car off on the base. None of the others were there when I arrived, and so I tried to get my head down in the terminal for a bit, though I didn't have much success. Shortly after five, I spotted Goose wandering in. He sat down, and I asked him what this was all about.

"A load of shite," came the reply. He, too, had driven from the north through the night to get here and wasn't at all impressed.

We learned from one of the RAF staffers that Mike would be flying back with us but hadn't arrived yet, though we were expecting him there soon enough—and in fully pissed off mode.

At five-thirty, I spotted him walking towards us, and we chatted over a brew, but I could tell immediately that he was irritated. All of us were. Mike wrote about it in his book, though he had found out about what was going on later than both Goose and I had as he couldn't be reached.

"'We had no way of contacting you. They're coming to get you. Quick, quick, there's no time to lose!' Mum was still jumping around. What the hell has got into you? Nasty pictures of ambulances with doctors in white coats wielding straightjackets flashed through my mind. I managed to calm her down enough to get some semblance of sense out of her. Ten minutes after I'd left for London some staff officer in Wilton had rung up and said that a disaster had blown up in the Balkans.

Rose was returning to theatre at six in the morning from RAF Brize Norton. A staff car had been dispatched to scoop me up and was arriving at four, within an hour. My parents hadn't been able to get hold of me. Dad had gone to bed and poor Mum had stayed up fretting. She was right. There wasn't a moment to lose. The most pressing problem was the motorbike. It couldn't be left on the street for fear of being stolen and there was nowhere to garage it.

At half past three on Sunday morning a curious observer would have seen a seventy-two-year-old woman and her cursing son manhandling a Suzuki down a narrow garden path and into the front room of a two-up two-down terraced house. Our exertions left me quite weak and flustered since there was only a quarter of an hour to go before my lift arrived. I threw off my jeans and climbed into uniform while Mum waited in the street to flag down the staff car. I'd just laced up my boots when a young girl appeared at the front door chaperoned by Mum.

'Yes, that's right, Major Stankovic, this way my dear,' I could hear Mum cooing at the girl who turned out to be a very lost,

and now mightily relieved, Lance Corporal. We gave her a cup of tea and with a peck on Mum's cheek we were off. There hadn't even been enough time to say goodbye to Dad. I was still in a state of shock as we sped out of Farnham. The only thing I knew for sure was that Rose really was jinxed. The driver knew nothing of all this. In fact, it had been her birthday and some bloke in Wilton had put her on duty. She'd been drinking Coke when she was suddenly tasked to Farnham.

We sped quickly through the darkness, down the M4, up to Oxford and across to Brize Norton where she dropped me off at the departure's terminal. The first person I spotted was Goose looking red-eyed and really grumpy. Next to him sat an equally ruffled Glen.

'What's this all about, Goose?'

He just shook his head. 'Dunno, got a call at six yesterday evening and I've been traveling down from the north ever since.' There was no sign of Rose and there was no one to tell us what to do.

I went over to the counter and collared an RAF type and explained that we were Rose's personal staff and would be flying back with him. This did the trick. We scooped up our bags and were led off to the VIP lounge where Rose was pacing up and down in full camouflage gear, looking more manic than I'd ever seen him. Some senior crab sycophant was standing next to him wringing his hands, clearly unable to engage the General in mindless small talk. Rose spied me and barked, 'It's war, Mike! It's fucking war!' There was no time to try to get any sense out of him as the HS125 had arrived and we took off immediately.

During the two-hour hop to Zagreb the General rattled off something about Serb aircraft and NATO. Goose looked bored.

Glen was asleep. The General spent the flight squirming in his seat. By the time we reached Pleso and had been whisked off to HQ UNPROFOR I was still none the wiser. Whatever it was must be bad to have us scuttling back so fast. The base was pandemonium. Squads of UN guards were scurrying about in helmets and flak jackets. The UN right across the Former Republics of Yugoslavia had been put on red alert. The tension and air of panic across the HQ was enough to tell us that this was serious.

Up in the Chief of Staff's office it all became clear. The situation around Bihac had deteriorated. The Serbs had not only regained lost ground but were hard up against the River Una and very close to entering the Bihac Area. The Krajina Serbs had been flying jet sorties from their airbase at Udbina in support of the BSA. NATO had flipped and was going to strike Udbina with a multi-aircraft attack at half past twelve. This left us with barely two hours to get back into Sarajevo before the strike went in and before the Serbs closed down all their checkpoints and the airport. Time was against us. Being a Sunday there were no airlift flights into Sarajevo.

A crew of sleepy and hung-over Ukrainians were reluctantly woken from their beds and ordered to fire up their ancient looking twin-prop AN26, an old flying box originally designed to drop a company of paratroopers. None of us had any faith in the aircraft: Rose, L-P and Spicer had recently flown down from Zagreb in one, piloted by a crew who couldn't map read and who had flown around the city for half an hour while they tried to lower the landing gear with a hammer. As the four of us sat in this droning heap I kept glancing at my watch trying to calculate the timings and managed to convince myself that we weren't going to make it in time. If Serb fire from the Ilidza flats didn't bring us down then the faulty landing gear was going to kill us. I felt sick. We banged down hard on the threshold at Sarajevo at half past twelve. Instead of a hail of bullets and the expected fireball we were met by the vehicles and taken to the residency.

There the bubble burst. The NATO air strike had encountered bad weather and was being postponed twenty-four hours until midday the next day. Less than twelve hours earlier I'd been in a bar in Fulham. The residency was alive with rumor and speculation as to how the Serbs would react once Udbina had been struck. Consensus suggested that at the very least they'd freeze any UN movement over their territory, close down the airport and generally make life thoroughly miserable for all of us. Some even speculated that they'd go further and embark on a sustained shelling of the city. Whatever the reaction, there was only one place to find out—Lukavica barracks."

We were positive we were going to get blown out of the sky, most likely as we came into land in Sarajevo, so while we were on board prior to landing, we prepared as best we could. The General was given all of our body armor to protect him from rounds penetrating the cabin, though we couldn't do much if the plane was shot down. We got very lucky, and although the aircraft was hit with some small arms fire, it was nothing major and if any did go through the cabin, they missed us. We landed to be met by the rest of the team, and it felt good to be back with them. We then sped off to the residency. It had been a crazy last twelve hours: the night before I had been with family and preparing to meet some friends at a bar for a night out; the next I was receiving the call to get back and, a few hours later, I had found myself on a private jet with

General Rose, heading to Zagreb, to be met by troops in helmets and body armor before flying onto Sarajevo and preparing to either be shot out of the sky or crash-land.

If it hadn't been so absurd, we would have laughed; in fact, I think we did as we circled over Sarajevo expecting to get shot down. Goose, Mike and I didn't even know we were heading to the UN Headquarters in Zagreb until we'd taken off from Brize Norton; we thought we were heading straight back to Sarajevo. The following day, Mike and Geordie headed over to Lukavica Barracks, home of the Serbs, to find out what was going on. The strike on Udbina did go ahead, but it didn't seem to bother the Serbs one bit, despite a lot of damage being caused. It seemed that, no matter the consequence of their actions, nothing was stopping them, and so it was a constant dangerous game that they played. General Rose was losing patience with them.

We'd been back in the country for around ten days following our shortened Christmas break. The General wanted to be on the ground over the holiday period to show his commitment to the task and to support the troops. He really was that type of General. On Christmas Eve, he dragged all of us off to Midnight Mass at St Josephs—the huge Catholic Cathedral in the city. The place was packed, and we just hoped it wouldn't get hit—not tonight with all these people here. It was cold inside, and with snow outside falling without any sign of stopping, Mike wore a tracksuit underneath his suit just to stay warm.

On Christmas Day, we were out with the General visiting every single United Nations base and observation posts along the Sarajevo confrontation line, wishing the troops made up of different nationalities a Merry Christmas. Lunch at the residency followed, which was focused on the staff that worked there, as well as their families. They all ate in the dining room and were served by the General and his commanders, as well as those of us who lived there. It was a special time for them. After eating and unwrapping their presents, everyone went outside for a huge snowball fight with the children. We all ate later in the day, with Adie and his team doing an excellent job with catering to everyone. He certainly had his hands full that day making sure there was not only enough food but food of great quality, too. Then, in the evening, we all hit the bar—and even the General popped in for a drink and to socialize with the team.

Following Christmas Day, the powers that be were busy working on a new peace agreement with the Serbs and Muslims. We were back and forth to Pale and the Bosnian Government HQ throughout, and it seemed to be a sensitive time between all. New Year's Eve was soon upon us, and Mike and Geordie had been away in Pale on behalf of the General for the last day or so but were hoping to get back to join in with some of the planned evening fun. With the ongoing discussions not seeming to get anywhere and with the heavy snow falling, their chances of getting off the mountain to join us were fading fast. This was a day of extreme importance. In the office there was the General, Jamie, Jeremy and Tim, all frantically writing up a new peace agreement, which they were sending back and forth to Mike and Geordie. Their job was to get the Serbs to agree to it, but they weren't making progress.

We held off on the evening festivities until we knew it was safe to do so—and it was a good job we did: at eight that night, the General had to go to Pale for the signing ceremony, with the agreement finally approved by the Serbs. Although only ten miles away, with the checkpoints we'd have to clear, as well as the treacherous weather on the mountain, it would take some time for us to get there; however, it was returning that took our focus as it was New Year's Eve, after all.

Off we went in the two Range Rovers, as well as the backing Land Rover, reaching Pale just before nine. As soon as we arrived, we saw it was a hive of activity. The General went straight inside with Goose and Jamie, but we'd only just turned the vehicles around when they came back out again. We were done, it seemed. The General must have walked in, signed on the line, shook hands, and then walked straight back out again. We figured that he was eager for a drink with his team, but it could have been that he just wanted to avoid having a drink of the dreaded slivovitz with the Serbs.

We were chuffed to bits with the quick turnaround as we'd had visions of sitting on the side of a mountain in the freezing cold as the clock struck midnight, while everyone else was having fun back at the residency.

Back down the mountain we went. The roads were slippery, and the snow was posing a problem with the visibility, but we eventually made it back safe. The General and his team retired to the outer office for a well-deserved drink, while the rest of us hit the bar. Mike and Geordie had to stay behind in Pale to tie things up and have a drink with the Serbs, but we knew they wanted to get back to celebrate with us in Sarajevo. They eventually arrived with five minutes to spare before midnight. They fully deserved a drink by then.

General Rose had called for his whole team to celebrate the New Year with him in the foyer of the residency, and so we finished up our drinks, grabbed some new ones, and headed over. While standing alone at the top of the stairs, the General made a brief speech of thanks and toasted to the peace of Bosnia. The place was packed with familiar faces; Adie and his team, flight operations staff, the Signals team, SAS, French Foreign Legion, Captains, Majors, Colonels and Generals—all seeing in the New Year together and hoping for one thing: lasting peace in Bosnia.

When we stepped outside to make our way back to the bar until the early hours, we could hear the sound of gunfire echoing around the city. We could only hope it was celebratory.

A couple of days later, we were out visiting one of the outposts when disaster struck. With no improvement in the weather, the road conditions were becoming treacherous. Goose was driving the Range Rover when it suddenly hit ice and careered off the road, and down a bank and onto its side. It looked serious enough for fatalities. The backing vehicle quickly came to a stop to help, and Mongo managed to pull open the heavy armored door of the Range Rover to get everyone out. Goose and the General were okay, but Jamie Daniell had dislocated his shoulder. General Rose, however, was more concerned about misplacing his own beret! As far as he was concerned, he had an important meeting to get to, and so we left Jamie at the side of the road, waiting to be picked up by a British unit in the area. General Rose wasn't one for sympathy.

On another occasion while off-roading, Frank was driving the Range Rover with Goose in the passenger seat and the General in the back. Frank was encouraged to power through a water-filled tank trap. He should have followed the lessons acquired on the civilian police advanced driving course and the numerous years teaching anti-ambush and off-road driving at Longmoor he'd done.

He buried the Range up to the axels in deep viscous mud, so much so that we had to call in a Norwegian helicopter to pick up the General and Goose to get them back to Sarajevo before nightfall.

The General had been going on for some time about skiing and now, with the weather the way it was, it seemed as good a time as any for him to put his plan into action. What that exact plan was, we didn't know for sure, however, but we all guessed. I mean, we'd been camping in a war zone, so why not add skiing to that, too?

We soon learned that General Rose wanted to finish his time out here with a blast down the Bjelasnica Olympic downhill run. The more it was mentioned, the more we all became concerned, particularly Goose.

When the General chose the day, word soon spread and a number of people, including Mike, made every effort to be elsewhere. Most of us didn't really have a choice, though, and I was surprised that he got out of it.

We had all survived a long time in the war zone, and now it seemed that our time could finally be up as the run was not only an extremely steep one but, more worryingly, it was an unmarked minefield. Early in the tour, they had skied another run, but with Goose being a non-skier and carrying a big rucksack as well as his MP5, he'd encountered a lot of problems. Those he'd been skiing with were all advanced in level. He'd initially coped fine—for the first few seconds, at least—but then he fell and became a huge snowball.

By the time he got to the bottom, his skis and poles were broken and his MP5 had smashed him in the nose. By all accounts, he wasn't too happy. This time around, Goose tried everything to get out of it. He knew I skied, but I wasn't about to commit suicide going down an Olympic run that was littered with unseen mines. He knew he had no choice but to follow the General down. I took over driving the Range Rover when they all jumped out at the top of the run, while Clive drove the Land Rover with Mick and Mongo in the back as we headed to the bottom to wait for them.

Before we set off, however, and as Goose was putting on his skis next to the General, I tried to offer him some encouragement. "Good luck, mate. See you at the bottom, one way or another."

The General didn't know what all the fuss was about, but Goose just looked up and told me to fuck off. We all thought it was hilarious, but we could tell he wasn't comfortable. It wasn't even the hidden mines that were the issue—he'd have been fine with them! It was the skiing itself.

I don't know what the delay was but, by the time we'd parked at the bottom of the slope, they still hadn't even started their descent. We were in radio contact with Goose but decided we'd let him call us if there was a problem. Mick then spotted movement as these little figures in the distance started to make their way down. We watched intently and, although it was a bit of a laugh, there was also a very serious side, too; they could be opened up on by snipers, and then there was the small matter of the land mines they had to navigate around, not to mention one of them possibly falling and injuring themselves. I wasn't out of it yet: if something went wrong, I'd have to drive back up and ski down to help as the others on the team couldn't ski—or so they told me, anyway, but I figured that was a load of crap.

The General was off first and, being an expert skier, he took the lead, closely followed by a couple of others who had come along for the ride. Behind them, we could make out Goose, trickling down as best he could, and I didn't think he was doing too bad other than the odd minor fall. Everyone made it down unscathed and had enjoyed the experience, though Goose still wasn't pleased about it. If he was in the line of fire or faced with a threat, he was colossal; skiing this slope, though, forget it! But fair play to him for doing it, although he clearly didn't have much choice.

The most recent research places the number of victims of the Bosnian War at around 100,000–110,000 civilians and military killed, with a total of 1.8 million displaced. Research has shown that most of the 97,207 documented casualties during the war were Bosniaks (65%), with Serbs in second (25%) and Croats (8%) third. However, 8% of civilian victims were Bosniaks, 10% were Serbs, and more than 5% were Croats, followed by a small number of others, such as Albanians or Romanians. Shockingly, some 30% of the Bosniak civilian victims were women and children.

Despite the evidence of widespread killings, the siege of towns, mass rape, ethnic cleansing and torture in camps and detention centers, as reportedly carried out by different Serb forces, including the JNA, especially in Prijedor, Zvornik, Banja Luka and Foča, judges ruled that the criteria for genocide with the specific intent to destroy Bosnian Muslims were met only in Srebrenica or Eastern Bosnia in 1995. The court concluded that the crimes committed during the 1992–1995 war might amount to crimes against humanity, according to International Law, but that these acts did not, in themselves, constitute genocide per se.

Authorities missed arresting Radovan Karadzic in 1995, when he was an invitee of the United Nations. During his previous visit in 1993, he was handed a service of process for a civil claim under the Alien Tort Act. The Courts ruled that Karadzic was properly served and the trial was permitted to proceed in the

United States District Court. His supporters said that he was no guiltier than any other wartime political leader. His ability to evade capture for over a decade made him a local hero amongst the Serbs. In 2001, hundreds of supporters demonstrated in support of Karadzic in his hometown, whilst in March 2003, his mum, Jovanka, publicly urged him to surrender. In November 2004, a day after the General had a meeting with him in Pale, British Defence officials conceded that military action was unlikely to be successful in bringing Karadzic and others to trial, and that putting political pressure on Balkan governments would be more likely to succeed.

In 2005, Bosnian Serb leaders called on Karadzic to surrender, stating that Bosnia and Serbia could not move ahead economically or politically while he remained at large. After a failed raid earlier in May, on July 7, 2005, NATO troops arrested Karadzic's son, Aleksandar Karadzic, but released him after ten days. Three weeks later, on July 28, Karadzic's wife, Ljiljana Zelen Karadzic, made a call for him to surrender after, in her words, "enormous pressure" had been put on her. The BBC reported that Radovan Karadzic had been sighted in 2005, near Foča, thirty-eight kilometres down the road, on the edge of the Sutjeska National Park.

"Radovan Karadzic has just got out of a red Mercedes" and asserted that "Western intelligence agencies knew roughly where they were", but there seemed to be no political will in London or Washington to risk the lives of British or US agents in a bid to seize him and General Ratko Mladic. Accordingly, on January 10, 2008, the BBC reported that the passports of his closest relatives had been seized. Radovan Karadzic was eventually captured on July 21, 2008, having been indicted for war crimes by the

International Criminal Tribunal for the former Yugoslavia (ICTY) in The Hague, Netherlands. He was arrested in Belgrade and brought before Belgrade's War Crimes Court.

For some time, he had been working at a private clinic in Belgrade, specializing in alternative medicine and psychology under the alias of Dr Dragan David Dabic. There had been an outstanding international arrest warrant against Karadzic for more than a decade following Rule 61 of ICTY, which concluded that there were reasonable grounds for believing that he had committed war crimes, including genocide, against Bosnian Muslim and Bosnian Croat civilians during the Bosnian War (notably spanning 1992–1995).

The United States government had offered a US$5 million reward for his and General Mladic's arrest. In June 2006, there were reports that Mladic had suffered a stroke, his third one, and that he had a low chance of survival. Ratko Mladic was eventually arrested on May 26, 2011, in Lazarevo, near Zrenjanin, in the Banat region of northern Serbia. His arrest was carried out by two-dozen Serbian special police officers wearing black uniforms and masks and sporting no insignia. Security Information Agency and War Crimes Prosecutor's Office agents accompanied the police.

The officers entered the village in four jeeps in the early morning hours while most residents were still asleep. They pulled up to four houses simultaneously, each owned by Mladic's relatives. Mladic was about to venture into the yard for a walk after being awakened by pain when four officers jumped over the fence, broke into the house just as he moved toward the door, grabbing Mladic, forcing him to the floor, and demanding he identify himself. Mladic identified himself correctly and surrendered two pistols he had been carrying.

Mladic was arrested in the house of his cousin, Branislav Mladic, with Branislav having been identified as a possible suspect at least two months before and thus under surveillance right up to his arrest. After some initial doubt as to the identity of the arrested man, Serbian President Boris Tadić confirmed at a press conference that it was Mladic and announced that the process of extraditing him to the ICTY was underway. Mladic had been using the pseudonym "Milorad Komadić" whilst in hiding. Mladic did not have a beard, nor was he wearing any disguise; however, his appearance showed he had "aged considerably" and one of his arms was paralyzed due to a series of strokes.

For everyone concerned, the siege of Sarajevo was a brutal reminder that decades of calm and relative prosperity won't dull the murderous tribal instinct of the human animal. For Sarajevo itself, the surrounding of the city by Bosnian-Serb forces meant large-scale deprivation, hunger and death. We witnessed first-hand innocent people being picked off, one by one, by snipers in the surrounding hills, or slaughtered wholesale by artillery shells aimed at the thronging, under-stocked markets of the city. The encirclement of Sarajevo lasted from April 5, 1992 through to February 29, 1996.

As a result, the Serbs wanted to carve out their own Republika Srpska from Bosnian territory, for alignment or even reuniting with Serbia proper.

Estimates say that more than 12,000 Sarajevans were killed whilst 50,000 were wounded during the siege—almost all were civilians. By 1995, Sarajevo's population had dropped by a third when compared with pre-war levels, as a result of death and migration, to just over one-third of a million. On average, Sarajevo was hit by 329 shell impacts per day—with a record of 3,77 on

July 22, 1993. At the end of 1993, virtually all buildings in the city had been hit, and 35,000 were completely destroyed. The biggest single massacre took place in Markale market on February 4, 1994, during which 68 civilians were killed and 200 wounded by a mortar attack. The destruction of Sarajevo was so deliberate, so destructive, that a new word was coined to describe it; *urbicide*—a term that since then has also been applied to Gaza in Palestine and even New Orleans in the United States following Hurricane Katrina.

One of the grisliest developments of the Sarajevo siege was Sniper Alley, a street so exposed to Serbian firing positions that to walk it meant certain death, whilst running provided some chance of survival. In fact, there were several Sniper Alley equivalents in Sarajevo, and they were places we would purposely drive through with the General as a show of force and to show the locals to not be afraid. Whether it worked I don't know; we hoped it did without the increase of more innocent casualties. Driving through Sniper Alley in armored Range Rovers wasn't good enough for General Rose, though: we'd drive right into the middle of it, get out on foot, and walk, the message being very clear: shoot now, you bastards. We were all as one, from the General down to the lowest ranked person, which was me.

For us as a team, all good things must come to an end, and on January 24, 1995, we all left Sarajevo after General Rose handed over his reign to another British General, Sir Rupert Smith, who would be bringing in his own team. I met some wonderful people during my time there, mostly those who worked in the residency. One was the local barber across the street from us, where I'd pop over and get my hair cut now and again. We all got fed up with the General's hairdresser, who used to come in every couple of weeks;

we were sure he worked part-time as a butcher. We had mixed well with the locals, enjoying a coffee now and again in the park opposite the residency, or a beer and pizza in one of the nearby bars with some of them. They were nice people, just petrified of what was to come next. It was all they seemed to know.

It was rare that you would see a family walking down the street with their children; they would more likely be running from the snipers or the shelling or cowering in a doorway.

There's good and bad in many things. I came across a lot of good, but I also witnessed a hell of a lot of bad—we all did. It changed me as a person, of that I'm sure, and I remain thankful for the experience of working alongside some great people in a very challenging environment, and so doing on a daily basis. We witnessed people losing their lives, but we also played a part in saving many lives, too. Both of these experiences will live with us forever, as it's not just something that disappears with the passing of time.

As for the team, I know that each one of us was, and continues to be, affected in some way after what we experienced during our time there. It was a small, tightknit team that witnessed more than most people had in the region. The American Special Forces guys that were part of our team had to be rotated out after three months each. I later found out from Goose when we were in Iraq together in 2003 that they required counselling when they returned to their units. These were strong and solid guys, real good guys, but that type of thing can affect anyone, as we've seen with the rise of Post-Traumatic Stress Disorder. Lieutenant Colonel Jamie Daniell reportedly lost the plot on his return to the UK, although I'm not sure if it relates solely to his time in Sarajevo, but

I'm guessing it will have contributed. The following is a newspaper report from 'The Independent' in 2001:

"An Army Colonel who carried out a motiveless arson campaign against his neighbors was spared jail on Friday after a court heard he was suffering severe depression after 30 years' service, including spells in Northern Ireland and Bosnia. The court heard that, after falling seriously ill in 1997, Colonel James Daniell, 52, displayed symptoms of obsession towards his neighbors, who were making improvements to their home, a rectory near Taunton. Daniell, who was appointed an OBE after a five-month posting to Sarajevo, explained he was driven to set the house alight because he was angry at disruption and noise caused by building work.

The former Royal Green Jacket, who retired following diagnosis of his condition in 1999, complained anonymously to his local council and then delivered his neighbors matches and a live bullet as a threat, Taunton Crown Court heard. But a judge ruled on Friday that he would escape a custodial sentence because of 'extreme circumstances' only on the condition that he continues to be treated for his illness. Daniell also admitted stealing a credit card and attempting to obtain property by deception in 1997 while suffering from a depressive illness. Judge Graham Hume Jones told him: 'A depressive illness that could lead a man of your character and a man of your bravery and distinction to commit these crimes certainly does amount to an exceptional circumstance. This is the second time you have pleaded a progressive illness. I doubt you will get another chance.' Alan Large, for the defense, said that 'Daniell was still haunted by memories of his early days in the Army and they had been exacerbated by his Balkans experience. On his second tour of

Northern Ireland, aged 22, he was wounded by a gunshot and later praised for gallantry."

I liked Colonel Daniell. He was exposed to a lot of stress during his time in Bosnia, and it seemingly got to him in the end. Not long after we all left, Lieutenant Colonel Tim Spicer left the Army and found himself embroiled in the infamous "Sandline Affair" involving private military operations in Sierra Leone. Spicer was also reported to be involved in a political scandal that became one of the defining moments in the history of Papua New Guinea and particularly that of the ongoing conflict. He then went on to become the CEO of the private military contractor "Aegis Defence Services", which, in March 2004, was awarded a reported US$293 million contract from the Pentagon to protect United States Diplomats and support reconstruction efforts in Iraq. More can be read about this in Tim's book, "An Unorthodox Soldier".

Major Mike Stanley, AKA "Milos Stankovic", received an MBE from the Queen for his service in Bosnia, but was then arrested in December 1997, though later acquitted, on suspicion of treason and betraying state secrets. He then attempted to sue the Ministry of Defence for £1 million for the loss of his Army career, which was a terrible shame. The story behind his arrest and the backing down of the accusers and investigators was revealed in Parliamentary Answers. His book, "Trusted Mole", provides an excellent account of what he went through both during and after his time in Bosnia, and also goes deep into what his journey entailed.

Captain Jeremy Bagshaw returned to his unit and seemed fine, whilst Goose, Bob, Martin, Geordie and Jamie all returned to their SAS Squadrons. Bob left the Army in 2000 and went into the private security industry with a focus on media clients. We would go on to work together on two round-the-world trips, taking in twenty-four countries for an American reality television show some sixteen years on from our time in Bosnia. Geordie went on to head-up a private security company after the war in Iraq in 2003, whilst Jamie took up a lucrative position in London. Mick later left the Army and pursued a career in the telecommunications industry, whilst Clive and Frank served a full career before moving into the security sector. As for the main man, General Rose served a little more time before retiring from the British Army following an outstanding career. He became director of a risk management company before going on to become an international speaker and advisor to the media and business clients.

Our memories of Bosnia will never fade; even if we tried, they could never be erased. The stories we share and the experiences we gain are as clear as if it was only a short time ago. I hope to have the opportunity to revisit Sarajevo again one day; I feel I need to do that and—who knows—maybe other members of the team do, too, though it would be quite the story if we could all revisit for the first time together. Everyone deals with stress and problems in their own way, both good and bad, and I'm not exempt from that. For those who have suffered since—and I'm not exempt from that—it doesn't mean they made mistakes or were any weaker than anyone else. They weren't. They were all good, solid lads who were members of a small elite team during what was a very testing time.

It would be hard for anyone outside of our small team to fully understand what we went through. The highs and the lows, the shots fired, dodging snipers, the destruction and death we'd often come across, and the satisfaction of helping others—it's all ingrained. The camaraderie and spirit of the team couldn't be beaten, however; we were on a mission, and that mission was achieved. Over the twelve months that General Rose was in command in Bosnia, there were a number of assassinations attempts, four of which were of a serious nature. This was no playground—it was as real as it gets—and I was honored to have played my part.

I liken it to the heroic efforts of Seal Team 6, who, in May 2011, undertook a covert operation codenamed "Operation Neptune Spear", and killed "Osama bin Laden", leader of the terrorist organization "Al Qaeda", at his compound in the city of Abbottabad, Pakistan. The attack itself lasted thirty-eight minutes, and there were no casualties to the team. No matter how hard they try, those lads will never ever forget the build-up, as well as those thirty-eight minutes, and we won't forget our time together in Bosnia.

I wish everyone from our team good luck and hope that, one day, we can share the times we had in person because it was one hell of a time, and it gave me the platform to become a leader and international operator for years to come.

NEVER BE AFRAID TO
MAKE A CHANGE

I WAS REACHING A point in my Army career where I felt as though I'd done a lot, but I also knew that I'd need to make a big decision on my future. I'd joined up as a young boy and, since that time, I'd carried out four tours in Northern Ireland and spent a significant amount of time in Bosnia. All I wanted to do when I left Sarajevo was prepare myself for Special Forces selection. My time with General Rose and the SAS team I'd been working with was something I wanted more of, but as a badged soldier. Upon returning to my Battalion, however, I was thrust straight into a Northern Ireland tour, and then another one soon followed.

I was also starting to think long and hard about a career in close protection, which made sense after my time in Sarajevo. I arranged to speak with my Company Commander about it all with the aim of getting his thoughts on the matter. It came as no surprise that he told me he didn't want me to leave. It was June of 1998, and I knew that, if I applied for SAS training, it would be the next winter selection at the earliest. I felt ready at this point and, having spent time with the team in Bosnia and being encouraged by them to go for it, it was heavily on my mind.

The Company Commander asked if I was interested in being an instructor down at The Guards Depot where I'd gone through my own brutal training course nine years earlier. That piqued my interest, and I thought it would be a good idea to go away for a year and think it through. I could also use the time to train hard if indeed I was to apply for selection. I didn't have much time to decide, though I'd become accustomed to that over the years, as the Company Commander said he needed to get somebody in place as soon as possible, and that he thought I'd be a good fit for it.

Three days later, I made the hour drive to Pirbright in Surrey to take up my new position as a training instructor. It felt strange being there as staff, though I knew plenty of people there who were either instructors or staff members. One such individual was Bob, a Police Sergeant. We'd played in the same Infantry football team together. I met up with the other members of the training team, too, and in a few days' time, we'd be allocated a platoon of forty-two recruits who would be going through training together.

It took me some time to adjust but, after a while, I found myself in a good routine. Part of my role was to ensure that their fitness levels were improving, their weapons skills were up to speed, and to carry out drill, kit and equipment, room inspections and admin. I was finding it enjoyable. We spent some time on short exercises, and it was much more fun here, as an instructor, than it was as a recruit, where you'd be digging a trench to sleep in during the winter months. The fitness side was especially enjoyable and by this stage of my career, I was feeling exceptionally fit.

The recruits would carry 30lbs in their Bergens on an eight-mile run while I'd have double—and, to prove a point, I made them all feel the weight of my Bergen, both before we started and as soon as we finished. The idea was to spur them on, and it seemed to do the trick with a few but a number of others were not even able to handle the run, let alone carry the weight, even though we were only just building them up to get used to a more intense training schedule.

Halfway through my posting, I went away on a four-week close protection course in the south-east of England, which I'd chosen as my resettlement package. I'd decided it was what I wanted to do and had therefore made the decision that I'd see out my time before moving into civvy street. Despite enjoying being an instructor, though, I'd realized before I went away on the course that many things had changed since I'd gone through basic training, with the Ministry of Defence having made a lot of amendments to the curriculum of recruit training. As an example, the recruits couldn't be shouted at as much as they could when I went through it, and the fitness requirements weren't as intense as they were back then, either. It seemed much more laid-back, and I had a feeling that a lot of instructors were afraid to say or do what they thought was best. I found it to be quite different.

There was even a rumor that, if a recruit was shouted at and he felt it was unjust, he could show the instructor a yellow card, like a referee would do in a football game. If an instructor received two, he'd face disciplinary action. I only hoped this wasn't true.

Gradually, some of the recruits would be dropping out of training, though we did have some good recruits, those who seemed to absorb everything that was thrown at them and who always tried to make the next day better for themselves, but those were few and far between. There was still a decent level of discipline, however; it was just handled more in front of the Company Commander, rather than the platoon staff.

I'd been at the training depot for six months and, although it was a good challenge, I decided to get out of there before a young kid complaining of unfair treatment ruined my or someone else's career. The British Army continues to teach the best military tactics across the world, and yet that can often be spoilt with the restrictions imposed—especially when it comes to training. I won't win any fans in the Ministry of Defence for saying that, but they know it's true, as do countless others, including serving and former high-ranking officers.

Rather than going to my Training Commander, I called up my Company Commander back at my Battalion and explained how I felt about the place. He was now out in Northern Ireland and, while I could have taken the easy way out and wound down my time with a relatively easy number, that just wasn't me. Instead, one week later, I headed to "Bandit Country" across the water again. I handed over to my replacement by wishing him "Good luck" as we shook hands. I then left.

In early January, I boarded the flight from Brize Norton to Aldergrove in Belfast; a familiar route I'd taken over the last nine years, though I knew it would be the last time I made the journey out there. I was met at the military side of the airport by two of the transport guys I knew. Dressed in plain clothes, we headed to Bessbrook Mill in South Armagh, arriving just before eight in the evening. I threw my kit in my transit room and headed to the bar to catch up with some of the lads. The following morning, I'd have to jump on one of the helicopters to take me to the out-base where my company were. The headquarter element were out of Bessbrook Mill, again with the patrol companies spread out in smaller bases in Newtown Hamilton, Forkhill and Crossmaglen, also known as XMG, and where I was heading.

Crossmaglen is a village in South Armagh with a population of approximately 1,459, making it the largest village in South Armagh. The British Army had a major presence in the area over the years, despite being unwanted by most of the locals. During the troubles, the Provisional Irish Republican Army in South Armagh killed at least 58 police officers and 124 soldiers, many in Crossmaglen itself. Our biggest problem here was the South Armagh Brigade of the Provisional Irish Republican Army, which were operating throughout South Armagh—a predominantly Nationalist area along the border with the Republic of Ireland. It was organized into two Battalions: one around Jonesborough and the other around our area in Crossmaglen. By the mid-1990s, the South Armagh Brigade was thought to consist of about forty members.

The morning after I arrived, I went and grabbed breakfast in the cookhouse and headed over to see the transport lads, where I had a brew in their office and got up to speed with their pattern of life in Bessbrook.

I was familiar with how things were, having spent my last tour as one of the section commanders. Vehicle movement to the XMG area was restricted due to the threat; it was mainly helicoptering in and out only. The South Armagh Brigade of the IRA had been, by far, the most effective brigade in shooting down British helicopters during the conflict. They'd carried out twenty-three attacks, bringing a number of them down on separate occasions in 1978, 1988 and 1994. They weren't to be taken lightly when it came to attacks on the security forces—either on the ground or in the air.

I settled in quickly and was quite surprised how many new members there were in the company. I knew plenty there but, for many, this was their first tour over the water. I'd be working many roles, from Section Commander of a patrol team, to flying around in the helis with the Company Commander visiting various observation towers and the troops manning them. In 1986, the British Army had erected hilltop observation posts in South

Armagh; three of them were in our area of operations staffed with members of our company. At the height of the British military presence, there were eighteen watchtowers throughout South Armagh. One of the key reasons for constructing the posts from 1986 was to watch Thomas "Slab" Murphy, the then-IRA Chief-of-Staff whom MI5 once classified as the most dangerous terrorist in Europe.

Two of the posts overlooked the millionaire smuggler's farm that straddled the Irish border and would be a key focus of our operations over the next few months. The 1994 ceasefire was a blow to the South Armagh Brigade as it allowed the British Security Forces to operate openly in the area without fear of attack and to build intelligence on IRA members. We knew there was still plenty of activity going on; our guys in the watchtowers and the various covert operations that were being conducted could attest to that. We were busy and we took nothing for granted—peace process or not. Being here had us tasked with confronting some of the IRA's most deadly units in the heart of South Armagh—an area commonly referred to by many as "Bandit Country" because of its history of lawlessness.

Although it felt good to be back on operations, my time in Northern Ireland was, however, soon coming to an end, as was my military career. I had thought long and hard about leaving and had set my sights on a career in close protection. I knew fine well that the hard work would start here with a new career ahead of me.

On my final night in Crossmaglen, I reflected on my achievements and the ups and downs of my serving years.

It was appropriate that I had started out in the Army with a tour of Northern Ireland and then finished my career towards the end of my fifth tour there. I know that some doubted my ability to last five minutes in the Army, but ten years down the line and seven operational tours later, I was proud to have achieved what I did.

Throughout my Army career, I proved that, no matter what anyone thinks or says, it's possible to get out there and do whatever you want—and not only that, but to excel at it. For anyone reading this book that is faced with that challenge, my message for you is this: go out there and do what you want to do and do it to the best of your ability. To hell with what anyone else thinks. I know members of my family were proud of me for what I achieved, and some seemed disappointed I was now leaving, but I wanted to move on: I'd done a lot and was now focused on a career within the security industry.

Major risks were often taken during my Army career, but you can only take so many. Nonetheless, I learned a great deal about decision-making, and I felt well-guided throughout that. I believe that the decisions I made, as well as the advice I followed, have, to this day, benefited me and those around me. I wasn't sad to be leaving the Army—quite the opposite, in fact: I was excited for the next adventure.

I drove out of Victoria Barracks in Windsor for the final time, turning left and passing through the small winding streets before hopping onto the M4 motorway towards the M25, and then taking the M1 heading north. It was a route I was familiar with. I was driving home to Middlesbrough, but I already knew I had no plans to stay there for the long-term. Having finished my resettlement course a number of months earlier, I was now a qualified and basic trained bodyguard; it was time to pursue a new career. Despite the past ten years in the Army, I was still quite young to pursue a career in close protection, though I was determined to put the work and training in to succeed when given an opportunity. When that would be, however, I had no clue.

It felt strange being home for an extended period of time; however, I tried as best as I could to adapt, though it wasn't easy. Going out at the weekend was becoming a common occurrence, as was watching the Boro, but finding work was proving to be challenging. I found some driving work that I took on in order to bring in some money, but I had no interest in that as a career. This only made me more and more determined to find a position in which I knew I could excel, though I knew I wasn't going to find it where I was. I applied for several close protection related jobs; however, many were looking for those who had already gained some experience in the private sector.

I felt like I was in a Catch 22.

SADNESS, SORROW AND
ANGER FOR ALL

BREAKING NEWS FLASHED ON the small screen hung high up on the wall. It immediately caught my attention, as well as that of a number of others who had walked into the gas station on the I-10 freeway in Palm Springs, California. I'd been in the desert city for the past five days, having come over to see some friends, but any enjoyment soon disappeared as I looked up at the screen to see such devastation.

One of the famous World Trade Center towers in New York had been reportedly hit by a "small aircraft" and was now on fire. Rumors were already rife across the news that it had been deliberate. I watched intently as I waited for the shuttle bus to take me to Los Angeles, but I was early and still had some time to wait. I felt that this was more than an accident, and it didn't seem as though it had been caused by a small aircraft. And then suddenly, a second plane crashed into the second tower.

My suspicions were confirmed: The United States of America was under attack.

My ride had turned up but I was in shock, along with everyone else who sat on the shuttle bus. I just wanted to sit in front of the television screen and remain as updated as I could with what was happening, as shocking as it was, not stuck in a van for the next two hours. I was heading to Los Angeles to meet a colleague of mine. Steve was from the UK but was in LA for a while, working security with a celebrity. We'd arranged to meet up for a few days and catch up on what we'd both been up to. I'd worked with him for a few months when I'd left the Army; he was the head of a close protection team I had joined on a job in London, and when it ended, I'd returned to Middlesbrough. Work had been fairly quiet since I left for America.

Over the coming hours, we learned more about the atrocity on the East Coast. Nineteen hijackers had taken control of four commercial airliners en route to San Francisco and Los Angeles from Boston, Newark and Washington DC. At 8:46AM Eastern Standard Time, three hours ahead of me in California, American Airlines Flight 11 crashed into the World Trade Center's North Tower, followed by United Airlines Flight 175, which hit the South Tower at 9:03AM. Another group of hijackers flew American Airlines Flight 77 into the Pentagon at 9:37AM. A fourth flight, United Airlines Flight 93, whose target was thought to be either the Capitol Building or the White House, crashed near Shanksville, Pennsylvania, at 10:03AM.

During the hijacking of the planes, the hijackers used box-cutter knives to kill flight attendants, passengers and crewmembers, including the captain of Flight 11. Some passengers were able to make phone calls using the cabin air phone service and mobile phones, and provide details, including the fact that several hijackers were aboard each plane, that mace or other forms of noxious chemical spray, such as tear gas or pepper spray, was being used, and that some people on board had been stabbed. A flight attendant on Flight 11, a passenger on Flight 175 and passengers on Flight 93 mentioned that the hijackers had bombs, but one of the passengers also said that he thought the bombs were fake.

Reports were soon coming in of who may have orchestrated the attacks; the finger of blame was being firmly pointed at known terrorist leader Osama Bin Laden. Born March 10, 1957, Bin Laden was a member of the prominent Saudi Arabian Bin Laden family and the founder of Al-Qaeda. He was also associated with numerous mass casualty attacks against civilian targets. Bin Laden and fellow Al-Qaeda leaders were believed to be hiding in the border regions between Afghanistan and Pakistan. I knew they'd need to find the smallest hole possible before the biggest storm known to man descended upon them.

Over the coming weeks, the United States was to respond to the attacks by launching a War on Terrorism, attacking Afghanistan to depose the Taliban, who had harbored Al-Qaeda terrorists. Many other states also strengthened their anti-terrorism legislation and expanded law enforcement powers. The American stock exchange stayed closed for the rest of the week of the attacks, and posted enormous losses upon reopening, especially in the airline and insurance industries. The economy of Lower Manhattan ground to a halt, with billions of dollars in office space damaged or destroyed. Excluding the nineteen hijackers, 2,974 people died in the attacks. Another 24 were missing and presumed dead, whilst 6,291 were injured. The overwhelming majority of casualties were civilians, including nationals of more than 90 different countries.

We pulled into the driveway of the Beverly Hilton, a grand old hotel in the heart of Beverly Hills. I called Steve's room from the front desk but didn't get an answer, so I went and had a brew at the lobby bar where I was able to watch the TV. I thought Steve may have had to leave at short notice and so I stayed in the bar, watching the news. I ordered some food and, as hungry as I was, I felt sick with the images that were appearing on the screen in front of me. With the news streams broadcasting live, camera shots would often cut away as victims were seen jumping from the windows with no other way down; the pain and suffering clear as they jumped to their deaths from the high-rise buildings.

I was just finishing my lunch when I noticed Steve and a couple of other lads walk into the lobby. He was, at that time, part of the protection team for Madonna during her "Drowned World Tour" and was in Los Angeles where some of the shows were taking place, the tour having started in Barcelona back in June. They were due to have a show that evening at the Staples Center in downtown LA, but Madonna had cancelled it that morning out of respect for the tragedy that had occurred earlier on in the day. That evening, I asked Steve if he wanted to go out for a drink; he doesn't drink alcohol, and so I figured he probably wouldn't, and the fact that he'd hardly had any nights off over the last few months meant he chose to stay in the hotel to rest.

I fancied a walk around Beverly Hills, so I headed out to see what it was all about. The day's events were playing heavily on my mind. I fancied a drink, but I couldn't find anywhere open as I walked around. The place was completely deserted, clearly the morning's events had affected everyone. Throughout the day, emergency warnings were issued to the cities of Miami, Chicago and Los Angeles, and so I guessed people just wanted to stay at home for the evening. I couldn't blame them. I'd had enough of trying to find a place to get a drink and so I decided to head back to the hotel and call it a night.

Crossing Santa Monica and Wilshire Boulevard, I noticed what seemed like a bar that was adjoined to the Hilton where I was staying. The car park was empty, and I couldn't see anyone inside through the glass doors, although the lights were on and a TV was showing the news. I tried the door and found it was open, and so went inside to the bar. Sat down at a booth were two girls chatting away; I didn't pay much attention to them as it was quite dark and my mind was elsewhere. One of the girls got up and politely asked what I would like to drink. I ordered a beer of some sort and then a second a short time after. Trader Vic's was, by all accounts, a popular spot, but it seemed that nobody was interested on this particular night, which was understandable.

The girl who served me had said it was one of the top places in Beverly Hills, but she thought I'd be the only one in tonight because of the tragedy. We chatted away with her friend still in the bar and discussed what was happening. After a while, her friend left, and the hostess and I got to know more about one another. Although I hadn't been in the mood to meet anyone, she seemed nice. I told her I was only in town for a few days, visiting a friend, and she had kindly offered to show me around the following day. I knew Steve would be working and it would give me an opportunity to see the place.

The next morning, Michelle collected me from the hotel and we drove around. It was interesting seeing LA and all it offered. We then headed out to Malibu and sat on the beach. We were having a really nice time, and I felt there could be something between us. I certainly felt it was worth pursuing as we were having fun and really liked each other. Over the next few days. I spent time with Steve and caught up on all that he'd been up to for the past year. He was enjoying working with Madonna but said that it was heavy going: the strains of a world tour and the hours they worked meant that he didn't have much time off for himself. I was still new to the business of close protection, so it was good to learn about how he was doing things; he had a lot of experience.

I'd never really thought much about working with celebrities and had certainly not had any interest in moving away from England, but things with Michelle were moving at quite a fast pace, which was more to do with the fact that I lived in the UK. I think we both felt it a shame to go all the way back there when we were having fun, and so what had initially turned out to be a two-week American holiday soon turned into an eighteen-month stay.

I couldn't work legally in the United States during that time, and so it was spent with working away as much as I could with projects in Europe, Canada and South America. I would then return to the US on a ninety-day tourist visa. I was taking a chance, but I believed it to be worth it.

It was difficult at first, having to leave the country all the time, but we both got used to it. I was getting busier with training and operations and learning about the US market for close protection. I thought that, if I'd be staying out in the States, then I'd need to learn as much as I could. There were times, however, that I would go long periods of time without making any money, but that was to be expected considering the circumstances of being on a tourist visa.

BEING IN THE LINE OF FIRE

MARCH OF 2003 WITNESSED the start of the second Iraq war with a multinational force led by and composed largely of American and British troops. The military response led to the quick defeat of the Iraqi military and the eventual capture and execution of Saddam Hussein. Once the initial war was over, Iraq was fast becoming a haven for British, American and other foreign business interests, from electrical, power and building organizations through to energy and oil representatives, which then induced the need for a huge security requirement for the people that were visiting and working in the region.

There were an estimated 110,000 security contractors working in the country carrying out various roles, from convoy and personal protection, installation security, dignitary and corporate protection to ensuring all the news teams were safe. There were perhaps five or six companies I was looking at, the majority of them British, though two were based in the States. Having spent the previous six months instructing on a number of high-risk close protection courses in the United States, I was both fully aware of what was going on in Iraq and also up to speed with my personal and physical training. At this point, I fancied jumping on the bandwagon for a few months at least. The majority of those I'd been training were either on a break from the war zone—affectionately known as "the sandbox"—or were otherwise heading out for the first time and doing some deployment training.

In July, I reached out to some of my contacts and let them know that I was making myself available, having discussed this at length with Michelle. The risk versus reward for me was worth it; I could do six months over in the sandbox, which financially would be good for us and allow us to be able to have a nice holiday somewhere at the end of it. There was, however, a part of me that wanted the buzz of the high-risk work. It might sound crazy to some, but it's what I trained for, and I took an enormous amount of satisfaction from it. I received some positive responses from some of those responsible for putting boots on the ground; it seemed to be only a matter of time before I'd find myself amongst it. I knew the risk involved but, at the time, with being unable to work legally in the United States, it would offer me a great way to make good money while gaining some valuable experience for my career.

Two weeks later, I was in London sorting through all the pre-deployment paperwork for the company I was going to be working with. I was eager to get going and, once I had everything squared away, I met up with some friends for a few drinks. I woke early the next morning and had a quick wash before walking over to Hyde Park and going for a run, passing a number of Household Cavalry troops from the nearby barracks out doing their morning fitness. It felt good out: it was sunny, and the summer heat was already rising. As I ran, I looked up at the aircraft coming in one after the other on final approach into Heathrow, knowing I'd be up there later that night, on my way into a warzone.

Returning to the hotel, I grabbed a brew and cooled down while reading the paper in the lobby, before heading up to my room to shower and change before going for a good old English breakfast. My plate was stacked as I knew it would be a long day, and I had no idea what I'd be having for breakfast the following morning. There were a number of other lads heading out, who were all sat eating, all keeping themselves to themselves. I was fine with that as I was thinking of the day ahead and couldn't be bothered chatting much. The occasional "Hi, mate" was enough.

The British Airways flight took off on time at 9.20PM, and once we levelled, I started to doze off. Thankfully, I managed something that I always find hard to do: sleep on a flight. This one would be seven hours. I woke with only fifty minutes remaining—an amazing achievement for me. We arrived into Kuwait International Airport shortly after 6AM and, by the time I cleared customs and immigration, it was close to seven. I was looking forward to the day ahead, though, as I had a number of people to meet before going over the border and into Iraq.

As I entered the arrivals hall, the humidity hit me. I spotted a number of British and American military personnel milling about, waiting for people coming in from flights. I was met by one of the lads who worked at the company office in Kuwait, and so I fired loads of questions his way once we got in the car. The company had a villa that had been purchased around the time of their arrival on the ground in Iraq and was being used as the regional headquarters for all logistics and operational management. It seemed a good set up.

It was still early when I arrived and it was relatively quiet, with only a couple of admin staff and ops personnel to be seen. I learned that the three main locations where the company had a presence in Iraq were Baghdad, Basra and the port town of Umm Qasr, which was the closest to Kuwait just over the Iraqi border. The team in Umm Qasr operated in more of a logistics and admin role rather than a protective one, with regular trips down to Kuwait to pick up supplies. Thankfully, I was off to Basra, where the action was.

Perhaps Iraq's fourth or fifth largest city with a population estimated at just over one million people, Basra is located along the Shatt Al-Arab waterway, a total of fifty-five kilometres from the seas of the Persian Gulf and 545 kilometres from the capital, Baghdad. The area surrounding Basra provided substantial petroleum resources and many oil wells that became a target for insurgents. From March through to May of 2003, when the war had started, the city and surrounding areas witnessed some of the heaviest fighting. British Forces took the city on April 6, 2003, and the capture of Basra was pivotal in the fight against the Iraqi forces. It became the first stop for both British and United States troops deploying throughout various parts of the country.

One of the teams was on their way down from Umm Qasr to collect me in the afternoon; as soon as they arrived, I loaded up my kit whilst the driver popped into the office to drop a few things off. The drive to the border through the desert took only forty-five minutes and was of great interest to me. Heading out of the city on the Jahra Road, my thoughts strayed to the previous war, back in 1991 when I had joined the Army, and how it must have been in this area. Back then, this stretch of road will have been saturated with Iraqi armored vehicles, as well as tanks and troops on their way to invade Kuwait. This led to a massive response by British and American troops in what would be known as "Operation Desert Storm".

When we pulled up at the border checkpoint, we met up with another team, who were waiting to escort us the short distance to the base in Umm Qasr. No matter the distance or task at that time, it was forbidden to have only one vehicle traveling, such was the threat, so we'd need to have two vehicles with either two or four guys in each one. We stopped to get weapons from the lads in the waiting vehicle before heading across the border in our two-vehicle convoy. "We are now in Iraq!" the driver excitedly called out.

The drive from the border to the base was very short—no more than ten minutes—but, even so, no chances were taken: anything could happen on this route, I was told, as it was used several times throughout the day by security teams and coalition forces.

The environment and scenery were very different to where I'd come from in Kuwait. As we drove through a rundown village, I saw fires burning at the sides of the road, kids playing in the dirt with no shoes on their feet, and dogs roaming around barking aggressively as the vehicles sped by. The base at Umm Qasr was home to a British Infantry Armored unit, in addition to a number of support elements. The company I was working for were the primary private military company, also known as a PMC, and operated out of a hanger in the far corner of the base that was guarded by a team of Gurkha Soldiers.

It was very quiet when we pulled in, as a number of the teams were out on a task, and so we went to the cookhouse for a brew and a bit of food. On the way, I ran into one of the old Company Sergeant Majors from my Battalion and learned that he was the head honcho for the company in Umm Qasr. We chatted for a few minutes as he brought me up to speed with what was going on; this also allowed him the opportunity to blast off about a few things he didn't like. Mick told me to meet him after lunch at the armoury across the way and he'd sort out my gear, which I'd need to sign for. I was issued with a H&K MP5 automatic weapon, a Russian-made AK-47, as well as an Iraqi 9mm Tariq pistol and some body armour. I was assured by Mick that the Tariq was useless and that I would need to stick to the MP5 if I needed to kill a bad guy.

A separate team from Basra was on their way to collect me and would be arriving in the next fifteen minutes, and so I carried out a weapons check before leaving. As Mick and I stood talking, a couple of Mitsubishis SUVs swept into the compound, leaving a trail of dust behind them. My ride had arrived. I was to quickly find that the teams at Umm Qasr had the worst job as they didn't really go anywhere; I was bored within an hour of arriving. The teams in Basra and Baghdad were active 24/7, though the risk will have been a lot higher, I was sure about that.

I acquainted myself over yet another brew with the three guys who had come to collect me. We chatted for a while and I learned that they were a man down in their team, and so I hoped I'd be sticking with them. They all seemed to be fairly switched-on lads. Jim was the team leader and a veteran of many years' service in the Special Air Service. I'd be in the car with him for the drive back. He had long grey hair and a bushy moustache; he looked every part the old school soldier. In the chase car, there was Stu, who was a serving member of 21 SAS, and alongside him there was Shaun, who had recently left the Parachute Regiment.

As I loaded my kit into the vehicle, Jim returned from the ops room, having given them the information of our departure and the route we were taking. If we hadn't arrived at our destination by a certain time, a separate team would then be deployed to sweep our route, using the information Jim had provided to them. You couldn't take any chances here, they told me.

We pulled out of the base and headed West on the Basra Road. Along the way, Jim briefed me on the regional situation, any recent threats, as well as how life was for the teams in the city. I learned that one of the ongoing issues for the teams had been weapons—or, rather, a lack of them. They needed more AK-47s, as well as extra ammunition for the Tariq pistols; apparently, however, they were always malfunctioning. That evening, we'd be going out to meet a local contact to source more weapons and ammunition. I got to like Jim immediately. His friendly tell-it-how-it-was attitude made things easier, and, in this environment, there was no room for bullshit. I knew that before I'd spent any time in the place.

Forty-five minutes after leaving Umm Qasr, we swept into an old car park in the south-eastern end of town, with Jim pointing out our hotel across the street. I grabbed my bag from the car while the other lads covered me with their weapons in case of a sniper attack. The threat here was very real. The hotel was basic but, considering the environment, it was probably one of the best in the area. My room would be on the third floor of the four-storey building. It was small with two single beds, and a grubby shower and toilet area. Downstairs in the lobby and dining room area you couldn't see outside as all the windows had either been blown out, shot out, or were boarded up to prevent grenades from being thrown in. If the hotel was stormed by insurgents in the middle of the night, every one of us needed to know the layout; the location of the client rooms and the team members' rooms, the best places to take control of the hotel for fire positions, as well as access and escape routes.

The company had anywhere between twelve and eighteen lads there at any one time, all of whom made up the four-man close protection teams looking after six British Government people. We had our own recreation room and, although it was small, it enabled us to make tea and toast in the morning and also gave us somewhere to hang out. There was no gym. The best we could do was work out in our rooms with push-up bars and homemade dumb bells made up of buckets filled with water. On the fourth floor, I came across an access door that led to the roof, and so I pushed it open and explored carefully. It wasn't a very big hotel, but the roof offered enough space to relax, work out, and even do a little sunbathing if we wanted.

It also offered an excellent view of parts of the city, and, as the weeks went by, I found it very useful during my downtime to watch teams arriving or departing with clients when I wasn't out on the ground. By being able to look down directly at them, it allowed for the ability to see if anyone was watching them or being set up for an attack. Others did the same. Every time I went up on my time off, I would always take my backpack with weapons, maps and smoke grenades inside. I wanted to be prepared to the greatest degree in case something occurred outside, or the hotel got stormed, which was a high possibility. I assumed that, out here, anything could happen.

I learned that one of the most frequent trips we'd be making would be to the Palace of Saddam Hussein's notorious son, Uday, which was located on the banks of the Euphrates River, five minutes from our hotel. It was believed that the river running in front of the Palace was full of dead bodies, all executed at the hands of Uday. The Palace had been taken over by British troops when they entered the city back in April and was now home to a resident Infantry Battalion for their six-month tour of duty. It was also where the Coalition Provisional Authority or CPA was located and, more importantly to many, was the best place to eat, apparently. The CPA was established as a transitional government following the invasion of Iraq by the United States, Great Britain, and other members of the coalition, and was formed to oust the government of Saddam Hussein.

The remainder of my first day on the team was spent going over maps familiarizing myself with the various routes we'd be taking to the different locations, with a focus on both primary and backups. I also got around to meeting the rest of the guys once they were all back at the hotel. With a small bit of orientation with a couple of the lads around the city the following morning, I felt good to go. The whole unit was broken down into four teams led by Eddie, Jim, Carl and Steve who I'd worked with on another job previously.

When I arrived at Umm Qasr, it was Jim's team that had come to collect me, so that's where I'd be staying for now. Keith, who I'd also worked with previously, had arrived a week after me. It was good to have him here, though he'd be joining Eddie's team for now. Most of the lads were either current or former Special Forces or had served with elite Infantry units, and we also had a couple of medics on the team, which I appreciated.

Our area of operations would be wherever the clients would be handling business matters, though it would always be at our discretion with the various threats we could be facing in that particular area. The four towns and cities in Southern Iraq that would see us frequently visiting were Basra, Al-Amarah, which was an hour away, Al Nasiriyah, notably an hour and a half away, and As-Samawah, which was the furthest away at three hours, but all offered similar and very real dangers.

I was soon finding the job interesting. When we drove, it was always at speed and in a two- or three-vehicle motorcade. This was for two main reasons: first, to avoid, as best we could, any attack on our vehicles; and second, to take control of the road in an effort to deter anyone that fancied hitting us. The downside to driving at speed is that you don't have as much time to survey the road in front of you, and levels of awareness are lower, which is especially important considering the placement of improvised explosive devices, or IEDs, by the bad guys. I'd done a tactical driving course whilst in the Army, and so that was my main role on the team. Jim had known this when I arrived and asked if I'd drive the chase car. It was highly enjoyable, but it could be dangerous and stressful, too.

The role of the chase car is to protect the client vehicle—it's that simple. It acts as a buffer between that and the threat, and, if need be, it will take the hit, thereby minimizing any threat or impact from all sides. Should a vehicle try to ram the client car, the chase vehicle would get in-between them in order to take the impact and/or take out the attackers. That's the idea anyway. Meanwhile, the passenger in the chase should then, by that point, be firing on fully automatic through the windscreen, engaging the target.

Likewise, if a gunman appears and suddenly opens up on the client's car, the chase comes up on the threat side in an effort to block the client from getting hit whilst at once hopefully taking out the target. When this happens, the noise is immense, and the adrenalin is pumping; you really have to be prepared for that type of environment and threat. There simply isn't room for any delay or hesitation.

For those reasons, amongst others, the chase vehicle driver and the client driver need to know exactly what is going to happen with every scenario. Both must know what to expect whilst anticipating each other's every move, and both must have a lot of trust in the other.

There's a lot of high-speed driving and vehicle-blocking going on and making space in-between traffic for the client car to maneuver were specialties of mine. I had a fine knack of being right on the client's rear bumper, set off a little to the left or right, and then moving to block for him. As we approached traffic lights and junctions, a running commentary would be going on between the two vehicles, an example of which would be, "Traffic light ahead, two hundred meters", which would come from the client car whilst the passenger of the chase would respond with "Roger, traffic light two hundred meters, speed seven-zero". Should the lights be on red, we'd run them: stop for too long here and you may end up dead. Most of the lads had done basic driving courses and were learning on the job—never the easiest thing to do. Steve was my passenger one day and was amazed that I wasn't hitting the client's car in front. It was an exciting job, but one where, if you screwed up, it could be disastrous—even fateful.

After a few weeks, Steve traveled with Jim mostly and drove the client car while I drove the chase. This worked well as Steve had spent some time with me and knew exactly what to expect. If we were approaching a roundabout, he didn't need to look to see where I was or even have to slow down. He automatically knew I'd be flying by him before he reached the roundabout to block traffic coming from the left or right so that he didn't have to slow or come to a stop. As soon as he passed through me, I would swing the car right behind him and quickly block from the opposite side, it was a buzz to do but there was a very serious side to it: we had clients to protect and, ultimately, each other. We knew that enemy insurgents were constantly monitoring our movements and drills on a daily basis, looking for an opportunity to take us out; therefore, the better you are as a team, the harder you are to hit.

It was a fairly good group of guys, and most days we'd be out in our teams, although each team would have a separate itinerary and would have one or two clients each. Client A, for instance, might be heading to Al-Amarah for the day with Team One, whilst Clients B and C might be attending meetings in As-Samawah with Team Two, and then Client D could be going out in Basra for the morning and staying at the hotel in the afternoon. It varied each day, and if one team had to go to As-Samawah three hours away, another team would then do the next one, though often it didn't work out that way.

In our downtime, we'd all be doing various things; some would go to the Palace to use the gym whilst others would sunbathe, read a book, or have a brew on the roof. It was rare that any of us would step out of the hotel unless we were on an op, simply because, at the time, there was a reported bounty of US$10,000 placed on each of our heads by Al Qaeda. It was a huge amount of money in Iraq, and although we thought it was very nice of them, it was cheap all the same! I spent most of my downtime chilling out on the roof and reading. It offered everyone an escape from the confines of our rooms whilst not having to leave the hotel.

When you were up there, you could really hear the true sounds of the city; gunfire, explosions and car horns, all going off day and night. During the evenings, after our day's debrief and as we'd be going over the plans for the following day, we'd have a beer in the recreation room. Alcohol was prohibited in Iraq with it being a Muslim country but, as with most operational environments, plenty of it was flown in by both British and American transport planes for purchase out of big cargo containers on each of the bases. In the evenings, lads would be having one or two beers, and bullshitting away about the day and life in general, before tossing their cans of Carlsberg or Carling into the trash and retiring for the night.

If you've traveled a bit, you may have experienced the "excessive car horn" along the way. With some countries in the Middle East, you often hear it all day long before the call to prayer kicks in from the local Mosque. There is nothing that stops it, even during prayer time, and you can often find yourself going to bed with the noise of it thrashing around inside your head. It's part and parcel of some cultures where they don't necessarily know how to drive a car but sure as hell know where the horn is! This is the case in India, Vietnam and China as well.

As we chilled out on the roof in the evenings, it was all we seemed to hear; broken up now and again with the sound of an explosion or gunfire. Occasionally, we had to duck for cover as the rounds were a little too close for comfort. That was our evening entertainment; sitting up there and watching tracer rounds flying back and forth during a firefight whilst drinking a couple of beers. You really had to be there to truly appreciate how mad it was.

It had been a busy time since arriving in late-July, and I'd been working every day since I'd been there. I'd volunteered to stay out for Christmas, and so my break would be taken in the middle of November—in a week's time. A few days before going on leave, my team was tasked to go down to Kuwait for the night with a couple of the clients who were doing some business and a little shopping. Steve and Stu drove them down, whilst Shaun and I were in the chase. Stopping briefly at the base in Umm Qasr in order to leave our weapons in the armory, we then crossed the border and drove the short distance to Kuwait. An hour later, we'd dropped the passengers at a hotel before heading to the villa.

The clients were fine down here and didn't require any coverage, and so we'd see them again the following day for the drive back to Basra.

We made the most of our twenty-four-hour break from the warzone with the four of us heading to the local souk in the afternoon to pick up a few things before relaxing by the pool. In the evening, we headed to TGI Fridays for dinner—it was something we'd all been looking forward to: whilst the Iraqi chefs in our hotel were okay, the food was very basic, and so I found myself always eating the same thing for dinner as I had for lunch, which was pasta and sauce. Going on trips to the CPA at the Palace was an effort we tried to make every day because the food was great; the same when we were on the road, heading north to Al Nasiriyah or As-Samawah: we'd always stop off at one of the American bases as they did great food. They really look after their troops like that, and it goes a long way to boosting morale in environments that don't have much.

Arriving back to the Kuwaiti border the following morning, something seemed off as we were met by one of the armed soldiers. He asked if we could pull over into the car park. We found that strange as, normally, we'd drive straight through, but we noticed more than the usual number of vehicles parked up with people milling around. After a few minutes of trying to find out what was going on, one of our other teams pulled up alongside us, coming from the Iraq side into Kuwait. They informed us that intel just coming in was that American troops in the town of Tikrit had captured the Iraqi President, Saddam Hussein. If true, this was a huge deal. Stu made a call to our ops room to let them know we were with the clients at the border, waiting to get in. There wasn't much they could do as, for the time being, the whole country was on lockdown.

After an hour, the guard lifted the barrier to let us through— this after we told him we were only going to the base at Umm Qasr. The Umm Qasr bit was true; we just failed to mention we'd be hightailing it straight to Basra afterwards! As soon as we pulled into the base, we noticed Mick and a few of the other lads chatting, and so we went and joined them to see what was going on. The clients went for a brew; we advised we'd join them once we knew what was happening.

We were told that Saddam had been captured a short time before but, as the news was now filtering throughout the country, the threat level was at its highest. We could wait it out at the base in Umm Qasr, which would probably require at least twenty-four hours, or simply go for it and take the drive to Basra.

Stu went off to the ops room to get a brief on the developments while we went to speak to the clients to bring them up to speed with the situation. The longer we waited in Umm Qasr, the more chance we'd need to stay the night. If that was the case, we decided we'd head back to Kuwait and come back in when it quietened down. As it was, everyone, including the clients, agreed we should go for it and get back to Basra. We all knew and understood the risks of so doing. With the news of the capture breaking throughout Iraq, the following twenty-four hours would be lively without a doubt, and we wanted to be back there.

As soon as we carried out our weapons checks, we loaded into the vehicles and pulled out of the main gate of the camp. I'd informed those that needed to be aware of our departure and route in case we ran into any issues along the way. The team had also gone over the route we'd be taking, alternative routes, emergency rendezvous points, and a plan of action. If we were attacked between the base and the city, we would attempt to take out the targets and return to Umm Qasr or otherwise head south to Camp Shaibah, which was a big military base just off our route halfway to Basra. If our vehicles were taken out and we had no casualties, we'd find a place to get the clients into cover and hijack a vehicle if we had no immediate support from military or other security teams. The actions in the event of a casualty would be to administer first aid and head straight to the hospital at Camp Shaibah. With our plan in place, it was then time to go.

Our two-car convoy pulled onto the Basra Road and drove at speed towards the town, passing fires burning at the side of the road and kids waving in celebration; we knew, though, that this was the calm before the storm: although many in the country would be pleased with the former tyrant's capture, he also had many supporters. The insurgents who posed a constant threat to us all would no doubt use this as an opportunity to mount more attacks against the coalition forces and private security teams, which was something we were prepared for and were now expecting. As we drove, we could tell there was a strange feeling on the street; it was almost tangible in the air. People were honking car horns for fun, whilst many were hanging out and waving flags, with others dancing around. Only a mile or so further, we'd be getting the evil eye from groups of men squatting by the road, with on more than one occasion the sound of gunfire cracking around us, which kept us on our toes.

The roads were surprisingly quiet, which wasn't a good sign; that, in itself, can be a warning indicator that something may be about to happen. Locals may have been warned by insurgents to keep off the streets during a certain time due to a planned attack.

All we knew was: it didn't feel good, and we needed to get to Basra.

After twenty minutes spent driving, we had the city in our sights and, looking at my GPS, we had twelve minutes remaining before we arrived at the hotel—a long time when you're expecting to get hit at any minute. We'd earlier pulled our body armor from the back of the vehicles and had the clients wrap it around them—six pieces in total, including their own. We entered the city and, straight away to our right, came a volley of shots. We didn't get hit, but the rounds whizzing by felt exceptionally close.

It was all very tense and it was difficult to determine who was a threat and who wasn't amongst those on the street.

Military intelligence over the last week had provided us with reports of an increase in insurgent attacks; this was before Saddam's capture. They were using IEDs more, which was working in the insurgents' favor. Coalition troops and private security teams were constantly being targeted with this method due to its effectiveness at the damage it caused, bringing a growing casualty rate. That's why, when we drove, especially at high speed, everyone was focused on not only watching their arcs for anything suspicious but also for devices at the sides or in the centre of the road, on lamp-posts or even inside of dead carcasses. If there was something suspicious or out of place, we'd give it a wide berth—and if that meant going off-road, then that's what we'd do.

An estimated 41% of Coalition fatalities in Iraq were caused by IEDs whilst a later French study showed that, from March 2003 through to November 2006, of a total of 3,070 Coalition deaths, 1,257 were caused by IEDs. Typically, they explode underneath or to the side of a vehicle or convoy to cause the maximum amount of damage. However, as armor was improved on military and private security vehicles, insurgents began placing IEDs in elevated positions, such as on road signs, utility poles or trees in order to hit less protected areas of the vehicle. IEDs were very effective and became the terrorist's weapon of choice. We were always alert looking for things out of the ordinary.

The remainder of our drive through the city passed without incident, but you could tell that this was an altogether different day. With daylight fading as we pulled into the hotel car park, the clients thanked us for getting them back safe. After dinner, I grabbed a couple of beers and sat up on the roof with some of the lads watching and listening to the city around us.

The sound of gunfire was now more constant what with Saddam's capture, but there were also a number of firefights seemingly going on throughout the area. That was, once again, the night entertainment; it was something we'd all gotten used to.

My two weeks leave had finally come around, and I was ready for it. It had seemed like an age since I had arrived in Iraq, and I was glad of the break to recharge myself. I left Kuwait on a British Airways flight to London and had flown Michelle over from Los Angeles the same day. It felt strange to suddenly be back in London, having spent the last few months in Iraq. That evening, we went out to dinner and I ordered more than I could eat, unable to adjust so quickly to the food. I enjoyed my time off, though, and we had a few days away in Austria and then headed up to my hometown in Middlesbrough. What I hadn't factored into these places was the Winter cold; I struggled with it, having been so used to the heat in Iraq.

Upon my return to Iraq and throughout the Christmas period, we were kept busy with clients and the various schedules, though it passed without incident. Goose, who I'd not seen for almost ten years since our time in Bosnia, had come out to Basra for a few weeks to stand in for Jim who had gone on leave. It was good to see him and catch up on everything, and I ended up going to his team for his stay out there.

The day before Christmas, both he and I had a close call whilst on a trip to As-Samawah. We'd left Basra, heading out on the three-hour drive, and it was passing without incident until we reached the outskirts of our destination. There was a heavy build-up of traffic, but we could see the camp up ahead; it housed the CPA, as well as a Dutch military unit. All of a sudden, a burst of rounds cracked off around us. We were perilously close to it. We immediately grabbed our weapons to return fire; I was driving and was focused on looking for openings in the traffic whilst Goose focused on identifying the firing location. We pulled forward a little more and found ourselves right in the middle of a firefight between insurgents on one side of the road, taking cover behind an old bus, and the Dutch Guards at the camp to our right.

We could see the insurgents opening fire from behind the bus at the side of a road. If they got eyes on us, it was a safe bet they'd direct their fire at our vehicle. I was amazed it wasn't hit as others around us were. We needed to get out of there—and quick. I floored the accelerator, bypassing the camp as we weren't going in there now. If we were to pull in at speed, there could have been a high chance that one of the Dutch soldiers, already engaged in a firefight with the insurgents, would open fire on us, thinking we were a threat.

We passed the camp and reached the roundabout before taking a right. We were aware of the general area from our maps and needed to find somewhere to lay low for a while until the dust settled. We pulled off into a disused field, having made sure that we hadn't been followed. It was full of rubbish, and kids were playing around in it. No wonder disease is such a big issue in places like this; it was really dirty and festering.

We were only a couple of miles from the camp but pulled over to get a fix on our location. Goose jumped on top of the vehicle, using his binoculars to scan the area. If we were hit here, there would be nobody around to support us. Basically, the cavalry wouldn't be coming, and we'd be in the shit. We could hear the firing in the distance, but it soon died down, and so we took a chance on a drive into the camp thirty minutes later. The guards were understandably on high-alert as we pulled in. We didn't stay long; just collected the client and headed straight out of there, turning right out of camp to the roundabout and going back on ourselves at high speed, right past the insurgent location, but doing so without any issues.

Three hours later, as darkness was falling in Basra, we finally pulled into the hotel. We were both looking forward to some dinner and a beer.

On a separate occasion, I was with Jocky, who was the Team Leader. We were driving from Umm Qasr to Basra with one of our vehicles in front of us. As we entered the city, I noticed a truck parked up ahead on the side of the road. Shaun was driving the front vehicle and had pulled out to pass it, but as he did so, we noticed a car heading right towards us on the wrong side of the road. Shaun's car managed to pass the truck and pull right in order to avoid the car. I'd need to take evasive action, however, otherwise we'd be in a head-on smash, given that the driver wasn't slowing down, it seemed.

Jocky pulled up his weapon ready to fire through the windscreen. We didn't know if it was a suicide bomber driving to hit us or a clueless driver. We had a split-second to hope it was the latter, but I couldn't take the chance and so needed to take immediate action. I was approaching the parked truck and almost level with it when I suddenly pulled a hard right to avoid the oncoming car. I managed to avoid the truck by no more than a few inches. As we passed its rear, I sharply pulled left onto the footpath; if I hadn't, we would have ended up in the river, which was right in front of us. We then couldn't believe our eyes when, right in front of us, as I made the sharp turn, there was an elderly man on the sidewalk, praying on his hands and knees at the side of the truck. I don't know how, but I avoided him and got us back on the road. We thanked our lucky stars that day, and I hoped both the driver of the car and the truck driver thanked Allah as they were within seconds and inches of losing their life—as were we.

I'd decided to call it a day in Iraq as soon as the Christmas period was over with and would be heading back to Los Angeles at the end of January. The situation was changing daily and was becoming too unpredictable and volatile to enable us to fully protect our clients. There's nothing fun about being in a firefight and, although the majority of guys would stand toe-to-toe with you should you be in one, the same couldn't be said about others. It wasn't solely their fault as that responsibility must primarily rest on the shoulders of the many companies out there who recruited them. With the more contracts the companies working in Iraq acquired, the more people they needed to expand. That's business, but they've got to fill the slots.

I think the company I was working with had one of the best setups on the ground and, overall, the whole thing was good, offering solid operational, managerial and logistical decisions. The same couldn't be said for some of the other companies who we all had friends with and who we'd bump into on a daily basis. Driving around in soft-skin vehicles with one finger on the trigger and the others crossed for luck was a daily occurrence. That is *not* security, it's just playing at it. Those that know me—and especially those I've worked with—know I've been all for the high-risk work, but only as long as it's done right. That goes back to when I was in the Army with the number of operational tours I did—a feat no other soldier from my Battalion matched at the time.

This, however, was a different ball game. I'd spent six months on the ground in Southern Iraq, and had been shot at multiple times, survived a couple of potential vehicle disasters, took cover during mortar attacks, and had a bounty placed on my head. I'd had enough—for the time being, at least. Being in the line of fire can come in many ways for all kinds of people, but for me I was faced with the threat of death daily, and I was conscious that it could come at any time. If I'd have been single, I would no doubt have spent a year or two there or in Afghanistan, but I also wanted to make a name for myself in the American market and was starting to focus heavily on that side.

It wasn't to be the end of my high-risk jobs; rather, it was only the beginning! I was set to go on to work in places such as Russia, Mexico, the Philippines, and throughout South America— all working jobs that offered me greater flexibility for shorter periods of time.

The months following my return were spent working on a number of different projects, from instructing again on high-risk close protection courses to heading off on various jobs here and there. I went off on a skiing trip to Colorado for a week shortly after my return and found it extremely refreshing, though bitterly cold. It felt good to be back in the States, and a relief to not have to be concerned with taking one in the head—or indeed having it chopped off.

I also had another reason to return home safe as I'd be getting married to Michelle in September of that year—2004. We'd been dating since September 11, 2001, and during a trip to Vienna in Austria, I'd asked her to marry me. We were excited about the wedding, and as I returned home from Iraq, I was able to help with the planning of the big event, which would take place in Beverly Hills.

MISSION SUCCESS: ALWAYS HAVE A PLAN B

I'VE LEARNED OVER THE years that creating and having a Plan B can be extremely useful—both personally and professionally. There have been many times where I've needed to revert to an alternate plan; in the early days, however, I didn't really see the need because I didn't understand the benefits. Having a Plan B in the military is essential for operational success; in fact, there can be a number of alternate plans developed and executed, dependent upon the complexity of the task.

The most important part of any military operation—outside of, of course, making sure that everyone returns home—is carrying out the mission successfully; oftentimes, this may have to be done by utilizing an alternate plan. Only when I grew older and furthered my career in the private security field did I feel it had become useful. In fact, I'd view it as an essential tool for the international operator. Routes can be used as an example whereby having that Plan B that I developed through my advanced work could enable my client to avoid an area of high-volume traffic through construction, for example, thus saving him or her valuable time with a busy agenda ahead of them.

In the military, I was under the command of others mostly, and so the decision-making was theirs. In the security field, however, I went on to run complex international operations involving multiple clients, security personnel, drivers and business agendas. The larger the operation, the more complex your alternate plans become. Take, for example, a situation in your everyday life, such as your route to work: you could take steps to plan out a couple of alternatives as you just never know if, one day, you might have to use them. Or consider coming to choose a flight. Ask yourself: what's your Plan B if you miss it or if it's cancelled? You could think about a hotel you could stay at, and you might even ask yourself if you have an alternative just in case the *What if* scenario becomes your reality. On a bigger scale, what if you are leading a business team and your approach isn't working effectively? Do you automatically have a Plan B that you can execute, or do you scramble to come up with something that might, in turn, not prove to be effective because it's not well thought out? Think about what might be easier for you and your team. Again, your goal is simple: mission success.

Since the age of around thirty, I've developed a Plan B in virtually everything I've done, both personally and professionally, and I feel confident that I'm solid in my planning process. Sometimes, I've had to execute that plan, too, whether it was due to working in a job that I may not have been fully committed to, living in a city where I may not have been overly happy, or traveling across the globe where I don't have much time to sit down and lay out a new plan. Basically, in everything you do, it doesn't harm you to have a good Plan B should you ever need it. You just never know when that might be. I am, however, a firm believer that, if your Plan A is solid, you won't need a Plan B; however, some situations for me have indeed warranted it—and not everything is in your control, meaning a Plan B can be a good backup for changes caused as a result of other people and circumstances.

There have been a number of situations throughout my life that I could use as examples when not having or enabling a good

Plan B, but I'm going to use one particular operation in the private sector during a trip to Colombia as an example of how having a good Plan B is able to benefit the team. We not only didn't have a good one—we didn't have one at all and accordingly found ourselves in a dangerously critical situation as a result. If we'd discussed and developed one during our planning, we would most likely have avoided what then went on to become a major incident.

I'd been asked by a colleague if I was interested in heading down to Colombia on a training task. I'd be part of a four-man training team that would be working with a local close protection team, notably responsible for looking after a prominent businessman and his family.

The client had wanted his team to go through an in-depth training course, and so a US-based company was contracted to send a team down for four weeks.

My colleague put my name forward to his boss and, later that afternoon, I received a call from him. We discussed my military and security experience, amongst other things, though having some instructing behind me also helped. The following morning, I received the green light and, once I submitted everything to the company that they required, I made a start on packing for the trip. I'd be leaving in a few days' time and traveling to Bogota, where I'd meet up with the rest of the team.

I learned that it would be an experienced group I'd be joining, with two of the lads being former members of a highly regarded American Special Forces team, and then my colleague who had been with a government agency. All had plenty of training and operational experience, and I felt I'd fit in well with them. We'd have a couple of days down time together in order to sort out our gear and gel, before meeting up with the team we'd be training at a remote location in the jungle—around two hours away.

One of the major issues throughout Colombia at that time was the kidnapping of businessmen and women, primarily carried out by The Revolutionary Armed Forces of Colombia, also known as the FARC. They were a guerrilla movement who had been involved in the Colombian armed conflict, which had started back in 1964, ten years before I was born. They were a very serious group that employed a variety of military tactics in addition to more unconventional methods, including terrorism. The operations of the FARC were funded through kidnap and ransom, illegal mining, extortion, and the production and distribution of illegal drugs—lots of them.

The strength of the FARC forces was high, with an approximate armed force of around 18,000 men and women, whilst half were known to be armed guerrilla combatants. Colombia was known to be a high-risk country due to the threat they posed, and so it wasn't uncommon for business executives and those of a high net worth to have large private security details.

The FARC lost control of much of the urban territory, forcing them to relocate to remote areas in the jungle and the mountains. The greatest concentrations of FARC forces were in the south-eastern, northern and south-western regions of Colombia's 500,000 square kilometres of jungle, in the plains at the base of the Andean mountain chain and in north-western Colombia. We were well aware that our area of training would put us in somewhat close proximity of where the FARC were operating, and it was known for them to have their own training camps throughout the jungle, similar to the one we'd be working out of.

We couldn't be armed during our time in the country, but some of the local security team members we were training could be; still, it offered little comfort with such a great threat. We'd decided before heading into the jungle that, if the shit was to hit the fan, we'd do all we could to get our hands on some weapons and use them as we saw fit. We just hoped there would be enough of them when the locals arrived for training. It had been a specific request to the client that his team came with plenty of weapons as a course of security for us while we were training his people.

We soon found ourselves in a good routine once we left Bogota and settled into the encampment, it wasn't a bad set up at all though we'd be self-sufficient mostly. We had a load of food and items we'd need for the next ten days, then we'd be back in Bogota for a few days to replenish before the next rotation would come through the training.

The key aspects of what we'd be teaching were all matters related to close protection, complete with tactical driving, firearms, as well as patrolling operations. The client had a number of business interests in remote regions, and each location had a guard force to protect the facilities; so, all in all, we had quite a number of people to train.

I was enjoying it, and the team I was working with all offered something different. This meant I was learning things along the way, too. In the main, though, we were all on the same page, and we all felt that the training being delivered was of the highest standard, with those attending seemingly enjoying it despite some of it being challenging. We received a couple of visits from the client, so he could watch what was going on, and he'd fly into the camp on his helicopter and hang out for a few hours, asking plenty of questions and making notes on those he was watching. He took his security very seriously, that much was clear to us all, though he was also spending a lot of money to make sure he had the best he could get.

We were halfway through our time in Colombia when that Plan B I discussed earlier could have been greatly relied upon; instead, we didn't have one, and it could have proven to be very costly for us as a team.

We were to be heading out to a local area to conduct some work and had received clearance from the local police, helped by the client's connections with them. The morning went well, and the team were putting in some good work, but suddenly our training became an actual operation when we were ambushed by hostiles.

We'd been assured that the areas in which we were training were somewhat safe from the guerrilla factions, but we could only take the advice of the locals and police in recommending this. We'd seen no reason to doubt it initially, despite us going out to scout training sites prior to the training beginning, but as with most things down here, nothing could be guaranteed—unless money was involved.

We'd been out in and around the area a number of times since we had arrived and there had been no issues; in fact, our exposure to the general public had been non-existent once we left Bogota. We were in a remote location, and the nearest town was around twenty miles away; still, though, we were aware that FARC camps were scattered throughout these remote areas.

We were patrolling down a long dirt track when, in the distance, we saw a beaten-up truck pull out and drive away from us. We didn't think much of it at first but, in order to be safe, we went firm into the jungle for a while to wait out until the area had cleared of any locals. Moving back out, we patrolled in staggered formation along the track again and continued on, working our way through the jungle terrain before settling down for some scoff on a riverbank. It seemed ever so quaint being there, chomping away on our rations under the beating sun, but suddenly a volley of shots came our way. It was fierce and unforgiving as we all took cover and tried to identify from where we'd been ambushed.

I found what cover was available to me and just lay there, listening to the *pop! pop! pop!* of what was seemingly multiple weapons firing away at us. There had been no warning, just a sudden burst of fire that had forced us all to take cover where we could. After what seemed like a long pause, some of those we were training started firing back in order to suppress the fire coming our way. We'd welcomed those we were training bringing their weapons along for training purposes, but their ammo was to be strictly kept in their bergens. We'd considered not allowing them to have ammo at all, so it was a good job we'd changed our minds.

It's never nice being ambushed at the best of times, but when you don't have weapons—or very few of them—it obviously makes things a little more troubling. We were in the shit big time. We had no idea how many aggressors were there, but we were able to see that we were being shot at from across the river, just off to our right. The muzzle flashes and whiz of tracer rounds coming our way told us this wasn't a lone farmer who'd got pissed off that we were on his turf! It was an enemy force who seemed to know exactly what they were doing, which, in this area, could only mean the FARC.

Those who had weapons on our side were returning fire, whilst the four of us were doing our best to coordinate an emergency plan of action, and also directing the security lads with engaging the enemy, though it seemed they didn't need much help with that. We had one vehicle with us for medical and emergency reasons, with a few weapons in the back of it, and so we skirmished our way over to them whilst keeping low in order to avoid the firing; at this point, it had been ongoing for a few minutes.

As far as we were concerned, not being allowed to have weapons went out of the window, and the old saying of "rather be tried by twelve than carried by six" was a very brief thought as we grabbed the remaining long guns out of the back of the truck. Judging by the incoming rounds and the flashes of muzzles in front of us, we assessed that we had between four and six individuals across the river, but we had no idea who they were. Some of our folks were shouting, "*Seguridad Privada! Seguridad Privada!*" to let the aggressors know we were private security, but it only seemed to make matters worse as they continued firing. Mounds of dirt around us would suddenly pop up into a puff of smoke, and the noise of rounds smashing into the jungle around us was a frightening sound.

I'd no idea how none of us had been hit, such was the velocity of fire, but it seemed one on the other side had been, when a huge scream was suddenly heard. That was one less to worry about if anything, but we needed to get out of the area as we were rapidly running out of ammo. With only one small vehicle at our disposal, which was parked up just off the track a couple of hundred meters away, there was no way we could all just pile in and speed away once we got to it; the only thing we could initiate was a fighting withdrawal back to the vehicle and then proceed to camp a couple of miles away. We all acknowledged, though, that, even if we did that successfully, we had no assets besides a few locals who were keeping guard. We needed immediate help from friendly forces.

One of the lads was crouched behind a large mound with one of the locals, and they had the satellite phone out trying to contact the police; unbelievably, however, nobody was picking up after a few tries. Eventually, though, they made contact. I could hear the local shouting into the phone in Spanish, trying to get his message across, but he was panicking and kept having to repeat himself. The mound they were behind was receiving some serious fire from across the river, and the dust and debris were flying into the air around them.

When you're in a firefight, panic can set in really quickly, and that can apply to the most experienced of operators. None of us had time to think of it, though: one minute we were sat having a debrief and a bit of scoff; the next we were being opened up on from across the river. It seemed they were using heavy-caliber weapons but, thankfully, we had plenty of cover. Nonetheless, any one of us could be hit.

It was clear that letting them know we were private security was having no effect, and so we decided we'd get as many bodies into the vehicle, and the remainder would extract on foot alongside it. It was the only thing we could do before we found ourselves potentially overrun and out of ammo: if that happened, we'd no doubt end up dead, though I think I'd have preferred that than to being captured; these people—if indeed the FARC—were very serious well-trained soldiers, who specialized in guerrilla warfare. We had a battle on our hands with limited weapons and ammo, and so the only thing to do was fight and extract as aggressively as we could.

However, as I zig-zagged towards the vehicle in the distance, where we'd re-group and ready ourselves to extract, a volley of shots whizzed past and went straight into the bushes around me. I immediately went to the ground, took up a fire position, and returned fire with a quick burst. I knew from where the aggressors were firing, though they were hidden in the dense jungle; my only option was to aim into the immediate area of the flashing muzzles and hope I'd hit a target or two. I don't know if it was effective or not, but the shots coming our way suddenly slowed down to the occasional one. Maybe I'd taken one of them clean out or maybe someone else had, or maybe they were retreating just like we were trying to do. I didn't give a fuck either way: we just needed to get out of the area.

I chugged a load of water down my neck as we all regrouped near the vehicle. One of our lads would drive with as many in the back as we could fit, while the remainder would run back to the camp. Thankfully, we didn't have much gear, but what packs we had were thrown into the vehicle, and off we went. This had been the only time we could think through the incident, but we didn't know if it was over and so we needed to remain alert. I just hoped we wouldn't encounter an issue with the vehicle, like a flat tire. That would be all we needed.

It had only gone on for around eight, maybe ten minutes, but that's a long time when you're being fired at and in unfamiliar territory—unarmed, too. For all we knew, we could have been flanked and then opened up on by a separate group when we extracted away, but we seemed to be clear and, as we got to the camp, we immediately sent the local team out into positions of readiness to watch and warn if anyone approached the small camp. Contact had been made with the police before we got away from the riverbank, and we were assured they'd respond and meet us at the camp. None of us believed that, though.

I sat down for a minute near one of the lads and cracked off some unfunny joke; he, in turn, cracked off a couple of witty comments. It was typical humor you'd really only find within the military. I've no idea how I could laugh at a near-death experience like that, and it wasn't the first time I'd done so.

I've thought about this often, but it was probably my way of overcoming that dramatic nervous moment when all hell lets loose and you're a part of it. It's a bit like being involved in football violence but in a completely different setting. You're with your mates and other lads from your team in unchartered territory, and you've got rival fans coming at you, lobbing bottles and chanting away. You know the shit's about to hit the fan and you're going to have an off, albeit for a few minutes before the police turn up.

The adrenaline and nerves kick in, then you're in it briefly. Bang, wallop, whack. You've taken a few scrapes but, at the end of it, that rush is in you. You crack a few jokes and you're bouncing around with the adrenaline of what's just gone down. I know that because I've been in it, running around other towns or cities with the Boro Frontline, albeit not regularly given that I lived away. It's obviously nothing like being in a firefight where a round could crack through your skull at any second, but that same feeling of fear and nervousness, and the adrenaline that soon kicks in, is a similar thing.

Right now, though, I'd rather have been at the football, stood outside some pub in an unfamiliar town, with one hundred or so lads waiting for that off rather than being in a jungle in the middle of Colombia, being shot at by guerrilla fighters.

I hadn't asked for this or other situations like it, but I knew that I was in harm's way where the bad guys had rules, and yet we had to do our very best to stick to them. At some point, though, you've got to say 'Fuck this!' and fight back with as much aggression as you can muster. Failure to do so can see you dead, and I didn't train to be a solid operator to have that happen.

What I've learned over the years—and this goes back to my time as a young soldier in Northern Ireland and Bosnia—is there is always humor that can be found when fear presents itself. For some people, that doesn't work at all; for me, however, I found it to be the best medicine, so to speak. It's important, of course, to recalibrate your mind and think the 'What the fuck happened there?' thoughts, but if you dwell on it, then nerves can set in and that doesn't bode well for future operations or missions.

Being involved in situations like that is not really something you talk about in the pub with your civvy mates who don't have a grasp on such a situation or experience. How would they when they are in a completely different line of work?

"What have you been up to since I last saw you?" they might ask.

They'd think you're bullshitting with the truth, and so you may as well just make up some other crap and go with it! "Oh, you know, painted one of the bedrooms at home, took the girlfriend out to dinner, nothing much else, really."

The funny thing was, though, that, despite the risk and the near-death experiences, as in the cases of Bosnia, Iraq and Colombia, had I been home with mates or visiting family, I'd have just wanted to get back to that environment and do what I'd been trained for—what I was used to.

I was an international operator and former soldier, though to many I could probably be referred to as a soldier of fortune rather than a private security contractor. I've never been a mercenary, off fighting other people's wars for a load of money, where those conflicts had nothing to do with me. There's a line, of course, and I guess you could say I was right on the edge of it with some of the things I've been a part of in various conflict zones.

Before long, there was a response from the police, and we were soon out of the jungle and on our way back to Bogota. We'd managed to get some good training in while we were there, and also managed to do some work at an old warehouse in the city to finish things off, but it was very much thinking on our feet during the last part of it. We could have been more diligent when it came to planning out the training locations and not just been reliant on the locals letting us know. It wasn't their fault, as they knew the areas better than we did, but we should have scouted areas out more and taken the time to study and learn as much about those areas as we could.

All we'd focused on was delivering quality training to a particular team, and although that was exactly how it was, what we failed to do was look at an effective Plan B for all types of potential scenario. This could have been the need for alternate training areas, a medical situation, actions for in the event that we were ambushed, actions for if someone went missing in the jungle, and so on. It was stupid and foolish of us to have been in that type of environment with that particular threat level and not have an absolutely solid Plan B in place for all that we did. Doing so could have contributed to peace of mind in the event of the shit hitting the fan. It was a lesson learned, and thankfully we were able to look back on it and learn it.

This, of course, is an extreme scenario of when a Plan B would have been utilized to great effect, but it has been proven that many can rely on creating one for almost all of what they do. Whether in your personal life or career, it is always wise to utilize your mindset and make sure you've got yourself covered for any potential eventuality. After all, you just never know when you might need to use it.

DEALING WITH PRESSURE SITUATIONS

IN 2006, I SPENT five months on a world tour with Madonna, and had a great time traveling the world. Our final stop was in Tokyo and, as we prepared for the second-to-last show, I ran into Madonna's manager, Angela, who asked if I'd be available to travel to Malawi with her in around ten days' time. Steve, who was her head of security and a friend of mine, would be going, too, and I met with him immediately in order to discuss the possibility. Once the tour finished in a couple of days, I was due to fly back to my home in Los Angeles, while Steve would be flying back to London with Madonna, though once there he'd need to fly out to Malawi in Africa the next day to get everything set up. He'd have no time to get some much-needed relaxing in after a long world tour, but the trip would only be for a couple of weeks.

By the time I arrived home, I was tired after the long flight and the busy schedule we'd had for the previous few months, but I was excited to be heading to a country I'd not been to before and also to be taking another trip with Madonna, who I'd enjoyed working with. By the time I unwound and got myself sorted out, the next day I was packing again before heading back to the airport for my flight over to London. Nonetheless, I felt surprisingly fresh as I arrived early in the morning. The following evening, we'd be flying out to Malawi. Coming on the trip would be Angela, Madonna's masseuse Michelle, as well as Guy Richie, Madonna's then-husband. I always found Guy to be a very knowledgeable fella, and I enjoyed spending time with him when he visited his wife on the tour. He'd recently put together a documentary on the

Kabbalah faith, which he and Madonna were members of, and he was looking forward to showing me his work when we took off.

As we boarded the Gulfstream at RAF Northolt in London, I put a call in to Steve in Africa to let him know our flight and arrival time. He'd been expecting my call. I hoped to get as much sleep as I could as we'd be landing in Malawi at eight in the morning and would then have a full day's itinerary ahead of us. I squinted as the bright sunshine shone through when I awoke, having raised my window blind. The others were just waking, too, with the smell of breakfast being cooked by the flight attendant at the front causing everyone to stir from their sleep. I could make out the haze and desert below us; it looked hot. I'd been to various countries throughout Africa a number of times, and so I had a fair idea of what to expect.

As we came in on final approach, I noticed a convoy of vehicles lined up and Steve standing beside them on the tarmac. The early morning heat hit me straight away as I walked down the aircraft steps. Looking out into the distance, I saw a number of people gathered on the public viewing terrace; a few of them had long-lens cameras. Quickly I realized: it was our welcoming committee, the paparazzi. I handed over to Steve as he'd been on the ground longer than I and was set to travel with Madonna and Guy while I stayed behind to get the luggage sorted and secured. Louis Vuitton would have been proud as I watched a number of the locals unload the suitcases from the back of the aircraft.

Over the next thirteen days we would have a busy schedule, and only those in our small group knew of Madonna and Guy's plan to adopt a child during the trip. Outside of that, it was merely guesswork by the media. After we settled into the lodge and had a bit of lunch, we headed an hour south to Mchinji Orphanage and, upon arrival, got a taste of the shambolic conditions in which the children lived. The smell was horrendous. As we pulled into the parking area, the local children ran to greet us at first and then hung back, unsure of the strange people that had just turned up on their doorstep. Some of them had probably not seen cars before, never mind a load of White strangers getting out of them.

They quickly warmed to us, though, and although Steve and I had a job to do, we made time to kick a ball around with them. We still had our eye on Madonna but gave her a little much-needed space; she was busy chatting to the head of the orphanage and getting to know some of the children. Everything was quiet on the paparazzi front, thankfully; it seemed they didn't have any idea where we were staying, and we'd managed to leave the lodge without being followed. We hoped the rest of our stay would be the same, but deep down we knew it wouldn't be.

The following day, we returned to Mchinji, only this time we weren't so lucky with escaping the attention of the paparazzi. One car picked us up on the long road out of the lodge, and as we reached the main roundabout, we had another two on us. Steve and I both knew that the day's visit was important, and we could do without any unwanted attention. I made him aware on the radio that we had company. He was in the front car driven by Soldier, with Madonna, Guy and Angela inside, while I was in the rear vehicle with Michelle and our driver, Jarvis. I'd already briefed him that, if we had anyone pick us up along the way, we'd attempt to lose them before we got close to the orphanage. He understood, and so now that we had people following, it was time to put it to the test halfway to Mchinji.

I told Steve we would try to lose the follow vehicles, and that we'd catch him up when possible. He acknowledged straight away.

I then had Jarvis slow down to create some distance between our car and Steve's in front of us. I knew there was a village five miles ahead, and that's where we would try to lose the paparazzi.

By now, Steve's car was out of sight and, as we entered the village, I instructed Jarvis to take a left turn down one of the dirt tracks. It was a chance to take in the hope that those behind would follow suit. If they didn't, I'd not only look stupid, but they'd also be able to catch up to Steve's car.

As we turned in, I watched the first of the follow cars slow down and then turn, soon followed by the second and third cars. I breathed a sigh of relief; it had worked.

We drove a little further and, as soon as we were out of site, we pulled in behind a disused building, hidden from view. We listened as all three vehicles sped by and, as soon as they did, we pulled back onto the track and headed towards the main road. The plan had worked—with outstanding results. I was imagining the conversation in each of the cars as they realized what had happened. Sorry, folks, it was just business.

We managed to catch up to Steve as they entered the village of Mchinji before turning right down the long dirt track that led us to the orphanage. It was to be short lived, however; within thirty minutes of arriving, and with Madonna and Guy mingling with the children outside, I noticed we had company. The paparazzi had found us.

We knew they'd be in the area looking for us. We wouldn't have been difficult to find as this was the main orphanage in the area. There were only two or three of them at first, but soon that turned into fifteen. Some were locals, whilst others were from the United Kingdom, France, South Africa and the United States; we could hear them all talking to each other. Although most stayed behind the perimeter wall, there were a few that kept trying it on by climbing over and hiding in the bushes surrounding the orphanage. Steve and I had our work cut out, keeping them back and trying to restore some order.

We were surprisingly helped by a group of children who lived in the small village across from the orphanage, though that started to get out of control when they began throwing stones at the paparazzi. That didn't do Steve or I any favors as they thought we'd instructed them to do it. We hadn't and, thankfully, in a later press report, it hadn't directed the blame at us. Unfortunately, however, our trip to the orphanage needed to be cut short due to all the commotion. A small number of local police had turned up but, despite their attempts to control the situation, the paparazzi just ignored them. We had no choice but to leave and head back to Lilongwe and to the lodge.

By our own admission, we'd been doing an excellent job throughout the trip so far when it came to misleading the paparazzi, despite them turning up at the orphanage. By the middle of the trip, we had twenty-plus, who had been sent out to follow us everywhere and get as many pictures as they could. It was a complete pain in the backside for us as Madonna hadn't wanted any attention, especially as we were approaching a critical phase with the planned adoption.

The time was also spent visiting various organizations and villages in the area, where the attention from the paparazzi wasn't such a big issue as it was good publicity—though if we could lose them, we would still try. Sometimes we would see one or two cars parked up on the single track running out from the lodge, waiting for us, and although more often than not we'd lose them, they would all suddenly reappear wherever we were a short time later.

Steve and I, although suspicious at the best of times, were becoming even more so with it. During our downtime on an evening or over dinner, we'd go over the day's events and were fairly sure the paparazzi were being tipped off by somebody who had knowledge of our movements.

As the planned adoption gathered pace, both Madonna and Guy were scheduled to attend the local courthouse to finalize things. They had spent some time with a young boy at Mchinji, and he was the one they had planned to adopt. On the morning of the court appearance, tensions were somewhat high in our camp. On Steve's and my own side, we had to deal with making sure the paparazzi didn't follow us; doing so could disrupt the court process, and the judge could potentially take a dim view of the exposure the child would be receiving.

Angela had reiterated at dinner the night before that they definitely weren't welcome, and so we had a trick up our sleeve that we were mulling over. On Madonna and Guy's side, they were understandably nervous of things not going to plan, and that nervousness was evident when they both got into an argument about something or other just before we left. I was pottering around at the lodge, waiting for them to both come out. It was something I was used to with them, but as they were husband and wife, I left them to it.

Steve and I had decided earlier that, as Michelle was similar in size to Madonna, we'd arrange for her to wear a wig that had been used on the tour, and which we brought out to Malawi for such a situation arising. She would travel with Steve out of the lodge ahead of Madonna's departure around eight that morning. The paparazzi had been parked up on the road from early doors and followed them away from the lodge, as we'd expected.

According to Steve, they seemed hesitant at first, unsure if Madonna was actually in the car. All they would have seen as the car flew by them was a woman resembling Madonna sat in the back, complete with baseball cap, as she always did. The first stage of our plan had worked. Once they were clear of the lodge, Steve's car took a drive around the city until those following got fed up and realized something was amiss. It was at that point that I pulled Madonna and Guy out to get on the road and be on our way for the courthouse. We were free and clear to drive without anyone following.

As Steve broke away from the following vehicles, he then had his driver head straight to the courthouse, with nobody now following him. They were all on their way back to the lodge, realizing something wasn't right, but we'd already left. We assumed they'd be pissed off once they realized what had happened.

As we pulled down the street where the courthouse was located, I noticed Steve up ahead, waiting for us to pull in. He'd arrived shortly before us and had been hiding out of view until we appeared, jumping out to let us know where to turn in.

Madonna and Guy were escorted into the small courthouse, while Steve and I took a seat in the lobby. We had no idea how long they'd be in there but, after thirty minutes, they were heading back out. The child's Father, Yohane Banda, had also been in-attendance at the courthouse, as well as a small number of other relatives. We'd had no interaction with them until this point, and they followed us out as we left the building.

The mood between Madonna and Guy, however, didn't seem great, though we soon learned why. Rather than a full adoption being granted, as had been hoped for and expected, the judge had decided to award an eighteen-month interim adoption. This meant that the process would be more complicated than planned. At the end of the eighteen months, the situation would then be reassessed.

Once darkness fell that evening, Steve and Jarvis snuck out of the lodge and drove down to the Home of Hope Orphanage in Mchinji to collect the child, David Banda, as well as a local nanny, who would accompany him to the lodge. Given that the paparazzi weren't aware of the morning court appearance, they would most likely assume there had been no developments with the adoption, and so Steve was free and clear to collect the child without anyone following.

David would be housed in one of the lodges, where we were staying, and he'd be kept out of sight until our planned departure in a couple of days' time. I met them in the car park when they arrived shortly after nine in the evening; it was the first real opportunity I had to see the boy as we walked to the lodge. Shavawn, Madonna's stylist, was in Malawi with us, and would be taking care of David for the remainder of our stay.

We had been in the country for almost ten days, and both Madonna and Guy would soon be leaving to return to London. A Gulfstream jet had arrived into Lilongwe the night before and was scheduled to fly them home. Heading back would be Madonna, Guy, Angela, Michelle and Steve, while David, Shavawn and myself would stay behind until the adoption paperwork was complete. It had been too soon to get all the necessary documents completed since the court appearance and, given that Madonna needed to attend a scheduled engagement, the plan was for us to remain behind with David until we could fly out with all the legalities and finer details taken care of.

I left the lodge for the airport two hours ahead of the departing party in order to advance everything and get things set up for the departure. I allowed enough time for any unforeseen delays; we were, after all, in Africa, and I wasn't expecting it all to go to plan.

That would prove to be an understatement.

Once I arrived, I had a quick scout around to see if there were any paparazzi lurking about. They'd have no knowledge of the departure unless they'd been tipped off by someone at the airport, though Steve and I still had our suspicions about someone within our group. I then went inside to meet with the airport Chief of Police, who I'd spoken with on the phone earlier on in the day; he'd be assisting me with everything I needed for the departure. He was a pleasant enough chap when I met him, wearing his peaked hat and walking with a long stick. It seemed that everyone saluted him, everyone from the airline staff to the cleaners. He had the respect of others, I sensed.

We walked together to the immigration office and learned that the officers inside wanted the departing party to come into the office with their passports once they arrived. I produced them all from my pocket, at which point they told me they needed to see the passengers. I wasn't happy with this at all. I kept pushing the matter and said that it would be a lot more helpful if we could do exactly what we'd done when we arrived and have one of the officials at the aircraft.

"Not possible," one of the officers said. "I have no people to spare at this time." As he said this, I pointed to one of his guys who was sat in the corner, his feet up on the desk. I had made my point very clearly, but I could tell it went right over his head as he again stated, "Not possible, my friend."

As I turned to walk out, he stopped me. "For a good price we do."

Oh yes, everything comes at a price doesn't it, I thought. "How much?" I asked.

"One hundred pounds."

"I'll give you fifty," I said, pulling a crisp note out of my pocket and handing it to him.

He took it and had the nerve to hold it up to the window to check if it was real. I had to laugh. He asked me how long before they arrived and I told him in one hour, thirty minutes. Once they were ten minutes out, he would send an officer to the aircraft. He took the passports and stamped them, so all the officer had to do was match the pictures to the passengers as they boarded the jet.

I asked the Chief of Police if I could go out to the aircraft to speak to the crew without being escorted, and he said "Of course," but he wanted his palms greased, too. "And how much do you want?" I asked.

"One hundred pounds," he replied.

That's what happens when you front up a bit of money. It's not something I've often done in my career, but given the sensitivity of the situation, as well as the prowling paparazzi, I wanted no delays once Madonna arrived.

Happy that the crew were good to go, I stepped off the aircraft and walked back towards the terminal when, suddenly, I noticed something out of the corner of my eye. Three White males over to my left on the other side of the perimeter fence, next to the terminal, had flagged my interest. I knew straight away they were paparazzi.

There was no doubt they could see me and, having followed us around for the last ten days, I wasn't surprised they would know that Madonna was leaving. I was positive they'd been tipped off that I was here and that we had an aircraft on the tarmac, either by someone in the airport or, more concerning, a member of our team. Steve and I had been keeping a careful eye on a couple of people in the group for a few days, paying particular attention to the actions of one of the drivers.

The paparazzi hadn't followed me to the airport, and I'd given the area a thorough check when I'd arrived, but then they turned up. It could have been the airport folks; it could have been the driver; or it could have been both. If people know they can make some money from a quick phone call, they are going to do it. I've seen it the world over, so it wasn't really a surprise.

I reached the terminal and walked through the other side to get an idea as to how many had turned up. As I stepped outside to the drop-off point to meet up with Jarvis, I was approached by a number of people waving cameras and microphones in my face.

"Is Madonna leaving tonight?"

"Is she taking the baby with her?"

Ignoring the questions, I made my way over to the car to speak to Jarvis, who told me that the paparazzi had arrived around thirty minutes earlier. To a certain degree, I didn't think Jarvis had it in him, but I didn't really know him well enough. I'd worked closely with him over the last ten days, but he could have been tapped up somewhere during our time here. It was no secret that most of the paparazzi were staying at The Capital Hotel around fifteen minutes away from the lodge, so anything was possible. I knew how the paparazzi worked, and when money is flashed in front of you, especially when you don't have any, it's a different ball game.

Steve and I, however, were more suspicious of the other driver. Over the last few days, we'd set a couple of traps, and he seemingly walked right into them. One was when he was told that we were going to one location before we suddenly changed it at the very last minute. We watched from a distance as he fiddled around on his cell phone, for one reason or another. We weren't surprised, then, when the paparazzi turned up at our new location. When we set another trap the next day, he walked right into that one, too. Our suspicions had proved to be correct.

I called Steve to let him know that we had company and to get an update on his arrival time. They'd just left the lodge and would be arriving in thirty minutes. I walked over to the aircraft access gate and chatted briefly to the armed soldier on guard before walking out to the aircraft again to let the crew know they were on their way. As I approached the pilots in the cockpit, I sensed something wasn't right.

The lead one turned to me and informed me that they didn't have enough fuel to fly to London.

"What do you mean, you don't have enough fuel? Then get some," I replied half sarcastically. I couldn't understand how they hadn't known this sooner and why they hadn't told me when I had first spoken to them earlier. The pilot said they couldn't get any at this time of day as the person who managed the fuel supply at the airport had gone home for the evening. I'd initially thought he was winding me up.

They hadn't done themselves any favours by letting me know so late and so, rather than call Steve, who was now fifteen minutes away, I decided to wait until he arrived to let him know. The truth of it was the aircraft didn't have enough fuel to fly two hours, let alone the scheduled nine hours to London. The crew had requested to refuel from the airport supply, but were told it was broken and, as it was late in the evening, those that could do anything about it had gone home for the night.

I couldn't do a thing about it, and so I headed over to the access gate to wait for the cars to pull in and, after a short time, heard Steve on the radio giving me a two-minutes-out heads up.

I had the airport follow car ready on the inside of the gate and instructed the driver to head to the plane as soon as the cars came through so we wouldn't have any delay considering the paparazzi standing around. I heard the vehicles in the distance and, as they rounded the corner, the cameras began flashing away. I got Steve on the radio and told him to follow the car, pointing in the direction of the airport vehicle. Within a split-second, they were past me and heading straight out to the aircraft. I watched as the guard shut the gate behind us before heading out to meet them as they exited the vehicles. They seemed happy, but I knew the mood would soon change.

As everyone walked up the steps and seated themselves on board the aircraft, I pulled Steve to one side and told him of the situation.

"You are fucking joking," was all he said, but he knew I wasn't.

I briefed him of what I knew, and then the pilot walked down the steps of the aircraft to speak to us. Could we mention it to Madonna, he asked. I felt for the guy, but when someone has paid a lot of money for a flight, you expect it to be ready when you get on board. This was his problem not ours.

When Madonna was informed of the situation, she was understandably upset, though mad would be more appropriate.

Guy seemed more annoyed as he was tired. I'm sure he was looking forward to getting on board and getting some sleep, though I knew it would be a while before he could do that.

We let the group settle inside the aircraft while Steve and I ran through a number of options with the pilots. A request was even put to the airport official, who was at the plane, as to whether they could use the President of Malawi's private fuel supply, though I think that had been suggested by Madonna. The answer was no.

A decision was made to fly to Nairobi in Kenya, where they would then refuel. It was shortly after midnight when the aircraft went wheels-up from Lilongwe, three hours later than scheduled. Due to the waiting around on the aircraft prior to departing for Nairobi, however, the delay had taken up some of the pilot's flying hours. So, rather than flying from Nairobi straight to London, they would then need to fly on to another location in Europe, where a new crew would be ready to take over for the final leg. I was informed of this as I walked off the aircraft, having bid them a safe trip out of Lilongwe.

I'd have loved to have been a fly on the wall when that news was delivered to the passengers after the fuel issue. It was unacceptable, no doubt, and if things had been planned better, it wouldn't have happened.

I watched as the aircraft banked away in the distance and stayed at the airport, out of sight of the paparazzi, for thirty minutes. I always do this in case there are any issues and the plane needs to return, but thankfully this one didn't. There had been enough problems for one night.

The subsequent press reports were as inaccurate as they could possibly be. It was reported by some that Madonna had to sit on her plane for three hours while the pilots decided if the child could leave with her and Guy as they didn't have the right paperwork. The report stated that the pilot eventually allowed him to travel, though the fact that David was nowhere near the airport and was fast asleep back at the lodge didn't come into it. I'd denied the paparazzi an opportunity to get any decent pictures as the cars swept straight through the airport gates, but as the party walked up the steps to the aircraft, they assumed David was leaving as well.

With an early arrival into RAF Northolt the next morning, there was a heavy presence of paparazzi waiting to get a shot of Madonna walking off the plane with David. However, when they didn't see him, it confused them all and subsequently led them to report that he had actually been taken off the aircraft prior to leaving Malawi, which was the reason behind the delay. When they didn't see him leave the aircraft at Northolt, I'm sure calls were made to their colleagues in Malawi who were, by now, most likely preparing to leave the country. Once they all figured out that David hadn't actually left Africa, we started to get a little interest at the lodge, with a couple of fellas turning up trying to book a room for the night. Thankfully, the lodge owners, Guy and Maureen, a lovely couple from South Africa, had been on top of the situation and realized they were paparazzi, telling them that they had no available rooms.

The following morning, I woke and had breakfast with Philippe, who was with our team in Malawi. He'd stayed behind to help get David's visa sorted out and was about to head off into town to finalize that and to finish up a couple of meetings. Philippe had been instrumental in setting up and managing most, if not all, of the meetings out there for Madonna. He was also, in my opinion, the most valuable asset in taking care of all the legalities for David, and was always rushing around throughout the trip, as well as making calls.

Our job had been relatively easy compared to his. Philippe was a well-educated and friendly Belgian who, like Madonna and Guy, was a Kabbalist. He was also involved with the "Raising Malawi Foundation", which Madonna had founded, along with Michael Berg. Steve and I both joked that Philippe was a mix between a covert CIA operator and a British Military Officer.

The truth behind David not traveling back with Madonna and Guy was that, since the interim adoption had been granted only a couple of days earlier, there hadn't been enough time to get all the legalities taken care of. So, rather than stay there and wait for that, they returned to London as they had schedules to keep. This is where Philippe really stepped up and facilitated everything and, once done, those of us remaining would all fly back to London with David.

Many in the media seem to hold the belief that the public is more interested in the crap side of someone's life rather than focusing on the good, and I found it frustrating. Working with the rich and famous over the years offered me a great insight into what's true and what's not, with some things in the media often farfetched—and the case of Madonna and Guy wasn't the only example.

Later in the afternoon of the following day, Philippe was back and forth between the American and British Consulates, trying to get everything ironed out, but it wasn't a simple process. Shavawn and I walked with David to the small village near to the lodge to give the local children some presents, which Madonna had paid for. The kids were delighted when we turned up with footballs and gift bags for them. With my suspicions arising that the paparazzi would continue to sniff around, I hired a local security guard force, for which I had to get approval from London.

They were probing around the lodge, and so locking down the entrance to it and having regular patrols out would at least minimize any unwanted attention around the place. That evening, I took a walk up to the temporary gate where the guards had erected a metal pole on top of two big drums. I had a chat with them to make sure they had everything they needed, but they were happy with their little fire burning away. I kept radio communication with them throughout the night, just in case they needed to reach me, but thankfully they didn't. We were left alone for now.

At this point, we still didn't know when we could leave Malawi, but it needed to be soon as I was informed over breakfast that a local news channel had reported that a local militia group were planning on kidnapping David for a ransom. I called Steve straight away and then briefed Shavawn and Philippe. The situation had changed, and although we couldn't immediately confirm the report, it told us that we couldn't mess around. We needed the visa and we needed to leave. Philippe called me later on in the day to say that he was getting a visa from the American Consulate, which would enable us to fly to New York. We packed up immediately. We were prepared to fly to whatever country issued the visa; I didn't have the time or patience to piss around, especially with the reported threat towards David.

No sooner had Philippe arrived back at the lodge when he received word that the Consulate staffer had made a mistake with issuing David the visa. They retracted it after learning that it was an interim adoption and needed more time to complete a review. It was a major headache for us all while Madonna was getting frustrated with the delay whilst back in London. We found out from Philippe that the lady who had issued the visa hadn't sought higher approval from her superior, and so the Consulate had flagged it. She wasn't popular with us, to say the least. We couldn't take the risk of leaving with the visa we'd been issued, though such was the situation that we were close to doing so and had actively discussed it.

Philippe's next stop was the British Consulate, and so it went on, back and forth. I tried keeping out of that side of things as much as I could. I was asked a number of times to where I thought we should fly, but the best thing, really, was for us to wait where we were, despite the threat. Philippe and Shavawn were suggesting all sorts of places, however.

"We should fly to Johannesburg and wait there."

"What about if we fly to Spain or Switzerland?"

These were just two of the suggestions. It all sounded great, but I reminded them that we would need a visa to get into those countries, too. If the American and British Consulates weren't willing to give us one, then we didn't stand much chance of any other country issuing us with a visa for the boy.

I couldn't see how David would be issued with a visa from, say, Spain when he wasn't connected to that country; it could ultimately end up bringing us even more problems if we didn't sit tight. I could just imagine Madonna being informed that we'd all arrived in Spain safely but were now in jail. I'm sure that would have gone down a treat! I could, however, understand their frustration, especially as Madonna was applying the pressure from the comfort of her home in London. Everyone was trying their best, but the powers that be just weren't sanctioning anything in a great hurry. It was a procedure where both Consulates had to make sure they were doing the right thing before allowing the child to leave the country.

I reached out to the Regional Security Officer at the American Consulate to let her know of the threat we'd been informed about. She kindly offered to move us to a safe house in the city but, having discussed it with Shavawn and Philippe, I decided against it: I reasoned we were better off where we were for the time being; at least here there were plenty of paparazzi hanging around. This was a time where I was okay with them being there and it was also useful to have the guards to patrol the grounds and provide access control throughout the day and night. It seemed to me that, if we moved to a house in the city, it could ultimately end up directing further attention to us if they followed us there—and that was the last thing we needed! The lodge was in a remote location and close to the Presidential Palace; if it had been anywhere else, I'd have made the decision for us to move. David was staying in Shavawn's room, which was next to mine, and we had connecting doors so, if she needed to pop out for a few minutes, I could keep an eye on him.

On the morning of October 16, we were given the green light to travel to London after the British Consulate granted David a visa. I was with Philippe, having a coffee at the lodge, when we received the call. Immediately, he raced into town to collect it as Shavawn and I got everything packed up once again.

While Philippe was gone, she called Madonna to make her aware while I was dealing with Johanna the assistant in London and arranging our flights. With a growing presence of paparazzi near the lodge, I told Shavawn to let Madonna know that we needed a private jet out of Lilongwe, and I made sure to relay the same to Johanna. I couldn't believe that Madonna seemed perfectly fine with having us fly out of Lilongwe on an Air Malawi flight to Johannesburg. From there, we'd then connect to an overnight flight to London.

I was strongly against the Air Malawi flight and I made this clear to Madonna. We wouldn't have stood a chance with the paparazzi at the airport in Lilongwe. I was sure that, once they knew we were checking onto an Air Malawi flight, they'd be booking onto the same flight. It wasn't something I felt comfortable with at all. Thankfully, however, she came around and authorized for a jet to come up from Johannesburg to collect us and return us there for the flight to London. It would have been easier if we could just have a private plane to fly us to London, but this was better than the original commercial plan.

Johanna had booked us on a British Airways flight from Johannesburg to London, leaving at eight-twenty that evening, though then I was rushing around trying to get a jet to get us out of Lilongwe. I spoke with a company in Johannesburg that I'd previously earmarked prior to the trip in case we needed to call one in. I'm glad I did that. Lilongwe didn't have a suitable aircraft, and although the company I spoke with did have an aircraft available, it would take them more than two hours from the point of payment to come and get us. By the time we'd be all sorted and heading to the airport, however, this would actually be a viable option.

We then called Shari, who was one of Madonna's people in New York. I hoped she had her phone on as I needed to wake her up to get her to pay for the plane. Shavawn and I were sat on the balcony while David slept in the bedroom as I put the call in. Meanwhile, Philippe was on his way back to the lodge from the Consulate, David's visa in-hand. We were almost there.

I dialed Shari's number from my phone and hoped she'd answer. After a lengthy ring, I was in luck.

"Shari, it's Glen. We're in Malawi and M has authorized us to get a private jet to South Africa. We need it payed for now." I provided her with the details of the aviation company; my fingers were crossed that she didn't fall back to sleep thinking it had been some sort of strange dream. I'd asked the aviation office in Johannesburg to call me back as soon as they received the fax with payment details from New York.

After thirty minutes, I'd not heard anything. I called them back and the wait continued. I told them to expect the payment authorization any time, and as soon as they had it in their hands, I needed the aircraft in the air. With us all packed up, I went and had a brew in the lodge and called Steve, who was in London, in order to bring him up to speed with everything. He was busy preparing a team for the following morning to secure our arrival into London. We knew we'd have some attention when we arrived. As I hung up with him, a call beeped in from South Africa: the aviation company had received the payment and the aircraft would be taking off within minutes, I was told. Thankfully, they had mobilized the crew and aircraft whilst waiting for the payment and would be arriving into Lilongwe within two hours.

I made the decision to go to the airport ahead of the group; this was a decision made based on the good support I had received from the American Consulate. I made sure everything was covered for the drive with David, having first spoken to Shavawn, Philippe and the drivers. Jarvis loaded the car with everyone's bags while I called my contact at the Consulate to give her a brief of what we were doing. She offered to drive our group herself, and it was something that I gratefully accepted.

I arrived at the airport and met once again with the Police Commander. I had no doubt he'd be asking for another fifty pounds, and so I was prepared with a wad of money.

I gave him an overview of what was going on, being careful to not give too much away knowing there could be a mole within the airport—and, for all I knew, it could be him. All the passports were stamped straight away upon arrival, and I was given approval to walk out to the aircraft as soon as it landed. It was going well so far although, after the events of Madonna's delayed departure a few days before, I hesitated to get excited and instead took a more reserved approach.

I then called Shavawn to get an update from her. They'd just left the lodge, and she told me that nobody had followed them as far as they were aware. That was, in fact, not true, as what the group didn't know was that I had authorized for a couple of lads from the Consulate to follow them at a distance. The Regional Security Officer had mobilized them quickly in order to provide some additional security, and with me having to go to the airport ahead of them, it was a big help, which it provided me with extra reassurance.

I walked over to the side gate where they'd be driving through to make sure the guard had been briefed to let them straight in; he hadn't and so, once again, I had to chase down the Police Commander. It came as absolutely no surprise when a group of paparazzi turned up: they were quickly setting up tripods and carrying out test shots on me—something I had always hated. I noticed a couple of them by the gate whilst up on the public viewing balcony; there were at least twenty, all setting up, and they knew exactly what was happening, it seemed.

I was expecting the aircraft landing anytime. I'd noted the wheels-up time from Johannesburg and, as I checked my watch again, I had them arriving in less than five minutes; Shavawn and the others were ten minutes out. Scanning to the west, I noticed a small shiny dot in the distance. It had to be our aircraft. It was too far out to tell, but a few seconds later I realized it was a small Air Malawi plane; however, there was another one following close behind. *Definitely ours,* I thought. As the passenger plane landed and passed close by me before turning towards the terminal, I looked to my right to see the Citation XLS coming in on final approach. Within a few minutes, it was pulling up to me, out in the middle of the pad.

There was no doubt the paparazzi would get a shot of us all getting on the aircraft, but I wasn't too fussed about that: I was just glad it had gone as well as it had so far. As the aircraft came to a standstill, Shavawn called; they were now two minutes out. I stayed at the aircraft and watched as the guard lifted the gate in the distance to let them straight through. Rather than wait for the airport follow car—which, unsurprisingly, never showed up—I instructed them to drive straight out. Flashes could be seen from the public balcony and from the gate where they had just driven through. The paparazzi were trying to get as much as they could.

The doors of the aircraft opened, and I quickly hopped on board to introduce myself to the crew as the car pulled up. I had everyone get on board first before Shavawn carried David up the steps. I looked back and gave a thumbs-up to the drivers and the Regional Security Officer as a show of thanks. I didn't have time to chat to her, but decided I would email at a later date. As soon as everyone was on board, the door closed immediately. It was that quick of a turnaround that we were still settling into our seats when we pulled out onto the runway.

A few minutes later, we were in the air, and a feeling of relief washed over us. We were leaving at last. I looked across at David, who was sat on Shavawn's knee opposite me, thinking that he was a very lucky kid. I wondered how he would adapt to the environment he'd be going into compared to the one he'd just left. I'd witnessed first-hand the conditions he'd been living in, and they weren't good at all. This little guy had just won the lottery. It wasn't long before media reports were hitting the news and, no sooner had we reached cruising altitude, when Philippe found an article online detailing David's departure. It was about to get crazy, I could feel it, and I had my concerns with arriving into Johannesburg.

"Despite the attempts of a coalition of Malawian rights groups to challenge an interim order granted for Madonna to adopt a 13-month-old boy named David Banda, the Material Girl's bodyguard has been spotted at an airport in Malawi with an African baby, believed to be the child she is hoping to adopt."

www.askmen.com

We landed in Johannesburg shortly before 6PM and were met at the aircraft by a driver who transferred us to the rear side of the international terminal. It was very quiet with no members of the public around as he led us inside to an immigration desk with only one officer working.

"Oh, so that's the famous baby," he commented. We ignored him as he stamped our passports upon entering South Africa, but his comment registered with me, though.

We didn't have any airport officials escorting us as we cleared immigration and made our way down a long corridor, assuming it would lead us to the main terminal where we were connecting to the British Airways flight in a couple of hours. However, as we came through an electronic door and rounded the corner, I noticed two individuals: a man and woman stood near the wall and immediately seemed out of place; we'd gone as far as we could without being spotted. They'd been tipped off, no question about it, and they knew exactly where we'd be coming out of. My suspicions from Malawi resurfaced.

There was a slight pause as they quickly figured out who we were before hurriedly reaching inside their backpacks for their cameras. I'd expected a couple of people to spot us, but not so soon. What followed, however, was nothing short of madness.

We walked faster, not knowing where we were heading as we made our way through crowds of people mingling in the airport. Not only was I dealing with the two paparazzi in front of us and trying to shield David, but I was also looking for the British Airways desk. It was proving difficult as the airport was packed with travelers. With flashes continuously going off, we started to get a lot of attention from everyone, which really didn't help matters. It felt like someone had just announced on the public address system that we were there: all eyes were seemingly on us.

It turned out to be the calm before the storm as, within a minute or two, we had a few more paparazzi turn up. We then had passengers waiting for their flights joining in and taking pictures as well. I took off my grey hooded top and handed it to Shavawn to shield David and, by the time we reached the elevator to head upstairs to the check-in desks, we had at least thirty paparazzi surrounding us. Shavawn was holding David against the corner of the elevator to keep him out of sight so as not to expose him to all the flashes, whilst Philippe and I tried to get the doors closed.

The horde of photographers stood in front of the elevator five-deep, and every time the door closed, one of them would put their foot over the line so that it would open again. There were two fellas in the elevator with us who seemed like rugby players. Thankfully, they lent a hand. Whoever they were, they have my thanks.

"'I saw White people with a Black baby. I recognized the bodyguard and knew they were the ones we were waiting for,' Ntsoma said. 'They went through the boarding gate for the flight to London.'"

Reuters

As we exited at a brisk pace on the next floor, I saw the paparazzi all running up the stairs to catch up with us. It was a situation we needed to get out of—and do so immediately. I wondered if there were any police in the place, and when I eventually spotted one through the crowds, he just had a look of astonishment on his face. I'm sure my own face was pretty much the same as I watched him pull his phone out of his pocket to take a picture.

We finally found the British Airways check-in desk ahead of us, through the crowds. As with any airport, you have to stand in line to check-in; in this case, however, once you had your ticket, you went past the desk, which then led you to the security check point.

For a moment, we stopped at the desk with a young lady sat behind it. "Good afternoon," she greeted us. "Could I see your passports please?" She didn't know what was going on as a swarm of people suddenly descended upon her, trying to get photos and videos of the people she was speaking with. We had no choice but to push straight through—it really was that bad—and the only time I could see it ending was once we were through security. As we bypassed the check-in, we didn't have tickets to get through but, thankfully, a switched-on supervisor recognized what was going on.

He escorted us through the metal detectors and put us in a side office where he allowed us to explain the situation. The supervisor went off to get an airline representative, which turned out to be the same girl who had been sat at the desk. I apologised for rushing past her, though once I explained the situation, she said she understood and that we had done the right thing. It had really been mayhem, and I was glad it was now defused. Taking possession of our passports, she went off and returned a short while later, our tickets in-hand, ensuring we didn't need to go back out.

Our luggage was transferred straight to the plane from the private jet we'd taken, but I had no clue how that happened or by whom. I was doubtful we'd see it again but was relieved we didn't have it when we were making our way through the terminal. I know I would have had no choice but to dump it.

It had seemed the dust had settled for now and, after a short time in the office, we were escorted straight to the plane by a number of people. In hindsight, I could have contacted the airline people before we left Malawi, but there really hadn't been the time. We had no internet and, with all the calls back and forth to London in dealing with the jet company and the Consulate, before we knew it, we were off to the airport. I would have thought someone in

London could have called ahead for us, however—probably Johanna, as she had booked the flight—but that hadn't happened. None of us had dealt with a situation like this before. Perhaps I should have taken it upon myself.

Once on board the aircraft, and with everyone seated, I met with the Chief Purser, who had been made aware of our presence. I explained everything to him, and he said his team would do all they could to help us during the flight if we needed anything. All I asked was that they keep an eye out for anyone with cameras—most notably anyone that could be paparazzi. I also asked if they could be strict on non-business class passengers coming up to the front for a nose around. With it being a night flight, it would be dark once we were in the air. At least this would help with being alerted to any flashes. Even so, I was glad to have the support of a great crew.

Before we took off, I called Steve to bring him up to speed with what was going and told him how manic it had been getting through the airport, though he already knew. It had been broadcast throughout the world already, with some stations even showing it live. Steve also knew, just as I did, that it would be just as bad, if not worse, once we arrived in London the following morning. We hadn't realized the magnitude of the story.

David slept for nine of the eleven-hour flight, cuddled into Shavawn, who sat next to me. When she felt uncomfortable and wanted some sleep, we switched over so that she had more room.

Rather than have three seats, we had to settle for two; I guessed it must have been expensive. We'd been given a choice when Johanna was booking the flight: one seat in Business and one in First Class, or two in Business Class. I didn't have the time or patience to get into it with the team in London; we were only bringing Madonna's new kid back. I told them to book the Business seats so that we were seated together. It would be the most appropriate thing to do. I felt sorry for Philippe, who had been booked in Economy; after everything he had done for Madonna and with the adoption process, I felt that was unjust. If I hadn't had David to look after, I wouldn't have hesitated in swapping my seat with him; after all, he'd worked harder than any of us. One thing I do know, however, is, being the gentleman he was, he would have refused the offer.

"David Banda has left Malawi with one of Madonna's bodyguards and her personal assistant, prompting charges from local human rights groups that she had used her celebrity status to bypass normal adoption rules."

OK! Magazine

Before we even took off for London, I was starting to get wind of some media reports harping on about the legality of us taking David out of Malawi. I wasn't concerned at all as everything had been done above board, but I could see that questions were being asked. The fact of the matter was that there was nothing illegal about the adoption: it had all been legal and was completely watertight, but it came as no surprise to be seeing those stories.

Whilst being served breakfast the following morning, the co-pilot came to see me and let me know that armed police would be meeting us at the gate upon our arrival. It wasn't the airline that had initiated this; it was the police themselves, deciding to do so based on the television and newspaper reports while we had been in the air. I looked down over London as we came in on final approach, wondering what delights would be in store for us. A short time later, the aircraft touched down. As the front door opened, I was met by a uniformed officer, with one hand on an automatic MP5 strapped to his chest. Standing behind him were three other officers, each carrying the same type of weapon.

"Good morning. Glen, is it?"

"That's right. How is it?" I replied, though I already knew the answer.

"Crazy," was all he said.

As we walked from the aircraft, I called Steve to get an update from his side. He told me that the police would bring us out to a side door where he would be waiting with the cars, and that we didn't need to worry about the luggage. I'd given up hope of seeing mine again, anyway. I asked him how many paparazzi we had.

"A hundred or so in the terminal, more at the house."

That was a big number of people to piss off if they didn't get a shot of David, which was obviously all they were hoping for. As with the paparazzi in Malawi and Johannesburg, that shot would have been worth a lot of money to a photographer, and so, to a certain degree, I could understand why we had so many trying.

We walked as a group down the long walkways towards the main terminal, though, unfortunately, there were three or four airport photographers shadowing us the entire way. The police told me that there was nothing they could do about it and that they'd be getting the biggest shots of the day—but if I had anything to do with it, they wouldn't be. I pulled my grey hoodie back out. David had it over him to protect him from the flashes of the paparazzi. In addition to the police with us, we also had airport and airline reps, all of whom wanted in on the big morning story that had suddenly descended on their turf.

As we walked, I gathered as much information as I could from one of the officers, and quickly learned that both he and Steve had earlier met to go over everything. We came into the large baggage claim hall and, at the far end, instead of going through the exit door into the arrival hall, where the hordes of paparazzi were, we headed for a door to our right. This led us straight into a covered service road where Mitch, Madonna's London driver, was waiting with a small passenger van. When we exited, I looked to my left and saw Steve with a couple of lads in the distance, watching out for the paparazzi.

As we scrambled to get into the van, we heard shouting and the sound of people running; some in the arrivals hall had figured out what had happened; a number of them came running around the corner and towards us, their cameras at the ready. We pulled away just as they reached us. Mitch had earlier put up a sheet inside the van so that those trying to get pictures from the outside couldn't see in; this worked a treat. We had no escort into London, and nor should we; after all, it wasn't an emergency, just a high-profile adoption, but it was funny how we had a police escort everywhere on the world tour. Madonna loved that stuff.

We pulled onto the M4 motorway, heading towards London, and soon noticed a number of vehicles and motorbikes following. As I looked back, I watched as drivers were frantically making calls, no doubt giving an update to their colleagues waiting at the house.

The morning rush-hour traffic was a problem and wouldn't allow us a smooth ride. We were stopping and starting every couple of minutes while the paparazzi in cars and on motorbikes were trying to get close up to get a shot. There really was no point.

David seemed to be doing fine. Having slept for so long on the flight, he was wide awake now, though it was only six-thirty in the morning. The same couldn't be said for us, however: Steve and his team had been up since three-thirty.

When we were a few minutes away from the house, the cars and bikes following us flew past to setup for us arriving, and as we pulled onto the street before turning into the private mews, the reality of it all was right in front of us. What seemed like hundreds surrounded the van, all pushing their cameras up against the windows. I heard the clatter of loosely swinging cameras hitting the vehicle. Steve had traveled with us in the van and had called the house to have them open the garage door as we pulled in. Mitch was doing his best to navigate around people, but he was being deliberately slowed down. When we pulled into the garage, Steve jumped out to keep everyone away from the sensors so that the door could close: it was like the lift situation in Johannesburg all over again—only when that was done, we were able to get out of the vehicle.

Madonna and Guy were inside waiting to see David, and so Shavawn took him straight in while Steve, Mitch and I hung out in the garage. I waited for an hour before leaving through the back door to walk the short distance to my hotel. I was glad to get in and shut the door behind me, even just for a few minutes. I took my shoes off, lay down on the bed, and closed my eyes to recalibrate myself. It had been chaotic to say the least. Rather than falling asleep, however, I took a shower and ordered food before going for a walk down Oxford Street, seeking out somewhere for a cup of tea. It was just a short break as I knew I'd need to be back at the house in an hour to head to the gym with Madonna.

It felt strange walking around London—even more so as I passed the newsstands with my own face plastered across the front of a number of British tabloid newspapers; the primary picture being of me, Shavawn and David boarding the jet in Malawi. As I stood in line at a coffee shop, I felt some strange looks from various people being directed my way. It felt odd. When I left with my tea in-hand, I was approached by a man and woman who asked if I could give them an interview. I learned that they'd been at the house and had then followed me to my hotel, waited outside, before then following me once again as I went for my tea. Ten out of ten for initiative, but I told them that I was making no comment. That pissed them off no end.

I was also receiving a number of calls from family and friends; they hadn't expected to see me flashed all over the morning news as they sat having their breakfast. Of course, what had gone on had been a big deal, but I hadn't thought it would bring that amount of exposure. None of us did. Some of those who called me hadn't known I'd been working with Madonna, let alone been out in Malawi and bringing her newly adopted baby home! I guess it was par for the course, and as I walked back to the house, it got worse as I was recognized by the paparazzi and news anchors who began hounding me. I scurried past them as I made my way to the front door and into the sanctuary of the house.

We left for the gym shortly after eleven, with Mitch and Steve in the front whilst Madonna and I sat in the back. We talked about how it had been in Malawi after she'd left and during the trip home, and she thanked me for everything. We had a number of vehicles follow us, as expected, and as we exited the vehicle, they were all over her. They, of course, wanted a shot of her with David, but that wouldn't happen for some time; in fact, it wouldn't happen for another two weeks when she left London to visit New York. For all the paparazzi attention in both Malawi and London, not one of them had got a clear picture or video of David. Steve and I were pleased with that. That was the result we'd hoped for.

The rest of the day was quiet as Madonna stayed at the house with Guy and David, whilst Steve and I relaxed at the hotel and went over everything from the last two weeks. The following morning, I accompanied Rocco, Madonna's son, to school in case there were paparazzi tailing him but, thankfully, all was quiet.

I arrived back at the house and said my goodbyes before heading to the hotel to collect my luggage. Surprisingly, it had arrived from Africa after all. I was heading to Heathrow to return to Los Angeles—forty-eight hours after arriving into London from Malawi—and I was looking forward to a break. It had been an experience for sure, but I was glad it was over with and that I could look forward to a rest from the manic time I'd encountered.

Six months later, in April of 2007, we returned to Malawi. I'd been busy leading up to the trip with visits to Europe and New York with another client. I'd been quite ill towards the end of the visit to New York, and by the time I arrived home at one in the morning on the Thursday, I was exhausted. With a heater on me to sweat out the bug I'd picked up, I woke at eight the next morning feeling no better. I went out for breakfast, hoping it would do me some good, but that hadn't helped much. That afternoon, I'd be leaving Los Angeles again—this time for Africa.

After breakfast, I returned home to unpack the business attire from my New York trip for more appropriate clothing for our visit to Malawi. I'd be leaving on an afternoon flight, which would take ten hours to London, where I'd then have a twelve-hour layover. If that wasn't enough, I would then have an eleven-hour flight to

Johannesburg, with a six-hour layover there, and finally a two-hour flight to Lilongwe. If I'd thought that I wasn't up to flying from New York to Los Angeles the night before, I was far from ready for this one.

I made sure to sleep as much as I could on the long hauls and get some much-needed rest, and by the time I arrived into Johannesburg at nine on the Saturday morning, I felt surprisingly fresh, though I wasn't overjoyed to find the airport nowhere near as accommodating as Heathrow. Having spent the best part of the six hours in Johannesburg bored and tired, I finally boarded the Air Malawi flight, and as we took off to the north, we skirted over Botswana before crossing Zimbabwe and Mozambique and eventually heading into Lilongwe. The flight was uneventful, and I was glad to finally arrive. Met by a driver who took me to the lodge, I soon settled in. It seemed as though we hadn't been away; everything was exactly the same—so, too, were the faces.

This time around, I went ahead to Malawi while Steve would travel on the jet with Madonna in a few days' time—a reverse of what we'd done for the first trip. I had quite fancied another couple of days in London to break the trip up a bit, but there had been no time. It was a long slog from LA to Malawi, but I didn't mind too much. At least I'd feel good when the others arrived. The following morning, I made a quick trip to each of the locations we'd be visiting, though it was more to make sure the drivers remembered everything, and despite my and Steve's previous reservations, we had the same drivers.

I was happy that everything was ready for the arriving party and, on the Monday morning, I headed out to the airport to meet the incoming flight. I'd once again been assisted by my airport contacts, though as before we had quite a number of paparazzi present. They weren't too happy when I had the large luggage van park at the bottom of the aircraft steps, blocking any opportunity of seeing Madonna getting off the plane carrying David. After the last trip, they needed to know from the start that we meant business. I knew they had a job to do, but they also needed to be reeled in if it was the same bunch.

The first couple of days, other than at the airport, the paparazzi kept out of the way and didn't follow us at all. Our group was more-or-less the same as the last time, though Johanna, who had recently resigned her position as Madonna's assistant, came along too, strangely. We quickly settled into our routine and went out visiting various places, including to the Home of Hope Orphanage in Mchinji, where David used to live.

We did a lot more fitness during this trip than the last one, and while we were at the lodge during the mornings, we would head out for a run through the farmlands. We had done the same a few times on the first visit, but now we were hitting it with Madonna every morning. As the sun was coming up, we hoped to beat the heat, but we never did. Steve and I would run with Madonna, and sometimes Angela would come along, too. Steve, however, soon had enough of Madonna's moaning over his selection of running routes.

In the end, he drove one of the cars as a backup vehicle in case of a medical issue while we went running. The risk of a snake bite was high and, as Madonna insisted on running the same route along the riverbank, there was also the risk of a crocodile or hippo attack. The thought of running along the river to be faced by a python or anaconda thrilled me no end.

Steve being in the backup car following behind offered some comfort, but the terrain wasn't great and, in some areas, he would have to detour around and meet up with us further along the route. I ran with my radio, water for us both and medical pack at all times as we plodded on through the trails—sometimes for as long as two hours.

Madonna was a fit lady and, although she would slow down a little after the first few miles, the only time we would stop would be to get a quick drink of water. We would always finish the run in a good time. On one run, Madonna and I left just after sunrise and ran six miles; Steve and Angela didn't come along for that one. With the temperature at just over a hundred degrees, we'd both been chatting and joking the whole way around. At the end of it, as we leaned on each other to stretch off, dripping with sweat, I asked her if she wanted to keep going. "Sure," she replied, "not too far though, Glen." We did another mile—it wasn't far, but it showed her determination.

Although miles of open land surrounded us, our routes were limited. On one side of the property line was great terrain for us to run, but a big stretch of it was along the river with the snakes and crocodiles hovering. On the other side of the property line, we would be running along the perimeter fence of the Presidential Palace. Although the terrain wasn't too bad, Madonna didn't seem to like it and had a go at Steve at the beginning of the trip for finding all the hills. It was one of the reasons he binned running with her. We had one other option, which would see us head out of the lodge and along the dirt road track. At the top before the entrance is where the paparazzi would park—a little way up from that was a small village.

The downside was the paparazzi hanging around, and so we didn't often run that route, at Madonna's request, which was a shame, actually, as when we ran through the village the one time, all the children would come out like a pack of dogs and run with us. It would have made for a good photo for her with the children, though Madonna didn't want to be photographed while she was out running—or anywhere else for that matter. The children didn't care less that they wore no shoes and ran in their bare feet, but they often got in our way as we ran. After a few hundred meters, however, we would pick up the pace and lose them all, apart from this one child who we could never lose. He probably went on to become an Olympian!

To avoid the possibility of running into the paparazzi, the croc and snake route seemed to be the preferred option most of the time, though I was getting pissed off with it. It's alright having a laugh and thinking nothing will go wrong, but if it did, we'd have been up shit creek without a paddle; in the middle of nowhere with the nearest hospital an hour's journey away. If you get bit by one of those snakes, you've perhaps got minutes to live. Once Steve knocked it on the head, I changed the whole thing; Madonna and I ran through the village more. I wasn't fucking about with it.

"It's a photo. It isn't life-threatening," I told her.

I've been to Malawi three times in all, twice with Madonna and once with another client. I found it to be a place of peace, surprisingly, and the majority of people I met were as down to earth as you could possibly meet. Granted, they didn't have much, but what surprised me more than anything was that they didn't ask for much either. I've been to some countries where you are constantly harassed for something—money, food, water, clothes, the list goes on—but in Malawi, not so much. We visited some really tough places, especially the orphanages, and to see babies and kids playing on dirty floors, often filled with excrement, was a sight that wasn't pleasant at all.

What Madonna did was a good thing—not only for David Banda but for the other children that she later adopted, and her funding of certain projects in the country has gone a long way to helping the locals in those areas. Yes, she may have had a plane load of Louis Vuitton luggage when she arrived in the country, but she also gave a hell of a lot and, from what I believe, she continues to do so. I was glad and thankful of the experience. It was both humbling and enjoyable, and I hope to have the opportunity to return again one day.

DECISION-MAKING: CONFIDENCE IS KEY

I RECEIVED A CALL from Mark, a colleague in South America, asking if I'd be available to work with him for an upcoming task he had starting in The Philippines. This would be for a new client of his, but I learned that the assignment would be a complex one due to the nature of the business needs and areas they'd be visiting. Mark and I went back a number of years, having worked with him in South America in 2002.

I flew from Los Angeles to Tokyo in mid-June of 2007, and then connected to a flight to Manila in the Philippines. Upon arrival, I was met by Mark, as well as a local liaison girl that would be working with us. She would be our local guide and provide valuable assistance and advice with regard to the various areas of the city we'd be out and about in.

The first couple of days were spent checking out various places we'd be visiting with the clients; they wouldn't be arriving for a couple more days, and so we needed to use this time to prepare evacuation plans and routes, and to get a feel for the local area. The Philippines is classed as a high-risk region, and terrorist groups operate in many areas of the country. Groups such as Abu Sayef, Al Qaeda, The New People's Army, as well as Moro Islamic Liberation Front were all very active and were known to be hitting random targets in the Philippines—and so doing on a regular basis. Mark and I, being former British Army, couldn't ignore the fact that we'd be a nice catch for any one of those groups. After spending a short time on the ground, it didn't feel right. With an environment like this, there's always a sense of paranoia—there has to be; that paranoia can save a life. We'd both been to many countries previously where the locals eye you up; here, however, it felt as if it was happening each and every time we left the hotel.

With the clients having arrived into the country, we soon started to settle into a routine with them, keeping it very low profile to not draw any attention to ourselves. If they were meeting someone in the lobby of the hotel, for instance, then one of us would sit out of the way and keep an eye on them from a distance. The same with the gym: one of the clients liked to work out, and so one of us would be in there working out also, keeping any interaction between us to a minimum.

After a few days, we got the feeling we were actively being watched and that our hotel phones had been bugged, and so Mark and I pulled them apart to have a look. We found nothing, but that didn't mean we were wrong. On the sixth day in the country, our suspicions were confirmed, though; with one client in the hotel, the other decided she wanted to go to the mall across the street for a walk around. Mark had been out of the hotel at the time, and so I got a message to him and let him know we were going on foot to the mall. Keeping it low profile and not walking with her, I maintained a fairly good distance. It was enough for me to see her yet far enough away for any watching eyes not to associate the two of us. Mark advised that he would make his way over to us within the hour to provide further support.

Stopping off at a coffee shop, the client sat down and read a newspaper. I grabbed a coffee and sat at another table on the other side. I was going through the motions of making mock calls while conducting my own surveillance; looking at who was walking by—a general routine. Mark called not long after he arrived in the area and sat out of the way and observed for some time; he had eyes on us but was positive he'd detected some surveillance targeting us.

At this moment, we had the advantage as far as the possible surveillance on us were concerned; they were either watching me, the client, or both of us, despite us not showing signs of being together. Mark, it seemed, remained undetected, which allowed him to watch those who were watching us. We needed to confirm that we had surveillance on us, so Mark called the client and told her to walk off again through the mall; he reassured her that we'd both be close by. By discreetly using shop windows to our advantage, we were able to look through a window as if looking at the contents of the store. In truth, we were using the glass and the reflection of people passing. Another call came in from Mark; he confirmed we had surveillance on us—more than one, as well— though it was unconfirmed as to the actual number. We got out of there and back to the hotel while losing the surveillance we had. They may have already known where we were staying, but if they didn't, we didn't want to draw them to it.

While Mark and the clients packed up their belongings, I discreetly left the hotel on foot, utilizing a side exit, and went to look at other accommodation options. I constantly checked over my shoulder and put in numerous detours along the way, ensuring I wasn't being followed. At this point, all we knew was that we'd detected surveillance on us; we didn't know if that surveillance was a hostile organization or a local team checking us out for some reason, but we couldn't take the chance to wait around and find out.

Returning to the hotel in the afternoon and under Mark's direction, I sent an email to our office manager back in the Americas. During all operations, they were aware of our movements and would be the first to be notified. I sent a quick email to let them know that things weren't okay:

Urgent: OPSEC
To: ******
Local Time: 13:10
Message: We will contact you in 6 hours, which will be 19:10 local time, 07:10 your time. If you do not hear from us by then, contact ****** *and establish incident procedure.*
Glen.

Although not going into great detail with the message, it was enough information; our team on the other end would know that if we hadn't contacted them by the time stated then something was definitely wrong. They would then initiate the contingency plan that had been put in place before we arrived in the country. We had to decide soon if we were going to move hotels, though it didn't happen straight away; in fact, it didn't happen at all. We bunkered down in the hotel we were at for the next twenty-four hours. All movements outside were completely restricted, but we still didn't feel comfortable.

After a week of being on the ground, Mark decided to pull the plug on the operation, having discussed this at length with the clients. We hadn't felt comfortable for the last twenty-four hours. At the same time, we had to ensure that the people we'd come here to provide support for were able to conduct their business, though we gave it as much time as we could. Their task had been to investigate various business goings on throughout the Philippines; our thinking was that the surveillance had been set up by someone who had been getting nervous due to the investigation taking place. If we hadn't done our job and detected it in the first place, the outcome could have been unthinkable.

Mark had made the call to extract out of there with the clients, and I think he made a brave and wise decision, but he did this with the confidence that he had, and I learned a great deal from it. It is, however, a classic example of well-trained security agents, who are not just there to protect but also to offer the best advice that can be given, supporting it with the most realiztic operational decisions.

That afternoon, we drove the fifty minutes to the airport and hoped we'd have no further concerns. Thankfully, we didn't, and we were able to get the clients on a flight to London. Mark booked himself on a flight to the US, and I was able to fly through Tokyo and back to LA. It had been an interesting trip, that much was certain; however, there had been some positive business conducted for the clients. For security reasons, however, the right call had been made to move out.

Working in areas that are classed as high-risk environments should be taken seriously, and often you can find yourself doing so unarmed. Importantly, the need for awareness and vigilance is high on the agenda, and the planning phase of each and every movement is essential. One wrong decision, one wrong turn, and you and your client can find yourself in a place you just can't get out of, so you've got to decide and often quickly.

We knew our limits on that particular operation and the decision was made to pull out for the safety of the clients and ourselves. We were on foreign turf and didn't know the area as well as the locals, and we had no idea if this was a local security team, government people watching us or, more worryingly, a terrorist group. It's common for many to not realize that the path forward may be better taken by walking away, recalibrating your thought process and, if need be, your operational approach, then going back to it another time. That's when mistakes are often made by not thinking it through. But if you have the confidence to make solid decisions, it can only be beneficial to you, your clients and/or your company. It really may be the best approach when looking for a successful outcome.

Remaining Humble in All You Do

MY LIFE IN THE private sector in particular has taken me to some wonderful places around the world, but that doesn't just mean to exotic locations where everything has been five-star luxury (courtesy of those I've had the fortune to work, with of course). When referring to wonderful places, my meaning relates to being able to experience different cultures, interacting with people from all walks of life, and taking in sights that are out of the ordinary. One thing I've learned during my travels with the rich and famous, though, is the importance of staying humble.

Whether you are rich or not, being humble is something we can all strive to be, though I look at some in the world today and struggle to see them understanding the word, let alone learning to carry it out. These are the ones who are constantly flaunting their wealth and possessions in the media and on social platforms, and although that might come across as impressive to many, to others, it can come across as showing off and downright arrogant. Fortunately, I've not worked with people like this, nor would I want to; it just doesn't appeal to me in any way at all. Yes, I've worked with some very rich and famous people, but in the main, they've all been quite humble people, whether that be in their business or personal lives.

This doesn't just apply to the wealthy and famous, however. I've come across people who have regular jobs and an average income, yet they portray themselves as being wealthier than they actually are or wearing an expensive watch that could be viewed as living above their means, for example. It's okay to treat yourself to things that you've worked hard for, but there's a fine line between showing off and remaining humble. I've spent the best part of the last twenty years traveling the world on private jets, staying in five-star hotels and visiting exotic places, but none of this was paid for by me.

Yes, I've had the ability to go on nice holidays and live a life that I probably wouldn't have been able to had I have chosen another career path, but I'd like to think that, throughout the course and no matter who I've worked with, I've remained humble. I was raised on a tough council estate in Middlesbrough—I never forget where I'm from, even though I left home at a young age—but, since the day I left, I've always returned to visit and won't ever forget my roots. It would have been easy to move on and never look back but, for me, I do so because it helps to keep me grounded in all that I do, and that remains the case, regardless of who I work with.

One particular well known family who are renowned for not being as humble as they could be, however, and who aren't people to whom many could seriously assign the word, is the Kardashian family. I struggle to see how they've gotten where they have in life, but a sex tape, a sex change, a television show and other strange goings on have led them to develop a huge fan base. I'm astounded at the lengths some will go to for fame and money—not just this particular family, as it could apply to many people today, but I use these as an example as, for me, they have led the way.

Kim Kardashian is at the top of the tree when it comes to not grasping the meaning of being humble, what with her constant exposure in the media and on social platforms. Make no mistake, though, she should count herself very lucky after being robbed at gunpoint in her Paris apartment in 2016 due to the constant flaunting of her wealth and luxuries. The upside to having millions of followers on social media and your own television show—if there is one—is that you have one hell of an audience if you need to promote yourself or a particular product. The downside, however, is that you're opening yourself up to a high amount of risk exposure, as Kim learnt that night.

She'd been to Paris many times before, but maybe she found herself in a comfort zone and thought this next trip would go smoothly, much like the previous ones. She was clearly wrong. The gang of armed robbers, acting as police officers, burst into her residence in the early hours and weren't messing around. They were very serious criminals who had clearly planned their attack for some time, possibly since her last visit to Paris. Maybe the robbers knew where she normally stayed, the type of security she had, and the places she liked to eat, to drink and to shop. That's all recognized as setting a pattern.

Regardless of what you think of Kim Kardashian, she is a human being and a mother to young children, and for her to go through what she did I'm sure will live with her for the rest of her life, whether it be the glamorous life, as she's been living, or a lower key one, which I would advise, though I've yet to see it. As a famous lady for—well, I'm still not sure for what exactly—she has in excess of 30 million Facebook followers, 60 million Twitter followers, and 130 million Instagram followers—that's a lot of people around the world receiving every broadcast you make of your movements.

When you advertise your wealth, your travel destinations, where you're staying, where you're having dinner, or the event you're attending, you open yourself up to unnecessary risk—especially when you're famous. Reportedly, Kim makes up to

$500,000 per Instagram post when promoting products. As much as I find that completely absurd, if it was presented to you or I, would we do the same? Of course we would but, still, there's a way to be humble in all you do, regardless of fame or wealth. Not everyone has money and mansions all over the place but, again, some are impressed with this because they are fans of the individual.

During her first day in the city and before being robbed, a Ukrainian prankster tried to grab Kim Kardashian as she walked out of a car and headed into an event. Her bodyguard, Pascal Duvier, who is 6 feet 4 inches and 264 pounds, moved quickly to stop him, though not quick enough to prevent the assailant from reaching his target. If the idiot prankster had been armed, it could have been a far worse outcome. This should have been a big enough warning that she was at risk given her fame, especially when considering it was carried out in front of the world's paparazzi.

Social media, of course, doesn't help matters, especially when you've got a load of followers, most of whom you don't even know, as former England and Chelsea footballer John Terry found out, too. In 2017, he and his wife Toni jetted off to Dubai, as they often did, and posted a number of pictures of themselves enjoying their time in The Emirates. It looked wonderful and you could tell they were having a great time but, unbeknownst to them, while they were snapping away on the beach, by the pool and at dinner, their multi-million-pound home in Oxshott, Surrey, was being burgled, and hundreds of thousands of pounds' worth of luxurious belongings were being taken.

John, with more than 4 million followers, and Toni, with 300,000 followers on Instagram, had innocently let everyone know that they were away, but it told those with criminal intent that the house could very well be empty, and so they made their move. Did they make any adjustments following that? Maybe at the house with security measures, but they still post regularly when they are away on holidays.

Going back to the incident in Paris, the robbers entered the apartment ever so simply and tied Kim up at gunpoint before stealing her high-value jewelry. Seemingly, it was a vicious, nasty and dangerous incident. This was Paris—a city that had been home to two major terror attacks before this, and a city that has a high risk level, albeit from terrorism. One would think that someone like Kim Kardashian would be a prime target for ISIS but, fortunately, others got to her first—and, thankfully, didn't physically harm her. One would also think that someone of Kim Kardashian's fame and fortune would have the best protection available to her, where this would be prevented to begin with. Imagine if this had, indeed, been a targeted attack by ISIS, though, or imagine if the robbers had decided to kill her. Things could have been very different.

Yes, Kim Kardashian is very famous, but she didn't help matters with her carelessness. This was a well-planned and effective operation carried out by a team who knew exactly what they were doing—just like the burglars who ransacked John and Toni Terry's home. They didn't just turn up and go for it; they'll have done their research, which wouldn't have been difficult with the victims posting about their whereabouts—and the bad guys will have formulated a plan to strike when the time was right. The attackers in Paris will have been following Kim around while she was in the city—on bikes, on foot and in cars, whatever it took to maintain surveillance on her—and it wasn't picked up on by her security, who were supposed to be trained for such matters. It was reported that she was tailed in Paris for at least three days before the robbery, and at least one man pretended to be a photographer and followed her on a motorbike to find out her whereabouts.

Another man pretended to be a plain-clothed detective to try to get a seat next to her at the exclusive Ferdi Restaurant on the Thursday night. But both men were fakes. The acting photographer tried to listen in to the conversations by other paparazzi but he was challenged by the genuine ones. And the so-called policeman fled when staff at Ferdi asked to see his credentials. Red flags? Was her security made aware of these incidents?

The five masked men, dressed in clothes with police markings, burst into the luxury apartment in the early hours and held her at gunpoint. They bound her wrists and ankles with zip ties and left her in a bathtub before stealing the jewelry.

The gang of robbers had been able to enter the exclusive l'Hotel de Pourtalès after the concierge mistook them for police and let them in. Could things have been different if Kim's security had been present? Absolutely it could, even if it was just one person—but he wasn't there. Having that presence would not only have posed as a potential deterrent, but he or she would have been able to contact the authorities and get urgent support.

Security obviously comes at a cost, and often a big one, but how much do you value your life when you're rich and famous and have millions of social media followers? A good security agent will protect you from harm, protect your property, valuables, image, brand and reputation, ensure your itinerary is managed so that you're on time to a meeting or event, and will handle all the logistics of a trip. If the need requires, there should be more than one security agent and, in Kim's case, being high-profile with high-value jewely in a city classed as 'at risk' are all reasons to increase her security presence. Nonetheless, she had nobody around when she was robbed. Not only that but, had she had adequate protection, Kim would have gone to bed that night with peace of mind, knowing that someone on her security team was in close proximity. If you have a multi-million-dollar ring and you're showing it off on social media, how much does it cost to get an off-duty or retired police officer, or pay to have a residential security agent that is trained to work a twelve-hour night shift? Anywhere from US$1,250 to US$1,600—that's how much. Quite clearly, Kim didn't value the jewelry or her own well-being this particular night.

I'm not going to highlight too many questions about Kim's bodyguard. The reason for this is that nobody knows in detail if he was under any restrictions from his client—it happens. I fully understand what it's like to work with a major celebrity and also know the challenges that security professionals can face, especially with working solo or with multiple clients, as he was that night. Kim's sisters, also very famous and wealthy, were in Paris, too, and as they hit the town that evening, Duvier was dispatched to be with them while Kim was apparently safe in her residence for the night. Still, somebody should have been overseeing where she was staying.

With fame and wealth come issues and security concerns, whether physical, threats from stalkers, or those with criminal intent. Many in the media and on social platforms subsequently went on to blame the bodyguard following the incident; however, his client(s) dictate his day-to-day role and responsibilities, both Kim and Kanye are his charges, but he was out at a nightclub with the sisters. This is where additional security personnel come into play because Kim should never have been left alone at that apartment; either the bodyguard should have been there and had other security with the sisters, or vice versa. He may have addressed this but came to face resistance from Kim and or Kanye, possibly due to cost. The finer details are not public knowledge at this point.

One thing I do know is that when you're a celebrity with the fame and wealth that Kim Kardashian has, her personal security is not a one-man detail. There are very real threats all the time from all manner of stalkers, pranksters, idiots and criminals. If fame, wealth or risk means increasing the budget to have more security personnel due to a specific trip or threat, then for me I'll address it, but sometimes that can be rebuffed, though it never has when I've run operations. As a security agent, though, you have a decision to make as to whether or not you can sign off on the vulnerabilities. It's important to note, however, that protection isn't cheap if done right; again, though, it's down to how much the individual values it. Working solo will not only burn the agent out but will expose the client to risks, as was witnessed in Paris.

Many may think that the life of a bodyguard is all glamour and five-star luxury, and that walking rear-right over someone's shoulder is an easy role. I assure you: it really isn't. There's extensive planning for each event and trip, drivers to coordinate, advanced work to be conducted, and itineraries to be reviewed and, if need be, changed. Technology may need to be implemented, and many other areas that all roll into the art of close protection, and of course there are the threat elements mentioned above. The role of the personal security agent is a thinking person's game: you've constantly got to be thinking of the *What if* and have a Plan B in place for everything. If that planning is bad and something happens, you could not only lose your job but your career too.

Close Protection specializts vary in background, physical shape, and method of operating due to the nature of their training; some have little to none, and can be hired based on their appearance alone; Others train constantly in their downtime, have extensive military, law enforcement or government backgrounds, and blend into their environment and client's social or business setting without standing out. This can often be the best approach, especially in the case of high net worth families and corporate executives, but often you'll see celebrities with those who stand out due to their size, but many are diligent and professional in what they do. There are times when a bouncer has been hired to be a bodyguard after a particular celebrity visited a nightclub, for example, but most don't have any formal training.

The media reported that Kim's security consisted of her bodyguard, but there may also have been others—contractors who were supporting him—though, once again, this is an unknown. Either way, Kim had people following her around, unbeknownst to her or anyone else. She and her people may have assumed they were paparazzi, as they are used to, though the robbers used that to formulate their plan based on her pattern and movements in the city.

On the night of the robbery, the robbers went to an exclusive place where Kim was staying. They knew exactly where to go, where to find the jewelry that Kim had been showing to her millions of social media followers and they knew that security was out with the sisters. It was set up perfectly for them.

A surveillance operation was executed, they followed her around and blended into the local paparazzi, and at the end of the day, they watched where she was staying. What could possibly go wrong for the bad guys? Well, nothing. When you are carrying a large amount of valuable jewelry, it's not uncommon for that in itself to have its own security, but it's clear that wasn't a priority, and neither was Kim's personal wellbeing. You're automatically a target when opting to wear that jewelry—but you're even more of a target when you're flaunting it on social media, along with where you are in a particular city.

All the robbers had to do at the point of knowing where she was staying was to sit and wait, watch the bodyguard leave for the hotel to collect the sisters for the trip to the nightclub, and then execute their attack. They didn't need much from the porter other than for him to guide them up the stairs and show them which was her apartment. Whether they forced their way in or knocked on the door is an unknown, but they got in regardless, before handcuffing Kim at gunpoint. She apparently 'begged for her life', telling the gunmen she had children at home.

In a situation like that, it doesn't matter what you tell them, and if she'd have seen any of their faces despite them wearing ski masks, I've no doubt they'd have killed her right then and there. If she'd been staying at a hotel, her security would have been appropriately accommodated in the same location, with at least one member of the team in the opposite or adjoining room. There would have been hotel security and plenty of CCTV cameras that also might have been some form of deterrent, too. Importantly, in the event of an incident, whether it be criminal or medical, she would have had an immediate response, but that wouldn't necessarily have been available to her at an apartment like where she was staying.

There's a good chance that Duvier had worked a full day with Kim, dealing with her meeting agenda, appearances, the paparazzi and fans, and once she was in for the night, he then had to go out with the sisters until the early hours before being up again for another full day. A giant he may be; a robot he is not. You simply cannot function as an effective close protection specializt when operating on a limited amount of sleep. Working with a high-profile celebrity, such as Kim Kardashian, soon saps a person's energy, and so you need to be on top of your game at all times.

Kim Kardashian didn't deserve to be robbed in such a manner—nobody does—but she should be thankful she can make changes so that it doesn't happen again. Her obsessive presence on social media, without a doubt, contributed to her undoing, especially when broadcasting her location to everyone. Now is the time, however, that she and her family can become smarter with their family protection. By having the right program, they will minimize the risks with their personal security. Failure to do so could see another incident occurring with the Kardashians, where the outcome might be very different. A lot of this boils down to the fact that being humble could have minimized the potential of such an attack happening.

Has something like this happened to Will Smith or Halle Berry, for example? What about George Clooney and Leonardo DiCaprio? It has not, and I personally put the reason to this down to the fact that each of them is a humble and down-to-earth person. They aren't out chasing the dollar every two minutes by promoting things that don't have much meaning to them. Each of them has wealth and fame but, for some people, being rich and famous is never enough and it opens you up to unnecessary risk—not only for just yourself but also for your family.

I've worked with each of the above people, two of them for a number of years, and although I learned a great deal about being humble from each of them, there is still always the chance of something happening. However, each of them also made smart decisions. I do not mean that by having me work for them—I know some very well qualified and experienced people that have worked for them, too—but they made decisions that meant safety wasn't sacrificed for money.

For Kim Kardashian's security lead, Pascal Duvier, yes, he will no doubt look back and think of what he could have done differently. He will have gone over this event time after time, and it won't have been easy for him to have it occur on his watch. But for his former charge, I fail to see how the incident she encountered has altered her way of thinking when it comes to being humble moving forward. I find that to be a shame as she had one hell of a warning. Let's hope it doesn't come back to bite her in that proverbial backside of hers that she proudly shows off, along with her wealth and luxuries.

COMMUNICATION:
AN EVERYDAY NECESSITY

MANY PEOPLE BELIEVE THAT the significance of communication is like the importance of breathing. Indeed, communication facilitates the spread of knowledge and forms relationships between people. Without effective communication, people fail, teams fail, missions fail, relationships fail, and, to a certain degree, businesses can fail.

Moreover, communication is the foundation of all human relationship. At first, strangers start talking and getting to know each other, and then relationships are formed when they have more interaction and communication. Communicating helps people to express their ideas and feelings; at the same time, it also helps us to understand the emotions and thoughts of others. As a result, we develop affection or hatred toward other people, and positive or negative relationships are created. This applies to both our personal and business lives, and the past and present proves to us that great communication is paramount in our everyday lives.

For me, communication has played a key role in my life since I was a young boy. Venturing away from home to join the Army, I learned hard and fast that it was extremely important—it was drilled into me. Communicating with my teammates, with my superiors, with my family via phone and letters home—these were all essential elements in the learning curve for me. This period of my life acted as the springboard for me to become efficient at communication, as well as later on in life, when I worked in the private sector. I learned different methods, from the corporate world, communicating with executives, with large-event staff and attendees, with media personnel, as well as those with whom I worked and those under me on operations.

What I did struggle with, however, was communication in personal relationships, despite my efforts in expressing to my partners, over the years, that this was important for our relationship success. There were times where relationships ended due to poor communication. It wasn't for the want of trying, but we are all very different people and, just like in business, we must work extremely hard at making communication absolutely paramount in all that we have and do. There was one recent relationship in particular that I wish I'd have done differently in terms of better communication with my partner. Yes, I said all the right things when it came to how I felt about her—I adored and loved her wholeheartedly—but there were deficiencies that I only learned of later, once the relationship had broken down. It was too late by then, and I have deep regrets in that regard.

Communication has played a big part in my personal, military and business life for thirty-something years, but none more so in the security side of things than on November 26, 2008. It was a day that would prove to be heavily reliant on effective communication, and if it had failed, the results could then have been catastrophic for one traveling family.

I'd been working in Long Island, New York, since April that year, adopting the role of Director of Protective Programs for a separate wealthy family. In June, I'd bought a new home in Texas and had gone there for a few days towards the end of November to get things arranged before Christmas. I was excited about my new place.

On the morning of Wednesday, November 26, as I walked out of the house and to my car to drive to the gym for a workout, I received a call from a driver who I knew in Los Angeles. Alfred worked with a well-known female celebrity in LA and, given that I did security for her on and off for a number of years, Al and I knew each other fairly well. Still, the call was unexpected—we'd generally only speak when I was in his car.

I answered the call immediately. "Hey, Al! What's going on?" I asked him.

"Glen, turn on the news. I need to talk to you about something," he replied. I figured it must be serious. I got back out of my car, walked to my front door, and unlocked it before stepping inside. I turned the television on straight away and watched as breaking news came out of Mumbai, India. Al went on to tell me that another of his clients, a wealthy LA-based businessman, was currently in Mumbai on holiday with his family, and he needed some help. He had desperately called Al to see if he knew of anyone who could assist him and his family, and that's when he made the call to me.

That afternoon in Mumbai, ten members of Lashkar-e-Taiba, an Islamic terrorist organization based in Pakistan, carried out a series of coordinated shooting and bombing attacks across the Indian city. One of the sites was the luxury Taj Mahal Palace Hotel, where the family were stuck inside their room. I'd previously stayed at the hotel during a visit with a celebrity client, and so I had some basic familiarity with the layout. Now, six explosions were being reported at the hotel, with one in the lobby, two in the elevators, and three in the restaurant. I could envisage the inside of the hotel from memory.

Al asked if I could speak with the gentleman as soon as possible, which I agreed to do. I quickly ran to my office and jotted down the mobile number Al provided me with before making the call. I tried five or six times before I was eventually connected and heard the man's voice on the other end. I introduced myself and asked how he and his family where. I then asked him to describe their current situation. What I was hearing was far from comfortable; I could hear gun shots going off and people shouting outside their room in the corridor. Remaining calm was imperative, but it really is easier said than done when you aren't in that situation yourself.

The family comprised the gentleman and his wife, who were in the room with their two young children. They'd placed furniture up against the door and were hiding under the bed and in the closet. They were scared and I could sense it—I could *feel* it. I put myself in that room as best as I could to try to be an asset to them, albeit from thousands of miles away. The call dropped suddenly, and so I called back another few times before being connected again.

"Are you okay?" I asked.

Nobody would be okay in that situation, especially when you have your family with you, but I needed to ask the question all the same.

There was no point in formulating any kind of extraction plan just yet: the priority was to make sure the family remained quiet and safe in their hotel room. The attack was ongoing, and so it was imperative that they stayed where they were. Venturing outside of their room to try to escape when there were terrorists roaming the corridors of the hotel could prove fatal, and so I tried to instill some calm as best as I could.

Given that the electricity was out at the hotel, so the gentleman informed me, we decided to speak again in thirty minutes' time, at which point I'd call him back. That way, he could conserve some battery life on his mobile phone. The last thing we both needed was for him to be unreachable. Time was critical right now. When we hung up the call, I immediately phoned a colleague of mine to loop him in on the situation. I'd known Mike for a number of years, and I both liked and trusted him. I needed to pull him in on this with me.

During the first call I'd had with the gentleman in India, we had briefly discussed some options of getting help to him, but it wouldn't be easy or cheap. He didn't seem to care either way: the personal safety of himself and his family was in danger.

I managed to reach Mike straight away and briefed him on the situation. We went through our contact lists of who we might know within somewhat of a response distance from Mumbai but, as we were going down each of our lists, we found that we weren't getting anywhere. Most were just unavailable or on other projects and deployed elsewhere in the world. We tried reaching out to both the American and British Embassies, but we weren't getting any joy from them either. We even made a call to the police in Mumbai but, with the number of incidents taking place, they were unhelpful. It was understandable: whilst all we cared about was this particular family of four, they were responding to a major terrorist attack involving multiple sites throughout the city.

Mike knew he could get a team in from another country, but that would be a logistical nightmare with visas and equipment, not to mention travel time, but it was what we were leaning towards, and so I presented the idea to the gentleman whilst Mike reached out to those of his contacts who were prepared to deploy. I made one more call to a team of lads I knew in Dubai who were within a couple of hours' flight time from Mumbai, but they were tied up on another operation, so that fell flat. We had to propose a team to come in from Johannesburg, but they wouldn't be able to arrive until the following morning. Unbeknownst to anyone at that time, was that the attack would, in fact, last for three days. As such, having presented the option, as well as the cost, to the gentleman in Mumbai, I was surprised when he approved it.

Mike and I immediately began the process of engaging the team to get to get out to Mumbai, but we knew it wouldn't be easy. The company we were using thankfully had a few guys who already had their Indian visas, which was a huge help: if they hadn't had them, it would prove to be far more difficult with getting anyone in. Communication throughout was absolutely key. I was speaking with the family, as well as their lawyer in the States, while Mike was dealing with and briefing the team who'd be going in to help them. There was, of course, a curve ball that we'd need to deal with, and that was the gentleman's mother-in-law was also in Mumbai, but the day before the attack she'd fallen and broken her hip, meaning she was in one of the local hospitals.

Throughout the remainder of that day, there were many calls being made, but I wished I'd have been able to be on the ground in person. I looked at flight options to get out of Houston, but it would have meant a long connection through London. Mike did the same, but he was currently in South America, which would make it a little trickier. We decided to both stay where we were and manage the team going in remotely. The cost hadn't been a factor but neither of us could have done it with being unreachable at such a critical time. We were fully focused on the family and the operation to rescue them.

The international news stations were reporting many casualties throughout the city, with attacks taking place in South Mumbai at Chhatrapati Shivaji Terminus, The Oberoi Trident, The

Taj Palace Hotel, Leopold Cafe, Cama Hospital and The Nariman House Jewish Community Centre.

By the next morning, there was no change on the ground, and it only seemed to be worsening. Police and military were all over the place; engaging with the terrorists but not getting anywhere—at least that's what we were seeing in the media.

Our four-man team would be landing in the afternoon, and the plan was for three of them to make their way to the area of the Taj Mahal Hotel where the family were, whilst one team member would head to the Breach Candy Hospital to locate the mother-in-law and secure her.

For that reason, I was on the phone with the hospital coordinating everything, but it wasn't easy. As far as they were concerned, I wasn't family, and so they weren't giving me any information of where she was; eventually, however, I succeeded through speaking with one of the doctors. I'd had to explain the whole situation to him but was thankful that he worked with me on making sure we could get our guy in when he landed.

Nothing ever goes smoothly, despite your best intentions. We should have known it wouldn't be simple and, when the team landed in Mumbai, that was proven to be the case. When they got off their flight, they'd decided to individually process through passport control and customs in case they ran into any issues. Four ex-Special Forces lads walking through together with tactical back packs was going to be a lot more suspicious than going through as individuals, but one of them was still stopped. He was asked to empty his backpack, but the problem was he was carrying two radios with spare batteries. It was a big red flag, especially when the city was experiencing a terrorist attack, and so he was detained until later on that evening.

The others were able to leave the airport, thankfully, but we'd now have two of them head to the hotel and the other straight to the hospital. Again, communication was key in making sure everyone was on the same page. I couldn't communicate with the family in the hotel as their phones had no battery, and so they'd need to remember the details I gave them in order to identify the team when they arrived— that is, if they could even get inside the hotel as the attack was still ongoing. The plan was for them to introduce themselves as high up the chain as they could with the local police commanders but knowing how sensitive the situation on the ground would be, both Mike and I weren't holding out too much hope. The team couldn't just wander up and walk into the hotel—we knew that much. We all had to sit tight and play the waiting game.

Early the next morning, on November 28, all sites that had been attacked, with the exception of the Taj Hotel, had been secured by the Mumbai Police Department and security forces. The next day, India's National Security Guards (NSG) conducted "Operation Black Tornado" in order to flush out the remaining attackers; it culminated in the death of the last remaining terrorists at the Taj Hotel and put an end to the attacks.

With the mother-in-law secured at the hospital, where our guy had found a room close to hers to hold out in, we knew that getting to the family would soon be upon the lads at the hotel. They were cleared to go in, along with members of the police, who were going floor-to-floor to take out casualties and those who had been stranded in their rooms.

Mike and I were relieved a short time later to be informed by the team that they'd got the family out; they were in shock but they were safe. They had no intention of sticking around and were taken out of the hotel and straight to the hospital to meet up with the mother-in-law. Their relief had been evident, according to the team with them on the ground. In speaking with the doctor who was responsible for the mother-in-law, they wanted to have her discharged, but it wasn't possible. The family didn't want to leave her behind, but they didn't want to stay in the city either. I posed the option of us getting them over to Dubai whilst maintaining a presence at the hospital until she was clear to fly. They would then all meet up in Dubai and fly home. The gentleman agreed to the plan.

We were asked to arrange for a private plane to fly them out and to keep one of the team at the hospital until the patient could fly. He would then fly with her to Dubai and then the family would head back to the United States, but that wouldn't be for another week—until the point at which she could be discharged from hospital. Still, they were all safe and that was the most important part.

It had been an intense and critical few days, but the communication between everyone had been key to ensuring a successful operation, despite the detainment of one of the team and then having to wait at the hotel until it had been cleared. I can't imagine how it must have been for the family, but I had a good idea. Given that I'd been on the phone a number of times with them, I heard first-hand what was going on, as well as their fear. It wasn't pleasant at all being so far away.

The attacks, which drew widespread global condemnation, began on Wednesday, November 26, and lasted until Saturday, November 29, 2008. At least 174 people died, including 9 attackers, with more than 300 wounded. At the hotel where the family were staying, 31 people were killed and many more were injured. The casualties were mostly Indian citizens, although Westerners carrying foreign passports were singled out. It was later learned that the attack had been planned using information compiled by David Headley—a Pakistani-American—who had stayed at the hotel multiple times.

The family may very well have been able to escape the attack unscathed without our assistance, but in a situation like that, it's important to have a person or team who can keep you calm and guide you through the incident. Could the family have done things differently? Absolutely, they could. They could have taken one or more trained security personnel on the trip with them.

As a high net worth family, they had the money to do so, but they weren't well-known, and that unfortunately plays a deciding factor for many. They had the luxury of having the choice, however, whereas many do not and could be caught up in an international terror incident, as we've seen over recent times.

Always remember, though, no matter your fame, fortune or position: having the ability to communicate effectively can sometimes be more important than many of us might initially think.

LEADING FROM THE FRONT

FOR A GOOD LEADER to succeed, one must be prepared to make decisions that have a positive impact on him- or herself and, if need be, a team or company. Decision-making for me was learnt at a young age when making the decision on my own to join the Army. I felt confident that the decision I was making was the right one, and even when looking back, I know it was. I'd learnt a hell of a lot during my service and always looked at others in regard to the way they made decisions. Granted, this was mainly all military-related, but there were some elements of that that I knew would benefit me outside of military operations.

I started to learn leadership at an early age when I began basic training for the Army. It started with simple things, such as maintaining a head count for my platoon amidst chaos or making sure my team was on time for a parade. In the private sector, where you might be working for a growing company, it is critical for leaders to lead by example. This means following the processes and procedures outlined by the company, not breaking promises, and not asking anything of anyone that you are not willing to do yourself. In combat, as in with business, the best leaders lead from the front, get their hands dirty, and show their team that they are willing to do what it takes in order to accomplish the mission.

In the military, leaders aren't born; they are made. That is no exaggeration: the armed forces invest well in those who they believe can become good leaders. In battle, leaders must make very serious decisions, often based on little-to-no information for which there may be no time for verification. This is a worst-case scenario when it comes to leadership, but it's one that has allowed me to build the foundation of learning; not only learning what it was all about but also everything that it entailed and what was expected of me. Military leadership plays such an important role when the troops are sent to handle conflict. Without it, operations will fail.

Troops will have no central coordination handled by a good strong leader, whether it a Section Commander or up the chain to the Commanding Officer, meaning that leader must be there to lead. "Business as usual" doesn't occur on the battlefield, and so being a unique and confident leader is paramount to mission success.

No good leader assumes they know everything, and the best ones surround themselves with incredible talent of varying types and degrees. The success of any sports team, military unit or business unit, for example, doesn't only come from great leadership and management; rather, it comes from excellent team members and a collaborative environment. It's important to provide parameters and to allow the team to operate somewhat autonomously within those boundaries, which fosters creativity, empowerment, and a sense of ownership when goals are accomplished. And then, of course, acknowledging team members for hard work is fundamental.

In the military, blood, sweat and tears is a part of the job, and recognition for that is not usually given—nor is it expected; in the real-world, however, recognition is an important part of good leadership and in maintaining high levels of morale. In the military, soldiers earmarked for leadership roles are provided with training before being thrust into the firing line; in the case of organizations, on the other hand, staff are rarely given the learning and development needed to allow them to excel in a more senior role. For military leaders, an error in judgement can have fatal consequences. In the business world, the stakes are much lower, with a bad decision potentially resulting in a profit slump or share price drop. The fallout for military personnel is potentially far greater.

I've worked with people across the globe in the business sector, and I've protected corporate executives, high net worth families and members of foreign royalty; I have been fortunate enough to have learned something about leadership from each of them. I've sat in on some of the world's biggest corporate meetings and events and learned many different approaches to leadership from the top executives of some of the largest companies in the world. Each executive I've worked with has adopted a different approach to leadership, but it's those different approaches that have enabled me to fine-tune an art of leadership that works for me, and which benefits those I've worked with across the globe.

A small number of those for whom I've worked, like me, had combat experience from the military; most did not, however. Many had a fine education behind them, of course, while I did not, yet I was able to mix in business and social circles where I had the opportunity to meet others who were leaders, too. What I found as a common denominator, however, was that most had developed a list of principles of leadership from which they work; this is something I'd put together for myself when I first started out as a bodyguard, though it was the military that helped me to understand and execute them. As such, although we were all leaders in our respective fields, the one thing we had in common was our list of principles. Some had them written down, whilst most, like me, had them instilled in them. It's just a part of our lives; part of our make-up.

Today, some thirty-plus years since leaving home at the age of sixteen as a nervous teenager, I've been able to work to my own guiding principles, which I've subsequently carried through everything that I've done. Mine combine motivation and leadership—things that are ingrained in my mind and in everything I do. I refer to this as "The Military Mindset", which is something I know works for me. You can create your own shortlist to work from, which can act as your own guiding principles that can help to push and encourage you, or which provide a starting point from where you can grow to become a strong and effective leader. No matter the challenges I've faced, whether in the past or those to come in the future, I will always try to stick to my principles on leadership and motivation and have found such an approach to be helpful.

You can, of course, ask others to help you put a similar list together, but remember that it's not their job to make sure you stick to them. You'll have bad days, you'll have good days, and you'll have so-so days which might not offer much motivation, but in order to be a good leader you need to maintain that positive mindset and motivation at all times. Remember that you are leading, meaning people are looking to you for guidance, for encouragement, for drive and for passion. If you have a negative day and you show it, you can bet those you are supposed to be leading will be feeling it as well, no matter the size of your organization or company. You could be the head of a small dental practice or the CEO of a multi-national company, and still leadership will be paramount to your company and to your team's success.

You need to know your principles inside-out, and the more you start to really get your head into it, the easier you'll find self-motivation—and that's exactly where you need to be. Being a leader is great, but being a motivated leader who sticks to his own principles is admired greatly, in the corporate world especially, regardless of whether or not you come from the military.

The Military Mindset:

1. Pay Attention: Leave no stone unturned with absorbing information. Identify good leaders within your personal or business life and aspire to be better than them.
2. Be a Solid Team Player: To be a good leader, you first need to understand the importance of what or who you are leading. Communicate well, respect others, and ensure you are a team player always.
3. Lead by Example: When you do something, you've most likely got others watching you. Have the mindset of leading by example, it's attractive and admirable when done with confidence.
4. Take the Initiative: This applies to all that you do with both your personal and business goals. Be confident in your ability to take the initiative, raise your hand or take the lead.
5. Attention to Detail: When you do something, do it at 150%, always. Success is attained by putting your all into everything that you do to make sure that nothing is missed.
6. Accept Challenges: Create your own or take them on, either way, you smash them. You should grow to reach the point of accepting all challenges that are in front of you.

7. Overcome your Fears: You can live with your fears or you can attack them and grow. Remember, without fear, there cannot be courage to overcome any fears that you have or will have.

There are a number of things that bring good leadership to light, and these come in many forms. I've found that, in order to be a good and respected leader, there is a need to have integrity. A leader can be well-liked and popular, and even competent, which is all well and good, but if he or she lacks integrity of character, they are not fit to be a leader.

When integrity is questioned, you've asked for it yourself. Character and integrity are not something you can bullshit people about for too long. The people with whom a person works—especially subordinates—will soon know whether or not a person has integrity. A person may be forgiven for a lot of things, such as incompetence, ignorance, insecurity or bad manners, but they will not be forgiven for a lack of integrity.

Another key fundamental of leadership is establishing the ins and outs of your area of expertise. This might seem obvious, but some managers do try to cut corners rather than mastering the knowledge they must have, and that is essential to the quality of performance. Leadership rests on being able to do something others cannot do at all or that they may otherwise find difficult to do, and so there is a need to get it down, nail it, and show that your leadership skills are driven by your knowledge.

One of the things I've learnt, which is extremely important to companies and to leaders, is to show commitment. All too often, I've seen individuals, teams, operations and missions fail as a result of a lack of commitment from those involved. You've got to be absolutely committed to all that you do: if you're not, then why are you even there? I've been around people who aren't committed and, to be honest, it's distasteful and negative. I've never wanted to be around that—and I've actually walked away from a couple of jobs when I've come to realize that some didn't have the same commitment as I did.

Commitment and sound leadership are paramount.

DEFINING WHO YOU ARE

WHO ARE YOU? WHAT are you about? Maybe you don't give too much thought to it, or just maybe you're at a point in your life where you are asking the above questions. We don't all rollout of school or college and land the job of our dreams. For the majority of us, we need to define who we are and what we want out of life; this happens at a young age and as an adult, too. There have been a number of times that I've personally asked myself these questions, mainly through a couple of tough periods in my life, but today I know exactly who I am and what I'm all about.

None of us were born to wake up at 6AM, have a quick breakfast, and then drive through the morning traffic to get to the office, building site or store you might work at. Once there, your routine stays the same and you become accustomed to it. Maybe you started working for the company five years ago and still hold the same title. Quite possibly you've had no significant pay increase, but it's security; you're in a job and you are used to your routine. Whether you are totally happy or not is debatable; you might have good work colleagues, sure, but you also aspire to grow in your chosen field. And if you don't, then you should!

Believe it or not, I've met and worked with people who don't want the promotion they've been earmarked for because they'll have to work on a different floor away from their friends. Let me be clear: there should be *no* friends in business. Whatever you do outside of work and with whom is all well and good, but at work you need to look at *yourself*; how *you* can grow, how *you* can benefit *you* as an individual and, most importantly, the company you are working for. If you aren't happy in that job, then do all you can to go after the one you know you'll be happy in, where growth and longevity are meaningful to you.

Defining who you are and what you are about is paramount to your successes. Identifying your vision and your goals, both in your personal life and career, are key elements of your happiness and what you are able to get out of life. We spend so much of our lives living by what is defined as normal, and pass judgment on ourselves and others based on this, whether we try to be normal, determine that we are better than normal, or condemn ourselves as worse than normal. Nonetheless, if we think about what is normal, we are usually living a life in a comfort zone, with no growth or vision of personal success.

Everyone struggles to figure out who they truly are—don't think that they don't. Often, when they define themselves, they focus on the negative or how they compare to other people. Nobody but you can define who you are; you know your limits, you know your mind, and you know what makes you tick.

One of the greatest challenges we face when we try to improve ourselves, whether as leaders, partners, friends or family members, is the challenge of changing the way we define ourselves. I must have heard this phrase a thousand times: "It's just the way I am". But as we keep saying things like this, we increase the probability of "It's just the way I'm always going to be". It's as if some people think they can't ever change, but we can all change who we are if we aren't happy with ourselves. We can all change our behavior and mindset by defining who we are.

Despite leaving school without much in terms of qualifications, I was able to define who I was and what I was about. For me, that meant taking some risks. To what level at that age I didn't know, but I let myself define my own journey through a willingness to do what worked for me. I could have easily gone on to college and pleased various members of my family, but would that have pleased me? Would it have even worked for me? I know it wouldn't have, so you have to do what works best for you. When it comes to gaining self-satisfaction, that starts with defining who you are and what you are about. You are the CEO of your own life; you make the key decisions as to what is best for the running of your life, so make sure to take the time to strategize both properly and effectively.

If you allow a relationship to define you, for example, and that relationship ends for whatever reason, you will end up losing your identity. Truthfully, if you have allowed a relationship to define you, you have no identity anyway. I've seen it and I very nearly allowed a relationship to define me, but it never did. Our self-identity should be all about positive traits, but it can also include negative ones. Nonetheless, if someone has hopes of replacing your identity, you need to give yourself a reality check and tweak any deficiencies you have instead of allowing others to take over. Define what your talents and strengths are, what you are passionate about, and focus on succeeding in that.

I could have given up when I felt some didn't think I'd last five minutes in the Army. I could have chosen a new career when some didn't think I'd succeed as a bodyguard. Okay, there were times during the early part of my career where work was slow and opportunities were rare, but I kept my identity and remained focused and committed—and *that* is what enabled me to continue chasing my dream. If I'd not defined who I was and lost my identity along the way, then I'd most likely not feel the satisfaction within me that I do now. When I'm around negative people, for example, I look for any excuse to get away from them. It's unappealing and unattractive, and so I ask myself: Why should I, as a positive individual, want to be around that?

I also faced a period in 2010 when I made the decision to separate from my wife Michelle. This was made even more difficult as she'd only given birth to our wonderful daughter three months earlier. I'd come to the realization that our marriage just would not work, despite me wanting it to. I'd never wanted to get divorced, but the bickering and arguments were continuous and it was very much on both sides.

The separation and subsequent divorce were difficult, especially knowing I'd not be living with my daughter; I'd fallen in love with her the moment she was born. As a protector, this tore away at me as I'd often think of how much effort I invested into protecting strangers, and yet I wouldn't be able to protect my daughter fully. Still, I simply could not be in a marriage that had grown to be toxic, and to this day I truly believe that the right decision was made for all concerned—most importantly my daughter, who I'm extremely close to. I will always be thankful to Michelle for bringing Poppy into this world. She is a true gift.

No matter the challenges you might face, whether you are stuck in a rut, have received poor exam results, not passed a particular course, are looking for a fresh start in life or in your career, make decisions that are based on your goals, your own vision, your individual mindset and your own objectives. Doing this by defining who you are will make all the difference when it comes to self-satisfaction. Essentially, you never know where you can go or the heights you can reach unless you make the effort to work on yourself.

MOTIVATION CAN BE
A WONDERFUL TOOL

ONE OF MY STRONGEST assets is my ability to self-motivate. I've never needed anyone to do it for me; I've always been more than capable of taking care of that on my own. This is something I've done from a young age, before even joining the Army. I didn't have anyone who would push me to succeed. I did it all myself and, looking back, I'm okay with that because it worked for me. I often wonder where it came from and how was I able to not only have a successful military career but also go on to work with some of the biggest names in the world.

My point is not to say I'm the "big I am" because I'm not; I was a shy and skinny kid who was raised on a tough council estate in the north-east of England, where opportunities for young school leavers was minimal, to say the least. For me, I had the choice of going to college, taking a Youth Training Scheme, or going in the Army and, as I wanted a challenge, it was the latter I chose. In doing so, I left behind the regular sound of police cars giving chase to youngsters from my area—those who would often steal cars or cause havoc in some other way.

Now, things seem much better in the region but, at the time, I could have easily fallen into that circle; in fact, I actually hung around lads who did that, but I made the conscious decision to steer myself away from the life they were leading. I knew it just wasn't for me. When I entered the world of the British Army, I found it to be exciting, dynamic and intriguing, and I knew I had to succeed—I *wanted* to succeed—otherwise, what was I falling back to? Going to the football every week, going out drinking every night, not experiencing fulfilment in whatever it was I was doing for work, and not having a pot to piss in when it came to money. Yes, that might be okay for some and enough for others, but it sure as hell wasn't the life I saw for myself—and I knew that at a young age. This, combined with some people's doubt, meant that only one outcome would come my way.

Throughout my military career, I was always pushing myself to be the best I could be. I'd identify one or two people who were more experienced than me and who'd been in the Army for a longer period, and I'd do everything I could to match them and eventually be better than them—whether that be taking a specialized course, being at the front on a run, or gaining further knowledge and ability in specific weapons systems. Yes, I recognized that these things would take some time, but I also knew I would get there. Unbeknownst to them, they were my mentors. I watched, I listened, I learned, and I invested maximum effort into making sure I was a good soldier—like they were. I knew the meaning of being called a "professional soldier", but I wanted to be the best I could be in order to show that. When I started basic training, I didn't see the point of just plodding along as I wouldn't have made it—and I sure as hell didn't go through all that pain just to be average when I passed out. I wanted to be the best.

And *that* is what I chose to do throughout the early part of my Army career. At some point beyond that, I started to notice that younger and newer soldiers were coming to me to ask questions; they were learning from me. I went on to become the senior solider in my company towards the latter part of my career, and I had a responsibility to show that I was a well-trained and responsible soldier—and it's something I enjoyed. It was the start of my journey of learning leadership, and it's something I found myself excelling in because it was a big part of soldiering and what I'd chosen to do. During my Army career, I would often visit home whenever I could and would see those who I used to hang around with; they were always just milling around on street corners or in the pub. For me, though, I was doing something I enjoyed—doing something that I was good at. It was meaningful and I was getting a regular paycheck.

If you are new to a company or have been in a job for some time, there is nothing stopping you from doing the same in identifying someone or various people you can look to.

Do you want to choose the laugh-a-minute person who is constantly fucking around at work as your mentor? Okay, he or she might be a popular character and might raise a few laughs, but the jokers surely can't be that professional. They do a good job? Okay, there may be some elements that you can learn from them, but you need to choose someone who you know you can learn from and who you can aspire to be. Be careful, though: you don't want to go down the route of trying to be better than anyone; that can often come across as arrogant, and I fell into that trap during my early days in the security field. They key is to find the right balance of showing enthusiasm and asking the right questions, mixing in with your team, and showing that you're a team player. That goes back to that "lone wolf" attitude; all that's going to do is piss people off.

One additional point to mention is that I've maintained a high degree of discipline since my younger years. Yes, I've run into some troubles, notably football-related, but I was never a notorious hooligan. I was, in fact, arrested on five separate occasions in my younger years, two of which whilst in the Army, so an angel I never was, but what I have done since then is learn lessons and motivated myself to be the best version of myself that I can be. I've gone from working with highly trained soldiers on the battlefield to corporate executives who run some of the biggest companies in the world, and I've learnt something new from all of them. I've also found that the three main things that have motivated them all has been pretty much universal: a passion for the job, a mindset that enables them to succeed, and the will to be good leaders. They have worked hard in their specific fields, but each of them has all had a high degree of self-motivation in them; it's what's enabled them to be driven.

Self-motivation is, in its simplest form, the force that drives you to do things, and I've always felt that the force behind me has been very much what has enabled me to succeed in what I've chosen to do. Self-motivation is far from being a simple topic; today, there are many books, websites and articles directed towards explaining self-motivation, and some top academics have dedicated their life's work to trying to understand, model and develop motivation theories. For me, however, the best form of expressing what worked for me is to tell it how it is through my journey to date, whether that be through this book or in some of the motivational talks I deliver. Some people may need family and friends behind them to give them that push, whether it be in going for a job interview or choosing a new career.

I never looked at my family or friends for that, and so I did it myself. I learnt to do it myself because I didn't have a choice. I spoke earlier in the book about the doubt from others that I felt before joining the Army, and it was this doubt that helped to lay the foundation for me to learn how to be self-motivated. I guess you could say I'm quite a stubborn person, and no matter the difficulties and challenges I faced through a gruelling basic training period in the Army, I was never going to just give up.

If I hadn't had the potential to be a good soldier, that would then have been another thing altogether, but that wasn't the case, otherwise I'd have been booted out! You can learn how to be self-motivated without anyone doubting you, however; I just used that to my own gain at the time and have built on it ever since. Some can find it hard to motivate themselves, and even when they have the support of others behind them, they can still experience struggles with moving forward. Yes, some may face personal, family or business struggles, but you can let these sink you or lift you. You have to make the decision, and there is only one choice: you aren't sinking. In the main, many are just pure idle, but I'm a firm believer that every single one of us has the ability to drive ourselves forward in order to achieve success.

How many times have you heard the words, "I can't do this" or "I can't do that"? What about someone saying, "It's impossible" or "It's too difficult"? I've come across some who have been presented with wonderful work opportunities—dream positions, really—and talk non-stop about it and how great it will be. With one such individual, when I later caught up with them, I asked how the new job was going, to which they replied that they didn't take it because they'd miss home. This was a thirty-eight-year-old man who had zero obligations, no girlfriend or wife, and no children, and had been offered an amazing job living overseas with an attractive tax-free package. Did I add that he was out of work when he received the offer? Miss home? He wasn't motivated! *That* was the problem! He just couldn't admit it.

On the flip side, I see some who are super motivated and who have found a good balance between personal and work life and who are constantly productive—both in themselves, whether it be going to the gym or having a hobby, and then with work, where they feel fulfilled.

A problem with motivation can also arise, however, if you become *too* motivated. In this scenario, you might want to impress people and show people you're on top of everything, and then you don't know when to switch off. That in itself can lead to health or work-related issues. First, learn how to motivate yourself. Don't rely on anyone to do it for you. Only when you feel you're able to do that, then learn to manage and balance it. Doing that will bring about positive results sooner than you think, and just remember what your alternative is if you aren't motivated.

In my capacity as a mentor and coach, I get to speak to a lot of people who talk to me about their goals and what they want to achieve. We discuss together how they can get there, but to do that I need to first understand their mindset. Nobody needs to take the path that I did because it definitely isn't for everyone, but if there is something you want to do, whether that be make more money, implement a change of job or career, progress in a current job or have your own business, one thing is certain: it can be done.

You need to have the confidence in that. I've found that too many people in today's world are in a comfort zone, and it's that comfort they have that restricts them from bursting forward and excelling. I completely understand it can be a risk to take but, without risk, there can be no reward.

I could have stayed at home as a young boy and had three meals a day cooked for me instead of eating boil-in-the-bag rations. I could have slept in a nice comfortable bed instead of in a trench in the field, piss wet-through and freezing cold. I could have stayed in jobs in the private sector which, although paying me well, didn't facilitate growth, whether in the company or in my position. Fuck that! I took the risks I felt were there to be taken to enable me to be a more well-rounded and happier individual. Self-motivation can be easier to understand when you consider some additional examples other than what has worked for me. Consider the following:

A man who goes to work every day just to pay the bills, keep his family off his back, and please his boss is not self-motivated, while a man who needs no external forces to make the trek into work every day and who finds fulfilment in what he does is self-motivated.

The student who only thinks about her homework when her parents remind her, nag her, or ground her for failing to complete it is not self-motivated, but the student who completes her homework with no prodding because she wants to learn and succeed in school is self-motivated.

The woman who only goes to the gym when her friends drag her there or because her doctor is adamant that she needs to exercise in order to get healthy is not self-motivated, but the woman who sets an early alarm and schedules time for the gym, regardless of whether or not anyone encourages her, is self-motivated.

You could question why I didn't motivate myself to do better in school or go on to college for further education. In answer to that, I would say I was simply young and unaware of how to be self-motivated until I started challenging myself in the Army's basic training. Although I was still young then, there were a number of combining factors that enabled me to learn. Self-motivation is all about where your drive comes from: if your motivation comes from within and it pushes you to achieve for your own personal reasons, it can be considered self-motivation, and then you aren't having to rely on others to motivate you.

It's possible to be self-motivated in some areas of life and not in others. As an example, I've always needed to run, and yet I hated it, but I've done it because it's been job-related. Nonetheless, it's an area I've always needed to work hard to motivate myself to do. If I can't motivate myself to do something that's important for my work, then I need to start thinking about an alternative career. If you find yourself in a job that you don't like or that you can't put your all into, then take the time to identify what it is you want and then put your all into it. There is nothing wrong with change; you just need to make sure it's positive change and something that you know can offer longevity.

Never be afraid to take chances or risks, but still recognize the need to be motivated to overcome challenges that you may face. If you can find that self-motivation within you, you'll feel as though you can attack anything—and not only that, but that you can come out on the other side feeling much more confident. For me personally, I feel as though I can do anything I want to do as long as I put my mind to it. And when I do, I feel a big sense of fulfilment and excitement. I don't particularly care what anyone else thinks when it comes to doing so, either: what I do and how I do it is because I believe in it, not because others want me to do it. You can do the same.

WHEN A DISASTER STRIKES

THROUGHOUT 2014, I WAS working as Director of Security at an exclusive residential resort in Cabo San Lucas, Mexico. My responsibilities included the protection of people and assets, with homes in the community ranging from US$3 million to US$35 million. I created contingency plans, handled all risk management, managed the guard force of more than 60, as well as the lifeguards, and provided close protection for designated clients.

As part of the senior management team, I hosted meetings and led the initiatives on all matters relating to the security and safety of all staff and members of the community. Within a period of six months in that position, I was promoted by the CEO to become Director of Global Security for the company, complete with a portfolio of other international communities. It was a role I enjoyed, which involved other properties in the Bahamas and throughout the United States, as examples.

During my time at the company, I was also fortunate enough to take in a new addition to the Burton family. Through the help of some folks in the entertainment field, I soon found that an 18-month-old black Labrador would be joining me. Despite a number of complex issues surrounding getting her from a shelter in Kansas, up to Chicago and then across to LA, Bella arrived in Mexico on George Clooney's private plane, where she would start her new life. Since then, she has continued to keep me on my toes on a daily basis.

Without doubt, the most notable incident during my time in Mexico was the arrival and aftermath of the devastating Hurricane

Odile in September of 2014. It was the first time I'd experienced such a catastrophic event, and one I hope to never experience again. In the week prior, I was planning on resigning my position in order to move back to Houston. I'd done a year down there successfully and felt it was time to move back, though that would be pushed back due to the inbound hurricane, which, of course, we knew nothing about at that point. I was in my office one morning when my number two, Carlos, arrived and asked to speak with me. He told me about some questionable weather that was forming off the coast and said I needed to be aware of it. I immediately pulled it up on my computer and transferred it to the big television screen in order to take a better look. At the time, it was a low-pressure tropical storm, about four days out, but it was clear it was forming and heading in our direction. We agreed to monitor it for the next twenty-four hours. I sent an initial email out to all members of the senior management team, informing them of the storm forming, and told them we'd be monitoring it. I told them that I'd provide further information over the coming hours.

The following evening, I left work and went home after monitoring the developments throughout the day. Pouring a glass of wine, I sat on my balcony and watched some of the golfers teeing off below me when Carlos called. He told me that the storm was rapidly forming and that we'd now need to pay close attention. It seemed that, in just three days' time, this thing would be hitting us head on. Not only Carlos but others, too, were becoming concerned with the trajectory of where it was heading. The worst-case scenario seemed to be that Tropical Storm Odile would make landfall, causing us to receive excessive rain and winds, meaning we had to be prepared for that as a very minimum. That evening, I compiled a weather warning email to send out to all staff. From that, they would then take the necessary measures for their respective departments, such as closing all villas, putting away garden furniture, and ensuring everyone had what they needed.

The next twenty-four hours passed, and we had come to face a hurricane Category 1 first before going to a Category 2. As luck would have it, though, the track of the hurricane shifted and looked to be heading away from our area. We thought we'd had a change in luck, but we would soon learn that we were wrong.

As a result of the change in trajectory, only minor weather alerts were posted by the local governments of southwestern Mexico. Unfortunately, however, through the course of the night, Odile unexpectedly took another turn—this time heading back towards us again. If that wasn't bad enough, it had gone from a Category 2 to a Category 3 hurricane just twelve hours before landfall, and we expected to be hit direct. The Baja California Peninsula was placed under red alert; this was the maximum warning level. A state of emergency was declared, and in Cabo San Lucas, 2,100 marine workers were set up to start evacuations. The ports of La Paz, Los Cabos, San José del Cabo and Loreto were closed, and all businesses, hotels and population tried as best they could to protect themselves and their goods. The local supermarkets were cleaned out with people getting their last-minute supplies; it seemed that mild panic was setting in with many on the streets.

I called an emergency meeting for 9AM that morning, with all senior management and department heads in attendance. Each were handed a disaster preparedness document pertaining to our property, and we went through it line by line. It was imperative that each left this meeting with the knowledge to allow them to ensure their staff and departments were fully prepared. The security team issued to all personnel a number of emergency items, including flashlights, candles, water and other items. Later, in the afternoon, all non-essential staff were instructed to go home and take care of themselves and their families. Once I knew we were clear of all those who didn't need to be there, I conducted a full tour of the large property to make sure I was happy with everything.

I'd gone to my apartment earlier in the day to grab some clothes, as well as a load of food for Bella. There wasn't much I could do to protect the apartment, as nice as it was, especially given that the whole one side of it was floor-to-ceiling glass. I locked up and headed back to the villa I was staying in at the resort.

Making the most of the electricity and anticipating we'd lose it through the night, I made a load of food and got it down me. I'd authorized Carlos and a couple of the maintenance guys to stay at the villa also, and so we had a few people on-site just in case.

I did a final drive around in one of the golf carts at 7PM, and as I drove along the beachfront, the waves were increasing greatly, and it was starting to rain heavily. I estimated that the next six hours we'd be seeing a major increase in weather.

By 11PM, we were starting to get hit hard, at which point I made a final call to our Chief Financial Officer, who was in Arizona, to inform him of the developments. He'd mustered a team at our company headquarters to ready themselves to support us in Mexico. What that support was going to be, though, none of us knew.

Odile made landfall near Cabo San Lucas as a Category 5 hurricane in the early hours of September 15, 2014, bringing with it winds of 125 mph. The noise outside was something I'll never forget; windows smashing, tiles falling from the rooftops, trees smashing against the villas, and doors and windows slamming. I remained in the villa with the others and tried my best to find somewhere safe to get my head down for a couple of hours, but it was impossible. Bella was smart enough to crawl under the bed in the master bedroom and crash there; it really was the only safe place. I tried popping my head out the door at 2AM but it was just too much; the wind and rain were unreal. It didn't let up all night.

The following morning, as daylight broke, the worst of the hurricane had passed and so I decided to go out and take a look around. I instructed Carlos to tour the west of the property, while I would take a look around the east side. The devastation was both shocking and saddening as I drove around on the four-wheel ATV. I called the CFO and gave him an update, sending to him mobile images depicting the devastation. He asked what our immediate need was, though at that point in time, I just didn't know. I needed to assess everything throughout the course of the day.

After making landfall as a Category 5 hurricane, Odile brought widespread damage to the Baja California Peninsula. I didn't know it at the time but all roads throughout the area were blocked in some way, and there wasn't one single building that hadn't suffered substantial damage.

I managed to locate my car on the property and found it on its roof, as were many others. The whole beach area of the property had been washed away, as well as the popular "taco stand". It could all be replaced, and so my immediate concern was those who were on the property, as well as our staff, who were at home with their families. It took some time to get through it all, but some of the staff went about trying to reach everyone who worked at the property. Thankfully, all were safe, but around 80% had either lost or suffered serious damage to their homes, vehicles or both.

I stayed on the property for the next twenty-four hours as I was unable to get out due to all the debris blocking the roads. The following morning, however, I managed to grab one of the company cars that was in a fit state to drive and headed to my apartment to take a look. Driving down the main road to the golf course community where I lived, I had to maneuver around downed telephone poles, trees and collapsed buildings. The area had been completely devastated. Before I even pulled up to the apartment, I knew it would have suffered severe damage, and when I walked in it was confirmed to me. It was completely destroyed. I stepped through the broken glass and over the flooded floor to grab the remainder of my things out of my closet. I was there for maybe fifteen minutes and never went back again.

Surprisingly, we had power immediately following the hurricane; however, it soon went off and caused even more of a problem for everyone. For at least ten days, we struggled when it came to the necessities of hot food, running water and electricity. I found myself going for a morning wash in some of the swimming pools at each of the villas. Each of them was trashed and littered with sand and debris, but it was the best that could be done. I was brushing my teeth with plastic bottles of water, but I knew I was one of the fortunate ones. Whatever we could find that we thought might benefit us, we grabbed it and used it in some way.

At least 239,000 people were left without electricity throughout Baja California Sur alone—some for weeks—which was equal to around 92% of the state's population. All flights in and out of the peninsula were cancelled and wouldn't resume for at least ten days as the airport in San Jose had suffered substantial damage. Thousands of military and police were brought in to provide support as the area resembled a war zone with the destruction of everything. Hurricane Odile had been the most intense land falling tropical cyclone on the Baja California Peninsula in history, alongside Hurricane Olivia of 1967. Unfortunately, the infrastructure throughout most of the area just wasn't substantial enough to withstand an extreme weather hit such as this, and so that made the damage worse. We managed to bring in a couple of private aircraft filled with supplies over the first seven days. It was much needed, but we'd require much more. Thankfully, we'd received a number of portable generators, which were very helpful, and I'd made sure to keep one in the villa where I was staying.

The effort invested by everyone involved at the community—from the security team to other departments, and the team in Arizona to some of our club members—was unbelievable. Over the following couple of weeks, we'd brought in around eight private flights with supplies, as well as aid trucks that had been sent down from the United States. It was all-hands-on-deck in the clean-up operation, too, and soon enough we had people out, taking care bags to our staff and their families, and helping them to rebuild their homes.

In December of 2014, three months after Hurricane Odile had hit, I left my position as the Director of Security and returned to Houston. I was thankful to have had the opportunity to spend the time I did down there, and I also got to meet some great people, but it was time to move on. I'd been visiting my daughter every three weeks throughout that time, but it just wasn't enough. I wanted to play more of a role in her life, and what with the sadness I had witnessed from the hurricane, now really was the time. I felt better for having made the decision. It was the first time I'd dealt with a major disaster on this scale and it taught me a hell of a lot. Now, I was looking forward to a fresh start in another job.

THE RISE IN
GLOBAL SECURITY CONCERNS

PICTURE THE MOMENT: YOU arrive in Colombo, Sri Lanka, and are taking in the wonderful sights and culture. You visit one of the local churches with your family and are looking forward to a fun-filled day ahead. You've all been looking forward to the trip, but suddenly it turns to disaster.

This was an attack that brought back memories for me personally when I helped to extract the family out of the Mumbai bombing attacks. On Sunday, April 21, 2019, a series of coordinated bombings took place in Sri Lanka. The explosions targeted Christians at Easter Sunday church services in Colombo, Negombo and Batticaloa, as well as tourists staying in luxury hotels in the capital. With the death toll at more than 350 and more injured, ISIS claimed responsibility within days of its occurrence.

Six of the eight bombings took place in Sri Lanka's capital. At 8.45AM, the city was rocked by simultaneous explosions at a large Catholic church, St Anthony's Shrine, and the Shangri-La and Kingsbury hotels. Five minutes later, another hotel, the Cinnamon Grand, was also hit. Police have not said which site was hit worse; however, it is thought that at least 160 people were injured in the congregation of St Anthony's Shrine.

Officers began to carry out raids across the city. At 1.45PM, there was another explosion in the suburb of Dehiwala, notably at a guesthouse close to the national zoo. At 2.15PM, a further blast occurred in a housing scheme in Dematagoda. These last two bombs appear to have been carried out by the attackers as they fled from police.

At 8.45AM, as the first explosions went off in Colombo, a bomb ripped through St Sebastian's Catholic Church in Negombo—a seaside town to the north of the capital. An Easter Sunday service was taking place, and it is thought that at least fifty members of the congregation were killed, though no official breakdown of the death toll has been released. On the east coast of the island at 9.05AM, the Zion Evangelical Church in Batticaloa was also attacked during its Easter service. The main hospital in the city received more than 300 people with injuries in the hours following the blast.

What would you do? How would you react or respond? Forget the bravado you see in the movies... When shots are being fired and bodies are falling around you, what would you be prepared to do? Bear in mind that a lot depends on your split-second decision. Yes, this could happen anywhere, but what if you were caught up in such an attack like the one that occurred in Sri Lanka? Clearly there isn't much you can do when gutless cowards blow themselves up along with innocent people, but vigilance must remain high for everyone.

The day turned into a sickening bloodbath where innocent people suffered at the hands of a cowardly and sickening act carried out by radical terrorists, though that's a common trend with them—spineless and sickening. The intention of causing mass causalities and panic amongst innocent civilians whilst facing minimal resistance was in effect that day in Sri Lanka.

The soft target approach was executed successfully, but so, too, were the attacks in London, Stockholm, Brussels, Munich, Hamburg, Madrid, Berlin, Barcelona and Nice. Will we see more of this? I see no reason to justify us thinking we won't, and that's the most concerning thing as we try to move forward from yet another shocking act of terror.

Don't be fooled into the idea that we've won the war on terror—far from it, as far as I'm concerned. There is still a long way to go when it comes to eradicating the global threat we've faced, particularly from radical groups such as ISIS, ISIL, Daesh, or whatever else they choose to go by these days. The next attack could come at any time and could be at any location. Don't be fooled into thinking that anyone is immune from being caught up in one.

In May 2017, we watched wounded children stream out of the Manchester Arena, where twenty-three people were killed and 139 more were injured. More than half were children—excited and happy to have been going to see Ariana Grande perform live in concert. Before that, in July 2016, a 19-tonne cargo truck was driven into people celebrating Bastille Day on the Promenade des Anglais in Nice, France. Eighty-seven people died that day, including a number of children and the elderly, with a further 434 injured.

We are still very much at risk, not only from radicalized lone wolves and groups, which notably both include men and women, but also kids, too. Yes, you really did read that correctly. Have you seen the pictures and news reports of the young boys holding a knife to the throats of those poor folk in orange jumpsuits or the ones pointing a 9mm at the back of the heads of others? It's not just for show, so make sure you understand that a would-be attacker in today's world could very much be anyone—regardless of age or gender. When it comes to international crime and terrorism, nothing surprises me. Some of these people will stop at nothing to inflict as much damage as they can.

It comes as no surprise when people ask me if it's still okay to travel. I'm a firm believer in traveling to anywhere you want—within reason, of course. If someone asks me if they should go backpacking in The Sudan or snorkeling off the coast of Yemen, then my answer to that would be a short and sweet "no". Some in the States that addressed their concerns with me suggested that they are now afraid to visit Europe and other parts of the world due to the threat, but your personal or business travel shouldn't stop, and let's not think that remote places are safe due to there being a smaller population because that isn't always the case.

I often speak to, and advise, individuals, families and business personnel in regard to their personal and travel security, and have found that, alarmingly, a growing trend is their fears for security and safety when traveling. I recently spoke with one particular family who do not go anywhere near high-populated areas due to their personal fears of being caught up in an attack, such as the one witnessed in Paris. They've restricted their international travel but, as I told them, an incident can occur anywhere, even in the United States where they live. We've seen it happen.

I understand their concerns; however, traveling should not put us off—or, rather, the threat from terrorists should not put us off; after all, it is this control they crave. Taking effective precautions both before and during a trip will go a long way to ensuring your security and safety, however, and will also provide peace of mind.

Because of this reason, our governments must, without fail, stamp down on the radical preaching and recruiting that has been allowed to go on in non-Muslim countries. These people have been able to increase their capabilities, increase their manpower and, due to the lack of action against these groups and individuals, it has allowed an increase in risk to us all. This is completely unacceptable, and it is now time to act because we have not done enough to counter the growing threat from Islamic extremism.

I don't want to hear that the attacks in Sri Lanka, Paris, Manchester, London and other locations have nothing to do with Islam because here's the thing: any man or woman shouting "Allahu Akbar" as he blows himself to paradise or opens fire on innocent people is an adherent of the same religion and scriptures children are forced to learn, repeat and regurgitate by radical Muslim clerics the world over.

Radical extremists have a clear strategy; it's a strategy that includes beheadings, crucifixions, terror and fear, and it all derives from a book—the only book they ever read. People ask if our strategy to counter the threat they pose is working. What strategy? Tell me what the strategy has been, and I'll tell you if it's worked. This has been the problem: extremists have a strategy and they've been executing it for way too long—and doing so successfully.

It's time that we all implement a strategy of our own to counter the risks we face, such as the terrible incidents that have taken place in recent times. We must implement such a strategy as individuals, as families, and as organizations. We all have a responsibility to protect ourselves and one another. Unfortunately, though, when people travel, many tend to switch off and focus on the finer aspects of their trip, whether that be for business or pleasure, but we must switch back on and stay alert to the possibility of the *What if*, regardless of where we are, as has been witnessed in recent years. Terrorists can be sneaky bastards in their method of operating, but if you see something out of the ordinary, if someone just doesn't seem right to you, then go with the old saying of "see something, say something". Trust your gut. It really could go a long way to stopping a major incident and ultimately saving lives—not only your own but also those of others.

ALWAYS MOVING FORWARD

A TOTAL OF 88 countries and 164 cities at the time of writing, and hundreds of flights. That's a lot of travel, and although I've enjoyed every bit of it and been thankful for the opportunity to work with some really great clients, I now appreciate the time I get at home. I never expected to travel as much as I have done, but it can wear you down after a while. I still enjoy flying off to take care of things now and again, but I'm not chasing the round-the-world trips like I used to do. Throughout 2018 alone, I did six round-the-world trips and visited China on twelve different occasions, as well as a number of other countries. That's an insane amount of travel in a year, but I must admit: I've loved every bit of it.

I'm often asked what my favorite country is that I've visited. It's a simple question from those who've known about my global travels. Surprisingly, however, I don't have one. I have had experiences, good, bad and indifferent, and I've stumbled across things I have liked and disliked. I've experienced the smells of the world, the different sounds—some strange. I've seen some of the most amazing sights there are to see whilst also finding myself immersed in extreme poverty-stricken countries.

Believe it or not, and despite my extensive travel, I have a fear of flying. No matter the type of aircraft, whether it be a Gulfstream or a commercial airliner, First Class or Economy, I'm not a fan, and I haven't been for years. I'm fine until we hit turbulence, and while I don't go all crazy, I still need to be left alone to get through it. Despite that fear, though, it hasn't stopped me from traveling the world to do the job I've loved doing. Yes,

I've had some scary moments from traveling on some questionable airlines to hitting severe weather, and so it's always good when I arrive at the other end safely!

Although I've mostly been in work mode during my travels, I've also been able to enjoy the places I've visited, either with those with whom I've been working or during any down time I may have had. I believe my travels have greatly benefited me, and learning about international cultures has, so far, been a great experience. When I first started traveling overseas, which really began when I was in the Army, I didn't pay much attention to the local culture or even to the locals, nor did I make any great effort to do so. Over the years, however, I've learned that I missed out on doing so, and have since tried to make up for it. Traveling to different places around the world and embracing international cultures can be a wonderful and rewarding experience. Yes, there are risks, but we can't allow those risks to put us off what could be memorable experiences. Besides, we face just as many risks when we walk out of our front door.

When I first visited Africa—Kenya, to be precise—during my Army career, I didn't want any interaction with the local kids who'd try to kick a ball over, nor did I want to entertain them as they looked at our uniforms. As far as I'm concerned, this was wrong. I did the same when I first visited the Middle East—Oman. It was only when I started to travel more, most notably in the security industry, that I really started to try to make a difference to not only the locals but to myself, too.

What have my experiences really been like? They've been great, and taking in foreign cultures has, I believe, benefited me greatly. I have, for instance, been on a trip to the Middle East and awoken to the sound of the call to prayer sounding through the city and, as it's another people's country, you have to respect their way, but by the same token, I'm also hopeful that our way is respected, too, as we go through some challenging times.

Without doubt, traveling has been able to provide me with incredible experiences I'm glad to have witnessed; the smells, the people, the culture, the food. All of it has been so worthwhile.

Take Jordan, for example; a place where I've found to be one of the most hospitable places on earth. Visitors are highly appreciated and respected in Jordan, and the locals are social and personable people who are interested in their guests and who similarly hope their guests will be interested in them. It's important not to stay in your little bubble when experiencing foreign countries and cultures. Sitting with a group of locals in one of their coffee shops and engaging with them in conversation can actually be very enjoyable.

Taking a trip to India can often be frustrating—the dirty streets, the excessive traffic and the poverty, can all take its toll. However, I've found Indian people to be extremely friendly and they will help you as best they can. The same can be said for many others all over the world. I've given my own food to those who have needed it. I've paid for the education of a few kids in Africa. I've held a young girl with Aids in my arms and learned that she died not long after. These are all things I've managed to embrace only because of being given the opportunity to travel as I have done. In the early days, I'd turn my nose up at Arabs, Indians and Asians, but then I quickly realized most were really nice people. They were helpful, they were interesting, and each had a story to tell or a personality that was something I could learn from. It's important to remember—we're all made of the same stuff.

Shaking hands is something that many of us are accustomed to; for the Chinese, however, it can often be viewed as highly uncomfortable. The Japanese tend to be straight-faced when happy, and smile to mask unpleasant feelings, such as anger or sadness. A tap on the shoulder, often done innocently by many of us, can be interpreted as threatening in some Northern European countries. During the course of my travels, I quickly learned of the different things requiring awareness so as to not insult my hosts but, believe me, I've done that, too, particularly in the early days. Doing something to which they are accustomed, especially when meeting them, I've found to go down well.

Don't get me wrong: I'm not off to become a preacher in some third world country, but I'm glad that I've been able to embrace international cultures, understand different religions, and spend time with some pretty interesting people, regardless of wealth, or lack of, and irrespective of their status in life. These are things that make me who I am today, and which have given me a much broader opinion of the world and the people in it.

At the time of writing, I'm running the Executive Protection for a Fortune 500 company based in Southern California. I can say, hand on heart, that it's the best job I've had in a lengthy and demanding career. The executives I travel with and the people I regularly interact with around the world have contributed to me being able to say that I've got complete job satisfaction. If you are unable to say that, then change your mindset and get yourself in a position where you can.

It hasn't always been the case elsewhere, of course, though in the main I've enjoyed my time with all of those I've worked with throughout the course of my diverse and interesting career. It always helps to have a great relationship with those I'm asked to work and travel the world with, and so I couldn't be happier with the personable approach to what I do with the people I work with now. They are busy executives who are damn good at what they do, and I continue to learn a great deal from them on a daily basis. The people I report to—great people—and those I work with in a support capacity, such as executive assistants, event staff and marketing teams, are all wonderful and personable, which really does go a long way.

With that said, this will most likely be my last full-time position in a global security capacity. Given my comfort level at working with the company and executives I currently support, I firmly believe that going to any other company would, in fact, be a step down, where I might not feel as fulfilled. I would, however, be foolish to say that I'll retire from this work once this job ends, whenever that might be. Hopefully, I've got some time left with them.

Some might think I'm so accustomed to flying off here, there and everywhere and that I'll keep doing that for the next ten or twenty years, but no, I won't. My daughter is far more important for me to be around than heading off across the world all the time. Yes, I will still travel, but hopefully I can find a good balance with that. If anything, I want to travel with my daughter and show her some of the places I've been to—something we can enjoy together—and so we regularly head away to some of the locations I've had the fortune to visit for work.

Around two years ago, I wanted to find a way to help others based on my global experiences of traveling the world, and I have a particular interest in personal and leadership development. I first became interested in this a number of years ago when I was asked to spend some time traveling with a young member of a prominent

New York-based family. Together, we discussed the future, his development goals, where he was now and where he strived to be. It was an enjoyable number of weeks together, especially as we also carried out some fun adventure activities. I've worked with other individuals in providing guidance and support on a number of matters and worked with them as a mentor and coach. Together, we formed a working partnership and friendship based on confidentiality, trust and truthfulness.

In 2018, I started a company that provides leadership development, mentoring and coaching, as well as adventure training for individuals, groups and corporate teams. I used the experiences I'd gained over the previous thirty years to develop a number of programs, courses and workshops, all of which prove beneficial to those interested in growing, building teamwork, achieving effective communication, enhancing confidence and developing motivated leaders. The company promotes *performance*, *motivation* and *mindset*, and the feedback I received prior to starting it was very positive, and so "Q Three Zero" was born and is something I am very excited about. With training locations throughout the United States managed out of our Houston office, and the same in the United Kingdom run out of our office on Teesside, we have the ability to work with people from all walks of life regardless of their geographic location. "Q Three Zero" gives people the opportunity to come to a company that they can rely on, where we work as a trusted partner rather than just another service provider. It's fun and challenging, rewarding and memorable, but, just like everything in life, if you put the effort in, show a willingness to learn and are prepared to take a risk, you'll soon see the benefits—and that's what we really focus on.

Running and managing "Q Three Zero", as well as carrying out keynotes and motivational speaking to help others, is something I'm embracing with great enthusiasm, though if some think I'll not be a success with it, they should really know by now that I'm cut from a different cloth. My mindset enables me to continuously push forward with what I believe in, and overcoming adversity and doubt is something I've used to my own advantage. I see no reason to change those traits within myself.

Abraham Lincoln once said, "In the end, it's not the years in your life that count. It's the life in your years". This is true, and I'd like to think that, although my life to date has been demanding and challenging, it has also been very rewarding. Moving forward, however, it's about more than just being "In Harm's Way".

For you, just remember that, no matter the challenges you might face, you can overcome and get through them. With the right mindset, you can achieve anything you want to.

Good luck and stay safe!

Up The Boro.

ACKNOWLEDGMENTS

FOR THOSE WHO HAVE been aware of the developing stages of the book, I thank you greatly for your advice, support and friendship.

For my mum and dad, who I know have encountered some sleepless nights over the years, thank you for your support.

I owe a great deal to a number of people who have directly or indirectly offered me support, most notably to my uncle, Martin, as well as to my brothers, Gary and Peter, with whom I haven't spent nearly enough time as I'd have liked.

Thank you to my friends Paul and Lisa, Ian and Amanda, Shelly, Chris and Danielle, Steve and Kathy, as well as Jeremy and Heather, and Swedish Pete. I owe a great deal to the team I served with in Bosnia—Clive, Mick, Frank and Mac, though sadly the latter has since passed away. It was in working with this great group of lads that gave me the platform to build on and develop a successful career for myself in close protection.

The executives I've had the pleasure of working with around the world and supporting in the past few years—Steve, Cristiano, Alex, Don and Brian—are a wonderfully committed group of hardworking and talented people from whom I've learned a great deal.

To the people I work closely with—too many to mention, but to name a few; Connie, Lindie, Kathleen, Sylvie, Gaby, Stephanie, and Indira.

Stew, Jim, Jeff, Chris, Kathy, Joe, Ron, and so many others within the company, I want to say: your friendship, advice and support is why I'm not only proud to be able to call you my friends, but my family, too.

Thank you to my publisher, Hayley Paige at Notebook Publishing, as well as the great folks at BBC Radio Tees, who have given me a wealth of support over the years.

To the good men I served alongside in the Army, it was an honor to serve with you. To the lads who gave so much, I and your brothers salute you. We will never forget.

And finally, to Goose, without whose leadership and guidance on the streets of war-torn Sarajevo and in the deserts of Iraq would not have helped me in the job I've done to date.

ALWAYS MOVING FORWARD

CPSIA information can be obtained
at www.ICGtesting.com
Printed in the USA
BVHW071609180619
551321BV00001B/180/P

9 780993 589898